CARRIED AWAY

Hélène David-Weill
President of the Union centrale
des arts décoratifs

Sophie Durrleman
Chief Executive Officer

Béatrice Salmon
Director of the Museums

Renata Cortinovis
Director of operations and development

Olivier Saillard
Director of programming
at the Musée de la Mode et du Textile

Editiorial coordination at UCAD
Chloé Demey, Claire Archer

Editorial director
Marike Gauthier

Photo research
Dalloula Haiouani
Anne-Françoise Bonardel

Designer
Juliane Cordes assisted by
Sandrine Bouet and **Charlotte Brétéché**

Originally published in France by
Union centrale des arts décoratifs
Le Passage Paris-New York Editions
Hermès

First published in the United States of America
in 2005 by
The Vendome Press
1334 York Avenue
New York, NY 10021

Copyright © 2005 The Vendome Press
Copyright © 2004 Hermès, Paris
Copyright © 2004 Union centrale
        des arts décoratifs, Paris
Copyright © 2004 Le Passage Paris-New York
        Éditions, Paris

ISBN: 0-86565-158-2

Library of Congress Cataloging-in-Publication Data

Chenoune, Farid.
  [Le Cas du sac. English]
  Carried away : all about bags / Farid Chenoune et. al.
    p. cm.
  Includes bibliographical references.
  ISBN 0-86565-158-2 (hardcover : alk. paper)
  1. Bags. I. Title.
  TS198.B3C4713 2005
  391.4'4--dc22
                                          2004017751

CARRIED AWAY

all about bags

Preface by Hélène David-Weill and Jean-Louis Dumas

General Editor   Farid Chenoune

THE VENDOME PRESS
HERMÈS

ACKNOWLEDGEMENTS

This book was published to coincide with the exhibition
"Le cas du sac" at the Musée de la Mode et du Textile
Union centrale des arts décoratifs in Paris,
October 6 2004 – February 20 2005.

The exhibition was created and designed
by the Musée de la Mode et du Textile and the Maison Hermès.

ADVISORY COMMITTEE

- Olivier Saillard, general curator of the exhibition,
director of programming at the Musée de la Mode et du Textile
- Monique Blanc, curator of the Medieval/Renaissance department
at the Musée des Arts décoratifs
- Roger Boulay, chargé de mission of the Direction des Musées
de France for the Oceanic collections
- Ménéhould du Chatelle, head of cultural heritage at Hermès
- Hanah Chidiac, assistant curator at Musée du Quai Branly
- Étienne Féau, chief curator at the Centre de recherche
et restauration des musées de France
- Viviane Huchard, general curator, director of the Musée national
du Moyen Âge, Thermes et hôtel de Cluny
- Katia Kukawka, heritage curator
- Pascal Mongne, art historian, Americanist,
lecturer in "Arts des Amériques" at the Ecole du Louvre
- Christiane Naffah, chief heritage curator, head of construction
of collections at the Musée du Quai-Branly
- Véronique Schiltz, associate researcher
in "Eastern and Western Archaeologies" (ENS ULM)

DESIGNER
Christian Rizzo

LIGHTING
Cathy Olive

The book and exhibition would not have been possible
without generous help and loans from the following curators,
museums, institutions, fashion houses, galleries, artists,
and collectors, to whom we extend our heartfelt thanks:

MUSEUMS AND INSTITUTIONS

- Collection Émile Hermès, Paris
- Conservatoire des Créations Hermès, Paris
- Ethnologisches Museum, Berlin-Dahlem
- FNAC
- Metropolitan Museum of Art, New York
- Musée Christian Dior, Granville
- Musée d'Art islamique, jardin Majorelle, Marrakech
- Musée d'Ethnographie, Genève
- Musée d'Ethnographie, Neuchâtel
- Musée d'Ethnographie, Tétouan
- Musée Dar Jamaï, Meknès
- Musée d'Arts asiatiques Guimet, Paris
- Musée Dauphinois, Grenoble
- Musée de Bretagne, Rennes
- Musée de l'Évêché, Limoges
- Musée de l'Hermitage, St Petersburg
- Musée de la Castre, Cannes
- Musée de la Castre, Cannes
- Musée de la civilisation, Québec
- Musée de la coopération franco-américaine, Blérancourt
- Musée de la Cour d'Or, Metz
- Musée de La Poste, Paris
- Musée des Antiquités nationales, Saint-Germain-en-Laye
- Musée des Arts et Traditions populaires, Tunisia
- Musée des Arts et Traditions populaires, Paris
- Musée des Beaux-Arts, Angoulême
- Musée des Beaux-Arts et d'archéologie, Besançon
- Musée des Beaux-Arts, Dijon
- Musée des Civilisations, Saint-Just Saint-Rambert
- Musée des Oudayas, Rabat, Morocco
- Musée du Château, Annecy
- Musée Galliera, Paris
- Muséum, Lyon
- Musée municipal A. Bonno, Chelles
- Musée national du Moyen Âge, Thermes et Hôtel de Cluny, Paris
- Musée Thomas Dobrée, Nantes
- Musées des Beaux-Arts, Angers
- Muséum d'Histoire naturelle et d'Ethnographie, Lille
- Muséum d'Histoire naturelle, La Rochelle
- Muséum d'Histoire naturelle, Toulouse
- Museum der Kulturen, Basel
- Museum of London
- Trésor de la cathédrale de Sens
- Trésor de la cathédrale de Troyes
- UCLA Fowler Museum of Cultural History, Los Angeles

FASHION HOUSES

- Bless
- Chanel
- Christian Dior
- Christian Lacroix
- Comme des Garçons
- Emmanuel Ungaro
- Goyard
- Hermès
- Jamin Puech
- Jean-Charles de Castelbajac
- Jean-Paul Gaultier
- Jurgen Lelh
- Lamarthe
- Longchamp
- Made in Utopia
- Martin Margiela
- Moschino
- Renaud Pellegrino
- Steven & William Ladd
- Vanessa Bruno
- Vuitton
- Yohji Yamamoto

GALLERIES, ARTISTS AND COLLECTORS

Christian Astuguevielle, Ballet Atlantique, Barbara Berger Cohen, Matali Crasset, Ina Delcourt, Karine Develay, Dominique Fiat, Galerie Yves Gastou, Françoise Lacroix, Stéphane Marcault, Hikaru Miyakawa, Marie Potvin, Raumtaktic & Post Theater

We would like to thank the following for their invaluable help:

Mohamed Abdeljalil el Hajraoui, Claude Allemand-Cosneau, Christine Athenor, Odile Babin, Isabelle Bardies-Fronty, Peter Barnet, Hervé Bathellier, Abderrazzak Ben Chaâbane, Béji Ben Mami, Pierre Bergé, Marla Berns, Christine Besson, Elizabeth Bonnel, F. Borel, Matthias Böttger, Monique Bussac, Peggy Canovas, Marie-Anne Capdeville, Marie-Andréme Chabon, Julien Chapuis, Christian Charamond, Antonia Charlton, Régine Chopinot, John Clark, Dominique Clémenceau, Michel Colardelle, Donald Cole, Christine Colin, Pascal Collet, Michel Coté, Marc Coulibaly, Marie Cuadros Pouget, Pierre Dalous, Roxanne Danset, Marie-Louise de Clermont Tonnerre, Xavier de la Selle,

Jean-Paul Desroches, Erica Deuber Ziegler, Georg Dressler, Laure du Pavillon, Jean-Claude Duclos, Jean-Luc Dufresne, Michèle Dunand, Carine Durand, Hafsa el Hassani, Fabienne Faluel, Francis Fichot, Didier Filoche, Géraldine Fonteilles, Max Friedmann, Coralie Gauthier, Andrée Gendreau, Marika Genty, Hayat Guettat, Desiree Heiss, François Hubert, Isabelle Jamin, Barbara Jeauffroy, Catherine Join Dieterle, Olivier Josserand, Sophie Jugie, Peter Junge, Ines Kaag, Christian Kaufmann, Sarah Kennington, Yoon Kyung, Mylène Lajoie, Touria Lamsaouri, Stéphane Laverrière, Cécile Le Faou, Philippe le Moult, Patrick Le Nouëne, Marie-Christine Lebascle, Rénilde Lecat, Leyla , Bruno Lobé, Christine Lorre, Stefanie Losacker, Xavier Luchesi, Mallory Marcourel, Jean-Philippe Martin, Annika Mc Veigh, Véronique Notin, Nathalie Ours, Henri Pailler, Patrick Perin, Soizic Pfaff, Mikhail Piotrovski, Sylviane Pochstein-Bonvin, Jean-Philippe Pons, Charlotte Potin, Michèle Prélonge, Benoît Puech, Éric Pujalet-Plaa, Bertrand Radigois, Bénédicte Rolland-Villemot, Pascal Roman, William Saadé, Jacques Santrot, Lydwine Saulnier-Pernuit, Patrick Scalon, Max Schumacher, Selosack, Jean-Michel Signoles, Stéphane, Marc Stoltz, Claire Stoullig, Laurent Suchel, Eric Tibush, Sylvie Toupin, Françoise Vallet, Ninian Hubert van Blyenburgh, Marie-Lucie Véran, David Verhulst, Lionel Vermeil, Marie-Bénédicte Verspieren, Nathalie Vidal, Marie Wallet, Marie Wurry, Père Zirnhelt

We would especially like to thank:

Marie-José Guigues, Jocelyne Imbert

Finally, this work could not have been successfully completed without:

Françoise Berretrot, Veronica Cereceda, Stéphane Deschamps, Yves Desfossés, Vincent Durand-Dastès, Françoise Labaune, Aurore de Lignières, Véronique Montembault, Dominique Quessada, Martine Plantec, Nicole Meyer Rodrigues, Philippe Sebert, Pierre Thion

There is of course the bag.
(Looking at bag.) *The bag.* (Back front.) *Could I*
enumerate its contents? (Pause.) *No.* (Pause.)
Could I, if some kind person were to come along and ask,
What all have you got in that big black bag, Winnie?
give an exhaustive answer? (Pause.) *No.* (Pause.)
The depths in particular, who knows what treasures.
(Pause.) *What comforts.* (Turns to look at bag.)
Yes, there is the bag. (Back front.) *But something tells me,*
Do not overdo the bag, Winnie, make use of it of course,
let it help you... along, when stuck, by all means,
but cast your mind forward, something tells me, cast your
mind forward, Winnie to the time when words must fail
– (she closes eyes, pause, opens eyes) *and do not*
overdo the bag. (Pause. She turns to look at bag.)
– Perhaps just one quick dip.

Samuel Beckett, *Happy Days,* 1963

Madeleine Renaud in **Happy Days** *by Samuel Beckett*, 1964, photograph by Thérèse le Prat

Conversation about bags....

By Hélène David-Weill, President of the Central Union of Decorative Arts and Jean-Louis Dumas, President of Hermès

1) **Jean-Louis Dumas**: You have to be careful of the bag, it is so familiar yet so badly understood... Having created, sold, revived and restored them for many years in Hermès, I thought I knew everything about them. I truly thought that I knew all the ins and outs concerning bags. I could describe some of our models without forgetting a single stitch of waxed linen, the loop open so that I can see they are *valorous* – a word one of our foremen likes to use – to check that the underside and topside are the same, cleancut, that the pouches are not stiff, the handles when held are soft and strong, handles that the painstaking work of an artisan's fingers may have spent two hours sewing.

2) **Hélène David-Weill**: When we decided that the Central Union of Decorative Arts and Hermès would work together, we had no doubt that it would be a wonderful adventure, filled with new experiences. The extraordinary beauty of bags from Papua New Guinea comes to mind. It was such a wonderful surprise, a bit like Alice's experience in *Through the Looking Glass*, to discover that the bag, ancient and useful, at the service of human beings to transport all they require, is in fact indescribable, libertarian, and escapes all the constraints and definitions available in our illustrated encyclopaedias. It is the most diverse and prolific of accessories, and never ceases to amaze us.

3) **Jean-Louis Dumas**: It's a story in itself! This exhibition and the book that accompanies it is, for us, yet another chapter in the story that links the artisan of fine leather goods in Paris to the bag. It is a story that has kept Hermès on the cutting edge for almost a century, flowing with ideas, punctuated with observations and ongoing research, patience and invention, changing with the times and the circumstances, with a sense of psychology and practicality, poetry, memory and audacity, and of course forever curious. It is a tale with many twists and turns, because, as you say, the bag, like a good storyteller, always keeps something up its sleeve, whether it be a piece of leather, canvas, feathers or hair, pearls or skin...

ill. II *"I didn't say there was nothing better"*
drawing by John Tenniel, from *Alice's Adventures
in Wonderland and Through the Looking-Glass and What
Alice Found There,* by Lewis Carroll
MacMillan and Co., Limited, St. Martin's Street, London, 1927
photograph by Philippe Sebert

4) **Hélène David-Weill:** That is what this exhibition and book are all about: to allow the bag, silent servant that it is, to speak for itself, by associating it with many specialists from the profession who have allowed us to exploit all its different facets, past and present.

ill. II **A bilum bag
for personal objects and betel nuts**

Papua New Guinea
Sepik region, Yuat river, 1959
bark cord string bag
top with cones and fragments
of large volute shells
Museum der Kulturen
Basel, Alfred Bülher collection

Mountain-dwellers in the center of the country live a long way from the sea, so shells like these are a highly prestigious reflection of their owner's savoir-faire and network of alliances.

5) **Jean-Louis Dumas:** Throughout this joint adventure, there has been so much emotion, moving encounters, mysterious meetings. For example the rider from the Asian Steppes who is so like Winnie with her frail figure in *Happy Days* by Becket, wonderfully enacted by Madeleine Renaud. You ask yourself what could these two possibly have in common? Both own almost nothing apart from their bags, an essential and reassuring companion in such existential solitude. Their hands slip into their bags feverishly, taking out of all the mess within, futile or decisive accessories, the inventory of their entire lives... An entire life, thirty years spent behind a shop till in Faubourg Saint-Honoré. It was a bit like this for Madame Baron, a cashier in Hermès, when she saw her worn handbag filling out like a balloon with the day's takings. For her it is a treasure and when she retired she decided to make Hermès a gift of it.

7) **Jean-Louis Dumas**: King's bags, or the rough pillows of vagabonds, the bag of Diogenes who gave up everything except his bag, vanity cases or working girl's bags, top-models' or vamps' bags, women's or men's briefcases, writers' and diplomats' valises, bags of fables and gods, riders' bags and car bags, hunters' bags, beggars' bags or merchants' bags, a plumber's, sailor's or schoolboy's bag, works of art preserved by museums, bags of anthropological or sociological use, gracious trinkets on a pretty shoulder or freed wrists, bags that are beautiful to look at, to touch and smell, they are all there. It's an amazing sensation! Twisting and turning, straps of all shapes and sizes intermingling!

6) **Hélène David-Weill**: When you suggested the project to the Musée de la Mode et du Textile, of emphasising the importance of meetings and people in order to discuss bags from the four corners of the planet, we were immediately convinced that we should take part in this exciting venture. It was high time to give homage to an accessory that is used all over the world since the beginning of time. Whether playful or intelligent, the bag completes the human body by decorating it, marrying itself to its curves and crevices, using a wide diversity of materials to envelop, lock or elegantly present the treasures it is required to carry. A bag has a million and one ways of being flexible but solid to protect the fragile belongings of its owner. When you open it, layers of life, intimate, past and present are to be found: ancestors' bones, souvenirs of loved ones returned to the earth, or a sleeping baby, all the future dreams carried within the soothsayer's bag.

8) **Hélène David-Weill**: I believe we both share the same desire: that all these bags inspire artisans everywhere to continue to add shapes, materials and new ideas to the world of the bag so that it will never cease to reinvent itself.

ill. iv **Shelter between Sefar and Jabbaren in Tinassoutine**, rock painting from Tassili, Algeria, undated

AUTHORS

Soumana Abdouramane, Advanced Graduate in Cultural
Heritage Management, Development and Promotion
of Tourism department, Ministry of Tourism and Crafts, Niger

Gabrielle Baglione, Curator of the Lesueur collection,
Museum d'Histoire naturelle, Le Havre

Edmond Bernus, Ph. D., geographer, Emeritus Research Director
at the Institut de recherche pour le développement
(IRD, ex-ORSTOM, Office de la Recherche Scientifique
et Technique Outre-Mer) *

Monique Blanc, Curator of the Medieval/Renaissance department
at the Musée de la Mode et du Textile

François Blary, Doctor of History and Medieval Archaeology,
archaeologist. Director of the Heritage Department,
Ville de Château-Thierry

Ménéhould du Chatelle, Head of Cultural Heritage at Hermès

Jean-Pierre Chaumeil, Research Director at the CNRS
(Amerindian Ethnology research team)

Farid Chenoune, fashion historian

Thomas Clerc, Assistant Professor of Modern
and Contemporary French literature, Université de Paris-X Nanterre

François Dagognet, philosopher

Emmanuel Désveaux, Director of Studies at the Ecole des hautes
études en sciences sociales, Project Director for Education
and Research at the Musée du quai Branly

Danielle Elisseeff, researcher at the Ecole des hautes études
en Sciences Sociales, lecturer in General History of Chinese
and Japanese art at the Ecole du Louvre

Étienne Féau, African Art historian, chief curator at the Centre
de recherche et de restauration des musées de France

Catherine Gouédo, Conservation Assistant in the
Medieval/Renaissance department at the Musée des Arts décoratifs

Laurent Goumarre, critic

Vivianne Huchard, General Curator, Director of the Musée national
du Moyen Age, Thermes et hôtel de Cluny

Kimiko Jurgenson, author of children's books

Djeli Mamadou Kouyaté, griot

Katia Kukawka, Heritage Curator

Stéphane Laverrière, assistant to the Emile Hermès Collection

Christine Martin, designer/editor, Co-Chief Editor
of La lettre du cinéma

Pascal Mongne, art historian, Americanist, lecturer
in "the Arts of the Americas" at the Ecole du Louvre

Charlotte Potin, assistant at the Conservatoire des Créations Hermès

Axelle Ropert, filmmaker, screenwriter, Co-Chief Editor
of La lettre du cinéma

Olivier Saillard, director of programming at the Musée
de la Mode et du Textile

Claude Savary, ethnologist

Véronique Schiltz, Associate Researcher
in "Eastern and Western Archaeologies" (ENS Ulm)

Marc Stoltz, responsable du Conservatoire des créations Hermès

Anne-Marie Vié-Wohrer, ethnohistorian, specialist in manuscripts
from the pictographic tradition of Central Mexico, Senior Lecturer
at the Université de Paris 8

* In July 2004, a few days before this book went to press, we learned of
the death of Edmond Bernus. We shan't forget his rather brusque kindness
and sensitive erudition.   F.C.

TRANSLATION

Carol Brick, Gail de Courcy-Ireland, Sally Laruelle, Juliet Mattila,
Robin Magowan, John O'Toole, Charles Penwarden, John Tittensor

REVISION

Natasha Edwards, Randy Holden, Gillian O'Meara, Elisabeth Robinson

CONTENTS

ill. 1 **Filippino Lippi**
Three archangels and Tobias

painting illustrating an episode
from the Bible, taken from the Book
of Tobias, Turin, Sabauda Gallery

The archangel Raphael tells Tobias
to catch the fish that had attacked
him in the waters of the river Tigris,
then guides Tobias and his faithful
dog to his cousin Sara, the victim of
a demon who killed her seven former husbands. On the evening of
his wedding to Sara, Tobias grills the
fish's heart and liver, whose smell
chases the demon away. Tobias
returns to his blind father's house
with his new wife, and restores the
old man's sight by smearing his eyes
with fish gall.

INTRODUCTION

ill. 2 **Egyptian wooden cosmetics spoon**
representing a naked woman
carrying an unguent vase and a bag with
lily petals, New Kingdom
Paris, Musée du Louvre

MAGIC BAGS FARID CHENOUNE

There's something odd about devoting an exhibition and a book to bags. Because the object itself is rather odd. A strangeness that arises from examining everyday use up close. The bag is one of the most widely used things in the world, probably the oldest and most universal object invented by Mankind as a way of transporting other objects—in the hand, on the arm, over the shoulder; in other words, within reach. This satellite object is so present, so obvious, that we often forget its singular existence. If the purpose of the bag is to transport all the little things of our lives, it is also more than that. Through it, life itself is conveyed, its realities and dreams, its harshness and illusions, its habits and utopias. The peasant in early rural society carries seeds, a guarantee of future crops. A bag is money, the purse strings, the safeguard of good fortune. For the African *griot*, it is the power of language, a bag of words. The Native American shaman's bag carries the creation myths of the tribe and is a link with the sacred. The craftsman puts his working tools, his expertise, and his professional secrets in his bag. And, as we know, the talent of a cunning man is to always be able to pull something new out of his bag of tricks.

Tricks, secrets, rites, wealth, and ceremony: the bag is therefore a microcosm of the values, tensions, beliefs, and conflicts of life in society. This book is a mosaic, examining the immense variety of shapes, the diverse materials, the luxurious details, the complex designs, the multitude of ways to carry a bag, and the sheer wealth of bags, through an overview of civilizations

ill. 3 **Attic red-figure cup**

Brygos Painter, circa 480 BC
Oxford, Ashmolean Museum

This young boy at the palaestra
is holding a net bag containing
knucklebones – a token of seduction.
The seducer – tutor? – is busy
with other games; he has put down
his stick, sponge and strigil,
and pushed back his cloak.

and a multifaceted approach to history, ethnology, archeology, aesthetics, and linguistics. Bags illustrate and identify diverse modes of perception, understanding, use and symbolization of the world, from delicate medieval marriage pouches illuminated with courtly scenes, through the beaded fabric bags of the Yoruba *babalawos* (priests) in Africa, whose colors seem to have emerged from the bottom of the ocean, and the *bilums* of Papuan sorcerers filled with bones, to the frivolous long-stringed reticules of the late 18th century, the first incarnation of the modern fashion bag.

There is also an astonishing permanence of certain forms, materials, and production techniques. Pouches, two-handled baskets, bundles, and string bags, to name just a few, pass from one period or one cultural environment to another. Bécassine's knotted bundle is similar to the bundles used by Pre-Columbian peoples to transport their gods. Just as the "four-knotted trunk" used by journeymen locksmiths as they set out on their apprenticeship tour through France[1] is similar to the Japanese *fukusa*, a square of silk that became a *furoshiki* once it was knotted, in which a visiting lady carried a gift intended for her hostess.

The carry-all bag, another quintessential archaic bag, has the ingenious architecture of a snare. It is flexible, almost fluid, and lends itself docilely to the odd shapes its holds: fat or sharp objects, bizarre volumes. They range from the knucklebone sacks carried by schoolchildren in ancient Athens to the *bilum* of Papua New Guinea, with its large openwork knit, and the much-loved shopping bag in the 1950s. The latter was elevated to the status of an *haute couture* accessory by Jean-Paul Gaultier in 2002 in a discreetly nostalgic tribute to a long lost, popular Parisian tradition. Something close to a repertory of archetypes developed intuitively with these overlaps and influences. The most recent of these archetypes could very well be the plastic bag; indeed, Martin Margiela adopted the model to create his white cotton shopping bag, a tribute, he says, to the now universal simplicity of this bag fashioned as a tank top.

THE POCKET, THE COFFER, THE BAG

I picked up my bundle: two shirts, two handkerchiefs, a half-loaf of bread, a notebook of songs, and as this was already a difficult process, without a word I left my traveling companions, pimps, hoods, thieves sentenced to three years, five years, ten years, or the banished, the crooks.

Jean Genet, *Miracle of the Rose*, 1947

What is a bag? Short of answering the question as simply as Jean Genet picked up his bundle, we could assess the unique character of the bag by comparing it to other objects used for similar purposes. A bag is not a solitary satellite. It is part of an invisible and complex dynamic with other objects, two in particular: the pocket and the coffer. All three, in different ways, are extensions, continuations of the individual.

A pocket is invisible, it is part and parcel of an item of clothing; it maintains an intimate relationship with the body that makes it almost an external anatomical appendage. The reason women did not carry bags for such a long time is precisely because they carried all their necessary items in independent cotton pockets under their dresses, sewn to a girdle tied around their waists. The pocket goes where we go, follows our movements, is mobile and supple. Bags often have the same suppleness and limpness as pockets. Indeed, in Toulouse, a bag is still called a "pocket" to this day. At the other extreme, the coffer or strongbox is hard and unmoving. It does not travel and is only taken out on rare occasions. It is confined to the home, often far from prying eyes, where it safeguards the precious, durable valuables that we don't need in the immediate future: seeds, savings, family objects, important papers. Bags some-times adopt the protective hardness of the strongbox; they can also be thick, stiff, hermetic, silent, and secretive.

The bag is both pocket and strongbox, yet neither of the two. It is not attached to the body or clothing like the former, nor rooted to the home like the latter. Its home port is its owner, it enjoys an independence that the others do not: it can (or not) be taken along easily. But, just as much or even more than this practical availability, the unique nature of the bag lies elsewhere: in its visibility. Of the three, only the bag is visible. The pocket, invisible, can only be guessed at; the bag, however, is on display, and, in the process, reveals that it holds something that it won't reveal. A bag is both the inside and outside.[2] The multiple social, societal, magical, religious, and erotic powers invested in the bag – and here again, its quasi-universality – resides in this dialectic of the visible and invisible, what is presented for view (without, however, being seen) and what is concealed.

SHALL WE OPEN IT?

She had no more money, and a terrible desire for a handbag.
Louis Aragon, *Residential Quartiers*, 1936

The handbag is a perfect example of this dialectic of showing that we have something that we will not show. Even if it is holding nothing, this nothing is a secret, something forbidden. The word "handbag" is just over a hundred years old, and in the 20th century the term spread as fast as the object itself became accessible to every social class. In Western culture, the handbag became an essential part of women's attire: the sign of a new independence, that of coming and going at will, of being able to leave home without answering to anyone. Indeed, fashion designers and labels soon set their sights on the handbag, once they understood that they were too lucrative and valuable to be left in the hands of the fine leather-makers.

With the handbag, we are brought around to the pertinent question of the sex of things, or rather the things of sex, those things that are the specific domain of each sex, the implements one needs to succeed most fully in one's gender, as you would succeed at your job: to be a woman, to be a man. The handbag-toolbox is a box of femininity; it contains personal instruments, the private objects of women, their intimate world. Like a detachable prosthetic device, it is as much a fetish as a secondary sexual attribute. It both attracts and repels, like an inviolable sanctuary, into which no foreign hand has the right to penetrate. You can't dig around in a woman's handbag, even with your eyes.

And anyway, what would you find? Showing that you have something that you won't show: but what is this something?

In the dual movement of the theatricality of the self and the revelation of the self that has marked recent decades, the handbag has become a stage of choice. Everything—transparent bags, X-rayed bags, celebrity handbags inventoried in magazines—rests on this illusion that the true nature of a woman lies within her handbag.[3] It's an illusion, as a mere list of the contents reveals nothing of the secrets of a handbag, no more than an autopsy offers a key to the mystery of a human being. Perhaps we need to look at the concept from another angle: what lies at the bottom of the bag is not the truth, but the illusion of a woman, her mirage, her impossible utopia, the enigma of her own femininity. Like Mary Poppins' suitcase, a woman's handbag is bottomless. This also explains all the gab about the bag, along with the burning desire to blurt out the magic formula from *The Arabian Nights*, with the unrealistic hope of finally figuring it out: "Bag, open sesame!"

1   Fernand Fillon, *Le Serrurier*, 1942, p. 34.
2   See Gaston Bachelard's analysis of the dialectic of inside and outside, in *La Poétique de l'espace*, Paris: Presses Universitaires de France, 1957.
3   See also the inventories of custom-made women's bags by watercolor artist Nathalie Lecroc as part of her "Petite Anthologie des sacs et sacs à main." This anthology includes 1001 inventories (*Libération*, January 24-25 2004).

carrying on

fashion

consumption

me

brand

pleasure

shopping

fetishism

hypermarket

intimacy

diversion

creation

collection

ill. v ***Remark on window-gardening***, Erik Dietman, 1965-66, plexiglass, screw, leather, Dominique Fiat collection, numbered copy 28/50

ill. vi **Urban scenes, view no 7,** 1997-2000, photograph by Denis Darzacq

ill. vi **Paris, 1967,** photograph by Raymond Depardon

ill. VII **House Bag,** Moschino, Spring/Summer 2003, leather, bamboo, beige interior, Moschino Italy collection

ill. VIII **Telephone bag** (accessories collection Spring/Summer 1996), **chess castle bag, armchair bag** (accessories collection Fall/Winter 1996-97)
Christian Astuguevielle for Nina Ricci, suede kid cover on a resin and fiberglass structure, private collections

ill. IX **Copacabana bag,** Shiro Kuramata, edited by Martell, 1988, leather, painted metal handle, three drawers of varying dimensions on each side, Galerie Yves Gastou collection

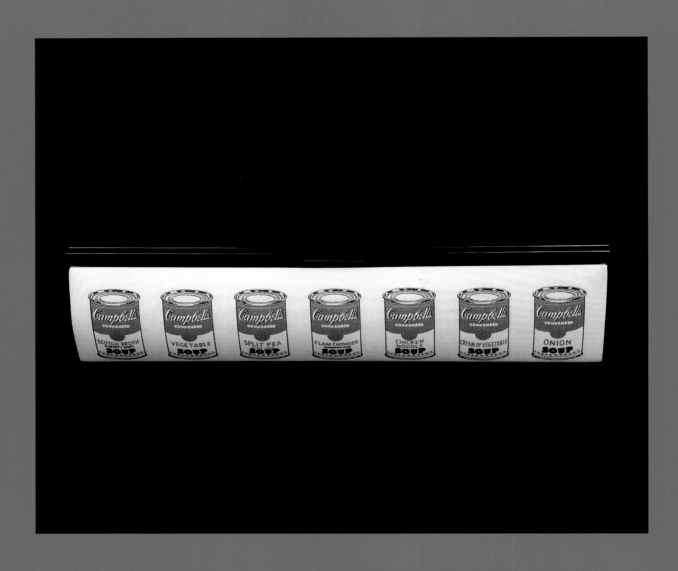

ill. x **Campbell Soup bag,** Philip Treacy, 2002, satin printed with Campbell Soup motifs in homage to Andy Warhol
interior lined in red satin printed with the same motif, lipstick case, metal clasp, private collection

ill. x **Twenty years old in Estonia**, June 1999, photograph by Claudine Doury

ill. 1 ○   opposite
Jean-Paul Gaultier glove bag
Fall/Winter *haute couture* 1998-99
black leather, pink satin interior
"Elégance parisienne" collection
Jean-Paul Gaultier

the high fashion bag

○ "Handbags – those signs of the times, those slightly mistreated little pets, those extensions of girls' hands – are witnesses to the sharing of secrets, adopted children of adorable mothers, bearers of delicious sensations."[1] Couturier Christian Lacroix readily admits that every collection he produces can be summed up as a bag: like pictograms of the seasonal succession of fashion parades in all their baroqueness or oddity, handbags are a small-format encapsulation in leather and ornament of what makes the latest collection tick. A hieroglyph of fabric, skin, and gold, each bag seems to open with infinite delicacy onto that distinctive, poetic world of haute couture.

Yet realism demands that this "extension of girls' hands", hatched by the couturier with stitching like some hasty sketch on paper, not be allowed to obscure the economic imperatives. A prisoner of its world's stylistic meanders, the fashion bag constantly runs the risk of staying permanently closed, and this at a time when its market presence makes it a vital accessory – to its maker's survival. From a 20th century that saw the disappearance of once-crucial satellite objects – parasols, fans, gloves (short or long, day or evening), muffs, and hats, little or big: all those accessories that have, so to speak, gone out the dressing-room window – the bag is the orphan survivor. It has managed to stay on the female wrist and even found its way onto the male shoulder. This means the prospect of vast sums of money, just as in the business of making and marketing cosmetics. Paradoxically for an object long forced to hide beneath petticoats and breeches, the bag enjoys an odd relationship with the visible, the invisible, and the intimate, evolving towards overexposure as the maker's mark on a wardrobe that no longer needs to flaunt itself.

ill. 2 ○   **Pair of detachable pockets**

France, circa 1910
white lawn, white cotton braid belt
Musée de la Mode et du Textile
UFAC collection
Chappée donation

ill. 3 ○   **Black cotton
detachable pocket**

coin purse in the same material
witha metal clasp, belt string
France, circa 1910
Musée de la Mode et du Textile
UFAC collection
Frantz-Jourdain donation

Purses, pouches, wallets, and pokes succeeded each other or lived side by side in the Middle Ages, when all sort of variations and ornaments could be tried out within a relatively static formal context. With the upper body corseted in rich fabrics, there was no choice but to externalize the containers that we're so fond of accumulating and dressing up with. Men and women wore purses, but the true ancestor of the handbag would seem to be the drawstring or flap-top *aumônière*, or alms purse. The latter may indeed have been designed to hold alms, but its function evolved as all sorts of objects eagerly sought refuge inside. Especially welcoming to keys, combs, scissors, jewelry, and tweezers, the *aumônière* "launched the jumble of precious and personal items"[2] in need of a container for everyday moving-about. There was, also, the belt-pouch, whose sophisticated versions, striving to outdo each other in the daring and imagination of their hinges and clasps, could end up looking like Gothic buildings or monumental sculptures. This taste for singularity, rarity, and eccentricity, which heralded in form and function the coming of the 20th-century fashion bag, hung on through the 15th century; but the 16th ushered in 300 years of hesitations, furtive entries, and even total exits on the costume scene.

The sheer voluminousness of clothes during this period meant endless little storage gimmicks and made the worn or carried bag superfluous. If the inside of a puffed sleeve, a hat or breeches didn't suffice, then the muff worn by both men and women would do the job. While the male silhouette became progressively slimmer in the 17th century and even more so in the 18th, thus generating external pockets with large flaps, the feminine wardrobe squeezed the torso, the better to spill generously outwards from the waist down, leaving little scope for improvised storage. It was out of this sartorial context that emerged the long-lived detachable pocket, made of patterned linen, cotton or, even, silk and fixed to the belt with a string. Access, via a slit in the upper skirt and underskirt, required an impish movement perfectly in keeping with the times. Each one a concealed, intimate drawer, these pockets – whose variants lived on into the 20th century beneath the skirts of governesses and housekeepers – are classed by many historians as underwear. Yet, even when hidden, they remain the ancestors of the modern bag: it was at the end of the 18th century that the cut and degree of transparency of women's dresses saw those internal pockets move outwards. While the strong point of the Middle Ages had been surface innovation and variation constant enough for contemporary fashion to continue to appeal, the pocket drove home the need for a "mixed bag" approach that would be closely related to social and cultural change over the two centuries to come.

the reticule and after

When not totally absent from the fashion magazines that made their appearance in the 19th century, pictures of handbags were so rare that the article in an April 1908 issue of *Fémina* has a touch of the pioneer to it.[3] Drawing attention to the revival of the reticule in forms quite different from those of its ancestors, the columnist takes an overview of the evolution of the handbag, which as early as 1901 *Fémina* had described as "an everyday item".[4] Using illustrations of well-known actresses with bags, the two-page article is the first of its kind in the feminine press in which the text can be described as being as influential as the images. Here we have a clear indication of how necessary the fashion bag was at the beginning of the century, even if some of the historical detail is a little cavalier. Interesting, too, is the connection between "reticule" – from the Latin *reticulum*, the little net carried by Roman ladies – and the "ridicule" suffered by those who first dared to carry their pockets in their hands.

The article's author is right on target in pinpointing the years of the Directoire (1795-99) as the birthdate of the kind of bag then coming back into fashion: "While the dresses of the *merveilleuses* [the trendy ladies of the time] reflected the whims of fashion, the bag reflected its very rationale."[5] The fit and transparency of dresses harking back to the simplicity of antiquity meant that pockets had to go; the logical consequence, as it was later with the new silhouette of the early 20th century, was the handbag. Rounded and slim, the handbag was back after a period of partial disappearance into the depths of crinolines. Like the *merveilleuses*, the women of the early 1900s carried their reticules low, in the interests of a slim silhouette.

ill. 8 ○ **Jean Béraud**
*La sortie des ouvrières de la Maison
Paquin, rue de la Paix*
1898, Paris, Musée Carnavalet

So the reticule reappeared twice at female fingertips after long periods of absence or of invisibility hidden in the depths of the underskirt. It's worth pointing out here that the Directoire years and the first decade of the 20th century saw the return of the reticule in an overall context driven by barely concealed nostalgia. In both cases, fashion was caught up in a cyclical process, drawing unrestrainedly on its own roots as a source of inspiration. Inspired by the antique *reticulum* and by memories of the *aumônière* or the waist-pouch, the reticule as ancestor of the fashion bag seems to have created itself from its own past. The impatience of the 20th century and the internationalization and structuring of fashion, which saw the number of couturiers double, the specialist press flourish, and the market expand, gave the handbag new status as an absolute necessity. Superfluously indispensable, usefully frivolous, the fashion bag in the host of forms the century would bring achieved real authority with the end of World War I and advances in feminine independence. A practical companion that rounded off the image of a determined woman – one totally unlike the subject of that 1908 article – the fashion bag laid the groundwork for its own modernity in the 1920s, with the appearance of the clutch bag, a kind of envelope that represented an extreme radicalization of the notion of a container. And the coming of the zipper – the Hermès reaction to the functionalist imperatives of the time – would likewise have an influence to be universally reckoned with.

the 1920s clutch bag: austere perfection

"But it's so infuriating, this lack of pockets in skirts that are too close-fitting, and all the precious things you lose – purse, notebook, handkerchief – that you end up resigned to the handbag, day and night. Wealthy women are still holding out – they can put all their bits and pieces in the car; but the others have made up their minds and the current thing is the handbag."[6] As the *Fémina* article indicates, the still-young 20th century was totally taken up with transporting "bits and pieces" and had made its decision: the appropriate accessory was designed to suit specific activities, the time of day and, in the evenings, the fortress of elegance that was the woman of the time. Yet can we see it actually freeing womankind of part of her burden? Hatted, gloved, bejeweled, corseted, and buried under kilometers of skirt, the elegant woman also had to hold her parasol, rearrange her hair, and hold up her hem to make walking easier. In a fashion landscape inhabited by such unreal creatures, holding a bag on your wrist to show off the strap was a veritable stylistic feat. So in 1911 the "all-purpose muff"[7] came back on the scene, with the same two functions as its ancestor: protecting your hands from the cold and holding everything you might put into a bag. "There's room for the lot: mirror, face powder, rouge, and even your purse."[8] It was "new and practical – it's so awkward going out with a bag and a muff. The muff-bag eliminates one of these accessories and the bother of having to carry it, not to mention the danger of losing it."[9]

ill. 9 ○ **Otto Dix**
Three Prostitutes in the Street
1925, Hamburg, private collection

ill. 10 ○ **Hermès muff bag**
France, circa 1930
calfskin decorated with cork, seal fur
interior lined with lambskin
muff lined with black satin
Paris, Musée de la Mode et du Textile
UCAD collection
Dreyfus-Barney bequest 1975

ill. 11 ○ **Madeleine Vionnet clutch bag, model 10133**

France, 1931
Documentation Center
of the Musée de la Mode
et du Textile

ill. 12 ○ **Madeleine Vionnet clutch bag, model 10134**

France, 1931
Documentation Center
of the Musée de la Mode
et du Textile

ill. 13 ○ **Clutch bag,** attributed
to the architect Robert Mallet Stevens

circa 1930
Documentation Center
of the Musée de la Mode
et du Textile

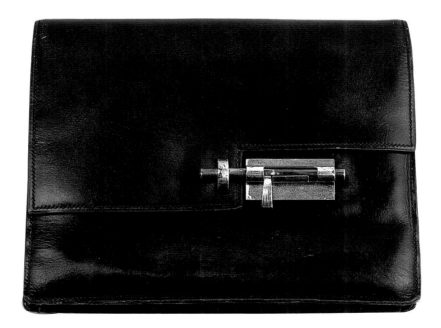

ill. 14 ○ **"Bolt" clutch bag**
that belonged to Ultra Violet
muse and friend of Andy Warhol

Hermès, 1938, black calfskin
dipped lambskin, silver clasp
collection of the Conservatoire
des Créations Hermès
gift of Ultra Violet

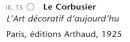

ill. 15 ○ **Le Corbusier**
L'Art décoratif d'aujourd'hu
Paris, éditions Arthaud, 1925

Despite these recommendations, the muff, ever bigger and more voluminous, never managed totally to eclipse the mobile marvel that was the handbag; however its convenience and ease of carrying had a distinct influence on the simplification of bags after World War I and the flat, clear-cut shape that reached its most radical form with the bags used by the flappers. Some clutch bags also had a flap on the reverse side: this revived the gesture of slipping something into an envelope and kept the muff's ease of storage while doing away with its furry shapelessness.

During the War "the dance card was replaced by the ration card"[10] and the new peacetime silhouette bore no resemblance to that of the beginning of the century. Comfort, spareness, and sobriety were the dress requirements of women who had no intention of giving up the social and professional advances they had won 1914-18. Short hair, flat chests, and skimpy dresses simplified down to squares of fabric held up by the shoulders: such were the defining factors of a trend often criticized as poverty-stricken. But as clothing abruptly went geometrical, the bag experienced the biggest change in its history. The clutch bag was the perfect complement to the purity of the square and an uncompromising retort to the pervasive sack dress. Gripped by the upper arm or forearm, or carried in the hand in line with the body, it was a traveling showcase that flirted with the decorative arts and architecture. As a kind of portable

painting imbued with the lessons of Constructivism and Cubism, the clutch bag represented a total break with the shapes of the past. Sonia Delaunay and Jean Fouquet, in particular, knew how to get the most out of an accessory in absolute contrast with a demandingly neutral wardrobe. For as the silhouette lengthened, simplified, and blurred under the influence of colors that could be discreet to the point of downright dullness, the accessory marched ahead triumphantly: cigarette-holders, vivid ostrich-feather fans, boas, and clutch bags with areas of clear-cut color sprang full-blown from a fashion scene that provided them with the perfect setting.

Only a few years before, in 1918, Emile Hermès, grandson of Thierry Hermès, founder of the famous firm specializing in harnesses and saddles, had come back from Canada with the zip fastener used for the tops of convertibles – and applied the same principle to the bag. There can be no overestimating the influence of the "Hermès fastener",[11] which quite simply brought the bag into the modern era. Alerted by the spread of the car, this family company had decided to diversify and use the traditional saddle stitch for leather luggage and, by logical extension, collections of everyday bags of stunning simplicity. Writing in the arts review *L'Esprit nouveau* in 1925, Le Corbusier had a few harsh words to say about ornamentation: "Trash is always – and excessively – decorated. The luxury item is well made, clean of line, pure and strong, revealing its quality in its very spareness... This influx of fake wealth brings shoddiness, but worst of all is the need to decorate anything and everything: this betrays a twisted state of mind, an abominable little perversion."[12]

To drive his point home he provided photos of manufactured goods or industrial furniture embodying the supremacy of function over form – and prominent among them was a range of Hermès leatherware: bolster bags, car bags, and wallets all sang the praises of plainness and all of them looked like offshoots of the Master's functional architecture. Simple handles, simple stitching, and the best clasps you could find inaugurated a generation of clean-lined models that consigned the bag of the previous era – soft, embroidered, made of velvet or lace – to the nostalgia department. Henceforth, functional bags whose true elegance did not speak its name – abstract or unconventional clutches resembling nothing so much as contemporary works of art – provided the foundations for an accessory whose modernity was rooted in those postwar years.

ill. 19 ○ **Elegant Spanish ladies on the beach**

photograph by Marcel Delius, 1930s

evoLution speeds up

For getting on ten years the clutch bag stayed a standard item, coordinating with gloves or clothes to become a fashion accessory in its own right. Until then a few big names like Henry à la Pensée and Hermès had shared a specialist market that also included a handful of manufacturers from Paris' rue de la Chaussée-d'Antin. Louis Vuitton, famous for luxury travel goods since 1854, tried to make a go of things in soft luggage, but the Keepall (1924), the Noé (1932), and the earlier Steamer Bag (1901) never set out to compete with the frivolity of the handbag. It was in the 1930s that top couturiers began to move into what had previously been a quite separate field reserved for leatherware. Madeleine Vionnet, Jean Patou, Gabrielle Chanel, Marcel Rochas, Jeanne Lanvin, Mainbocher, and Lucien Lelong all came up with their version of the ascetic handbag, a sort of negation of what the bag had once been. Apart from styles and motifs, the clutch was a good excuse to get the firm's monogram on things. Embroidered or stamped on a clasp it was a kind of signature whose future role would be enormous. Curiously, at the time no magazine commented on this ostentatious gambit, hitherto restricted to the customer's initials. Little by little the clutch got out from under the abstract influences of its early years and began flirting with more Surrealist inspirations.

The boldest and most inspired of all was Elsa Schiaparelli, who took the bag firmly on a journey towards weird shapes and, from the 1930s onwards, played an active part in its ever-faster evolution. With her piano-shaped bag of 1939, the Chinese lantern, the lifebuoy beach bag, the glass birdcage (1936), the bouquet of flowers (1938), and the umbrella bag (1949), artifice and trompe-l'oeil were the name of the game, sparking a playful urge to consume that had nothing at all artificial about it. Other couturiers were not far behind. Marcel Rochas came up with the hardbound-book bag that would become a running gag throughout the 20th century, and 1937 saw Robert Piguet's ball-shaped bag. This proliferating zaniness attracted new names and generated a whole new trade – neither leatherware nor haute couture – just for the handbag. Roger Model, first heard of in 1933, was the most interesting figure in this new vein, with creations that quickly stood out for their elegance and originality; very soon, however, he was working for other people – Elsa Schiaparelli, Hubert de Givenchy, Christian Dior, Jacques Fath – and did so tirelessly from the 1930s through the 50s.

The World War II put a stop to the excesses of a bag more for putting down than for carrying. Economic change brought a new balance to bag ideas, with an emphasis on practicality. Sporty stuff was no longer just a fashion whim: the gamebag, a compromise between lady's handbag and shopping bag was worn slung across the body, which freed the hands and was better suited to the bicycle, making a comeback as gas became a rarity. In 1944 two women

using the brand name Fernandes Desgranges brought out a leather rucksack: the versions that filled the streets in the 1980s were straight copies. But the sporty look was too closely associated with the dark years of war, and by the 1950s it was a thing of the past. Basque-topped, wide-skirted and transformed into a luxury giraffe, woman only had eyes for the handbag that went best with the style of the time: a time when mass-produced synthetic and plastic models rubbed shoulders with classics like Chanel's 2.55 (1954) or the Kelly bag, given official consecration by its *Time* magazine cover appearance on Princess Grace's arm in 1956. More than ever the handbag was subject to the feminine state of mind, which everybody kept trying to change to keep the consumer juices flowing. The vocabulary expanded, too: raffia and straw went colored, just like the imitation leather that got tried out every which way. In the United States strange plastic boxes made their appearance, sorts of flying chests of drawers for a greedy decade. These Plexiglas bags summed up 1950s taste: kitsch that was such fun you sometimes drowned in it.

The 1950s also saw the flowering of fashion mags, but in the 60s the bag was conspicuous by its absence from editorial offices, consigned to oblivion in the interests of a youthful silhouette wanting nothing to hamper its movements. At best there were models to hang off your belt, with Courrèges providing a miniature one. Then again, sometimes it swelled to the size of a shopping bag or a vinyl holdall. The sling bag came back, too, but hung from the shoulder this time, not across the chest. And in the 70s slings were everywhere. "We've got into the habit of using just one bag right around the clock. No more changing the color to go with the clothes, no more matching sets – bag, gloves, shoes, and so on… You fine-tune your bag with what you're wearing by adjusting the length of the strap… And don't forget, while the contents of your bag tell all about your personality – and identity – the look of it reveals your idea of what's beautiful, and your lifestyle." [13] To prove it, there were full-page photos of bags everywhere you looked. Ethnic or retro, new or used, the bag was there to proclaim the values of an existence based on rejecting uniformity. And at a far remove from all this

ill. 20 ○ left
Miss Lorraine Walter
An Elsa Schiaparelli design, photograph by André Durst, *Vogue*, May 1937

ill. 21 ○ middle
The elegant wartime bag
Photograph by Serge Lieb, 1943

ill. 22 ○ right
Baby sealskin bag
Roger Model
photograph by Sante Forlano
Vogue, October 1954

left to right, top and bottom

ill. 23 ○ **The 1910s**

The reticule
Photograph by Seeberger

ill. 24 ○ **The 1920s**

Fashionable young lady
Le Touquet, circa 1925
photograph by Delius

ill. 25 ○ **The 1930s**

Mademoiselle Doudou Moss
dressed by Blanche Lebouvier
photograph by Seeberger
Bibliothèque nationale de France
(Prints and Photography)

ill. 26 ○ **The 1940s**

Journée de l'élégance à bicyclette
photograph by Lapi
Paris, June 1942

ill. 27 ○ **The 1950s**

Woman wearing a suit
photograph by Toni Frissel
for *Harper's Bazaar*
Victoria Station, London, 1955

ill. 28 ○ **The 1960s**

Vacances, Saint-Tropez
photograph by Robert Doisneau

ill. 29 ○ **The 1970s**

Saint-Tropez
photograph by Elliott Erwitt, 1979

ill. 30 ○ **The 1980s**

Urban backpack
Bruges, 1988

ill. 31 ○ **The 1990s**

Paris, 1999
Photograph by Julien Lévy

ill. 32 ○ **Hermès handbag**
(the "Kelly bag")

mat black crocodile, fastener borrowed
from the Hermès "haut-à-courroies"
travel bag, created circa 1930

This bag was adopted
by the American actress Grace Kelly,
Princess of Monaco, in 1956.
It became famous, and was officially
named the "Kelly bag" » in 1959.

ill. 33 ○ **The Chanel
"2.55" handbag**

created in February 1955
padded bag with a shoulder strap

The lining was originally dark red,
with the double C stitched like a coat
of arms, and a fine gilt rectangular
revolving clasp.

ill. 34 ○ **Lady Dior bag**

France, fine leather
Fall/Winter 1995 collection

When the Princess of Wales visited
France in September 1995,
President Jacques Chirac's wife
presented her with a new Dior
topstitched handbag in padded black
lambskin with a canework motif.
Lady Diana adopted it,
thereby contributing to the success
of the bag which was then christened
"Lady Dior".

ill. 35 ○ **Dior Saddle bag**

cotton Jacquard oblique Dior logo
new edition of the classic canvas
Dior logo, gilt finish accessory
ready-to-wear Spring/Summer 2000
fine leather collection

ill. 36 ○ **Vuitton Speedy 30 bag**

multicolored and white monogram
canvas, Spring/Summer 2003

idealism, the emphasis it received in the magazines was an indicator of the economic stakes it would represent over the two decades to follow.

The "bag that goes with everything" might have been the dictator of the 1970s, but the 1980s would bring modification and diversification as part of a fulltime process that would really bear fruit in the 1990s. Natural leather coexisted with the colored canvas used for the belt bags and beach bags that were more and more in fashion. Transparent plastic, nylon, and polyamid came off the playing field and into the urban wardrobe as sports clothing became a massively popular dress style. In 1970 sales were running at four suitcases for one bag and by 1980 it was one suitcase for two bags.[14] And by then, to gain time at the airport, one short-haul passenger in every three had stopped checking his luggage. Small, practical items appeared, kinds of detachable pockets for sticking on your clothes. All kinds of fanny packs and backpacks made movement freer and dominated an otherwise supersize decade. The evening bag was caught up in the all-pervading creative baroque, the craze for haute couture as provided by Karl Lagerfeld, artistic director at Chanel since 1983, and Christian Lacroix.

With one of those reversals so typical of a domain ever ready to contradict itself, the functional bag of the 1980s was replaced in the 90s by one more concerned with style than practicality. Never were straps so short – or, if you like, handles so long. Vuitton, Fendi, Dior – the bag looked like a 50s clutch with a shoulder-strap added for convenience. Hoisted high up under the arm, the Fendi baguette bag and Dior saddlebag expressed a new-found femininity and with it a more feminine body language.

The decade was punctuated by personalization, as bags fell victim to the customizing and limited editions Vuitton instigated by working with artists. Overtly ornamental, badge bags and image bags pointed up a yearning for the rare and the unique previously focused on jewelry – with the danger, of course, of calling too much attention to the lucrative market they depended on.

"Little purses and reticules, those handbag substitutes, might not have done much for mobility, but they did introduce, insidiously, the idea of portable privacy."[15] At a time when fashion is facing a major paradox – more and more creators for creations less and less seen outside of a few capital cities, or when produced under license – the bag seems the last acceptably wearable signature. It is the first entry into a world described to us as luxurious. Curiously, after having gone through phases of total conspicuousness, it is returning, in the hands of today's most visionary designers, to its ancestral form: the pouch. In Yohji Yamamoto's ready-

ill. 37 ○ bottom left
Dress with a large metal bag clasp

France, Yohji Yamamoto
ready-to-wear Spring/Summer 2001
Yohji Yamamoto archives collection

to-wear range for spring/summer 2001, the bag as pouch is part of the garment and can be put away inside. For Junya Watanabe (ready-to-wear, spring/summer 2003), the bag, strapped up, and looking as it if has been inflated with hydrogen, is indissociable from the dress whose contours it imitates. At Comme des Garçons (ready-to-wear, fall/winter 2003), Rei Kawakubo offers finished clothes that look like improvised bundles. Elsewhere the multipocket look is flourishing. And the message is that while the bag seems to evoke mobility, its absence is synonymous with freedom.

1 *Connaissance des arts,* special issue designed by Christian Lacroix, Paris: December 2002, p. 101.
2 Geneviève et Gérard Picot, *Le sac à main: une histoire amusée et passionnée,* Paris: Editions du May, 1993. "Un accessoire indispensable de notre toilette, qui a de nombreux ancêtres", *Fémina,* 1ᵉʳ avril 1908, p. 148-149.
3 Camille Duguet, "Du réticule à la trousse. Un accessoire indispensable de notre toilette, qui a de nombreux ancêtres", *Fémina,* April 1 1908, pp. 148-149.
4 Fanchon, *Fémina,* February 15 1901.
5 Geneviève & Gérard Picot, *op. cit.,* p. 53.
6 Fanchon, "Fanfreluches," *Fémina,* February 15 1901, p.15.
7 "Le manchon à tout faire," *Fémina,* November 1 1911, p. 578.
8 *Ibid.*
9 *Ibid.*
10 "Étrennes utiles ou futiles," *Fémina,* December 1917, p. 26.
11 In 1923 Emile Hermès obtained sole French rights for the zipper, whose success was such that soon all Paris was calling it the "Hermès fastener."
12 *L'Esprit nouveau, revue internationale illustrée de l'activité contemporaine […] Arts, lettres, sciences, Directeurs Ozenfant et Ch.-E. Jeanneret,* Paris: Editions de l'Esprit Nouveau, No 24, 1924: "1925, Expo. Arts déco: l'art décoratif d'aujourd'hui", anonymous article reprinted in Le Corbusier, *L'Art décoratif d'aujourd'hui,* Paris: Collection de l'Esprit nouveau, G. Grès, 1925, reprinted 1959, Vincent, Fréal et Cie.
13 CB, "Les sacs compléments", *Jardin des modes,* March 1970.
14 *Jardin des modes,* July/August 1980.
15 Geneviève & Gérard Picot, *op. cit.,* p. 148.

ill. 38 ○ **Martin Margiela handbag**

France, ready-to-wear Fall/Winter 2002-2003, antique hand-painted handbag with a white cotton cover presented to the public in a plexiglass box, Maison Martin Margiela Archives collection

ill. 1 ○ *My father, my mother and her handbag*
early 1960s

my Life IN 128 CUBIC INCHES

○ "Look in my handbag!" Back when I was a kid, my mother's bag was a *handbag*, a word that made it seem like the ultimate shrine to femininity. At the time, it was carried, as the name indicates, in the hand, and with it came matching gloves and shoes – in those days, plenty of shoe manufacturers took the trouble to fit in with the season's models. The fetish to end all fetishes, there was always a stack of them in the cupboard, and never completely empty: traces of her comings and goings, her nights out, her forays into department stores – the whole thing designed to really put the school-bag and its kid owner in their place. Outside of the cupboard, the *handbag* was stuffed with combinations of the incomprehensible and the unusable: checkbook (you had to be able to sign your name), billfold (how did you actually earn money?), compact (still years away from zits, I wasn't bothered by shiny nose syndrome either) and lipstick (not a word to anyone!). The road to freedom was long and bumpy. I started out lugging the cool teen knitted tote bag, with the Greek fret and the signs of the zodiac banging against my knees and getting more and more out of shape as exam time got closer. Then I went virtual, with a crisscross elastic arrangement for my study folders, a kind of zero-bag, preliminary to the big step into my life as a woman.

Bag words. Will you hold my bag a minute? Hey! Keep an eye on my bag, will you? Please open your bags at the checkout. Excuse me, miss, your bag isn't closed. And when bagsnatching was on the rise, critic Serge Daney noted that movie houses were closing down even faster.

ill. 2 ○ opposite
Steve Miller
My Mother's Purse
radiography of a Chanel bag, 1995

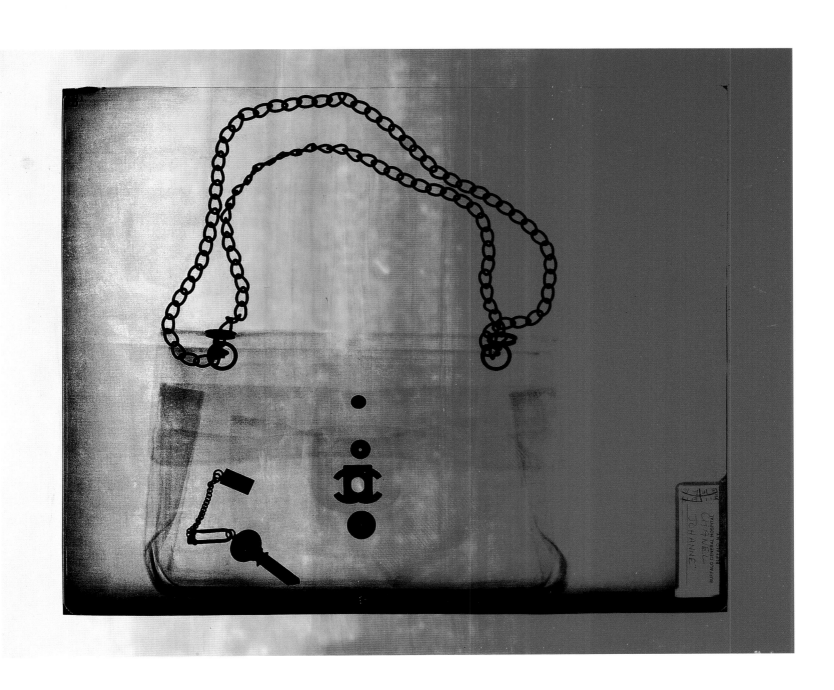

The opening exploits were dazzling: on Rue Tronchet, a big soft Bonnie and Clyde model and a brown and beige plumber's-toolbag style thing, saw me blow all the money I'd been given for my little brother and me to live on while our parents were away for two weeks. No sweat, we only liked pasta anyway. While I was at it, I filled out the collection with a fabulous emerald-green crocodile set – bag, billfold, compact – that my mother had gotten tired of. The billfold got stolen in the metro, the compact got given to Isabelle, a very beautiful friend, and my mother started keeping a close eye on her stuff: I couldn't hold onto a thing. Then the 80s: times change and saurians too. This time, it was a black lizard model with a magnetic clasp and an oh-so-delicate click, the bag closing as if by magic, no need for any pressure at all. And exactly the same size as my big black diary. Epaulettes were in, so you carried everything: tennis elbow guaranteed.

Bag drags. Where the hell did I put my bag? I'm sure I put it in this bag! I don't have it with me because I changed bags this morning. To find something that was in the bag, I'd sack the entire house.

After the handbag, the backpack. Very teen: nothing in your hands, nothing in your pockets. Positive: it's a sort of protection and keeps your back warm. Negative: when you need something, it's like getting half undressed: free one shoulder, free the other, twist your back... Now it's only for highschoolers, fabric version, slung down near the waist: not fashionable for women anymore – too *sensible*-looking. Waiting for it to come back into favor, I've made sure not to lose this one: a classic Gucci bought on the Croisette in Cannes, black suede and leather with two outside pockets and bamboo buttons. What I did lose, though, was the ultrasmart square box it came in. Stupid. And one of those typical little bag tricks: it was so pretty you didn't want it behind you, you wanted it to one side, so you could look at it now and then. So I wore it over my shoulder, hanging by the right-hand strap, which was the only bit to get pulled out of shape. And thanks to that bag, when the bamboo handle broke, I discovered the existence of a bag hospital. On Rue du Faubourg-Saint-Honoré, there's a little workshop where they pamper Italian models, and that's where I found my Gucci, curled up like a black cat in a zip-up dust cover. It still sleeps inside. Now I always keep these suedette sacks, security blankets for leather, with the brand on them in the same color as the bag.

Bag traps. The fanny bag: so hideously sensible no one can snatch it. Best when slung sexily at pelvis level, worst when it signals advanced travelers check neurosis. (My friend Sophie use to wear a fanny bag, so one day I gave her a clear plastic Miu Miu with braid edging. She meticulously chooses what she wants to put on show, and out of respect for her Prada bag, stuffs the rest in the pockets of her Zara coat.) Then there's the shopping bag: never easy. I remember recently convincing my mother – the same one who had the crocodile gear – not to go out, armed with a shapeless horror marked "Big Shopper." When it comes to shopping bags, Mary Poppins is still unbeatable.

A bag's life is a woman's life: everything summed up in a few cubic inches. So naturally you get attached. I make up my bag the day before, like a kid getting ready for school. I like a bag that can hold A4 paper without making you look like the postman. I only take the bare minimum, which as we all know, is a constantly expanding quantity. My bag used to be a mess, now it's tidy – at least that's what I think. But without me knowing it, my bag works, makes up, smokes and goes to the movies. It telephones without asking, taps out the numbers on my mobile with no help from anyone. It wears down my tampons. The keys get covered with lipstick, the pens open my mail. With a lighter inside, the bag's a potential arsonist. Year in year out, its contents and I have to make daily deals, and that's no easy matter. To know yourself is to know your bag. Inside out.

Want to look for something in your bag? The flamingo pose has a lot going for it: with one knee up to lean on, at least you can see what you're digging into. But to get something out of a bag still slung over your shoulder, you have to combine legerdemain with computerized fingertips: spot the difference in feel between the diary and the address book, not confuse the plastic cover of the driver's license with the plastic holder for your subway tickets. And so on. The slung bag demands a fast worker, with an archeologist's hands, if you're to bring up buried treasures like the ten cents needed to round off the price or the tobacco that gets under your fingernails (never enough to roll a cigarette with, though). And you have to do all this without pulling your shoulder up too high – ungainly, inelegant – or dropping it down too low, so that one of the straps falls (when it isn't your bra strap). Because once the bag strap falls, all the dead weight of the bag follows, and there you are, with the contents all over the sidewalk. (Question: why is it so hard for a right-hander to carry her bag on her left shoulder?)

That old sack magic. Stick your nose inside, breathe in hard: that inimitable, time-resistant mix of lipstick, tobacco, leather, paper. The handbag spray – the bag's very own little perfume – a bottle that won't stand up anywhere else and so has to add that subtle fragrance to your car license papers or, better still, the sandwich you bought for later on. And speaking of food: fruit if it's not too ripe, dried meat if you must, but fish – *nyet*.

My dream, frankly, is life with a bag that lets you forget its purpose – which is to contain what mustn't spill over. The bag of a more carefree life. No weight, no strings attached. A bag I could set off with in the evening, light-hearted and short-skirted. Let's try a sort out: what's the maximum minimum? A key, just one. A carefully folded bill (change is an absolute no-no). A lipstick. I can't go lower than that. At a pinch, I could skip the bag and stick them in the top of my boot. Ah, when I think of my friend Valerie, who seemed so emancipated, with everything she needed in the pockets of a heavy jacket! But how can you ignore those absolute jewels of bags, which are to the purse, what the Yorkshire terrier is to the Labrador: all those clutch bags, reticules and more. I bought a gilded satin one last summer, the last one left in the Prada factory near Florence. Take it out of its navy cover, check the shape of the opening – it's not the kind that gapes. Check the muffled sound of the velvety catch – just perfect to go dancing.

> Bag memories. Sometimes I come back to a bag I've given up, – a stain, maybe, or some microscopic fault. I take it out again, my heart goes out to it, I forget the little shortcoming that put it back on the shelf and I realize how time passes: the metro ticket has different printing, its color has faded. In an inside pocket are two tickets to the movies, colored card from the days when tickets were tickets.

Then there's always the latest bag, waiting to oust its predecessor. After a movie in Paris with Vincent the other night, around midnight I guess, there on the sidewalk, we come upon a heap of stuff that must have belonged to an old lady. A bottle of Schiaparelli's *Shocking*, some Magooly powder, a holy relic – a piece of cloth that had "touched Father Brottier", the menu from a 1978 family celebration with "Granny" written on it. And a tiny little bag, a "purse" as the English so charmingly say, when they're not using the word for a woman's pussy: a sealskin purse with all the hair gone, except for a few white bristles around the clasp, like a colonel's mustache. And inside, surprise, surprise, a pair of kid gloves, size 7: my size. Mystery woman, I'm wearing your gloves and carrying your purse.

IN PRAISE of a meta-OBJECT

INTERVIEW WITH FRANÇOIS DAGOGNET

ill. 1 ○ **Black, red,
and silver string bags**

Jean-Paul Gaultier, new edition
haute couture Spring/Summer 2002
"La Parigotte" collection
cylindrical black crystal beads
Jean-Paul Gaultier collection

ill. 2 ○ opposite
Martin Margiela boutique bag

France, used since the store opened
in 2002, white cotton cover

○ *As a philosopher of science and epistemologist, in your books you have been constantly engaged, to quote one of their titles, in "rematerializing the object".[1] Your publications include* Éloge de l'objet : pour une philosophie de la marchandise *(In Praise of the Object: for a Philosophy of Goods, 1989),* Le Corps multiple et un *(The Multiple and Single Body, 1992) and* Des détritus, des déchets, de l'abject. Une philosophie écologique *(Detritus, Waste and the Abject. An Ecological Philosophy, 1997). In a word, and quite literally, you are interested in a lot of things, including bags. But why bags?*

First, as you said, because I am interested in objects, in the most elementary and ordinary objects. But the bag has a particularity, a privilege even, in relation to other objects. It is a meta-object. It is used to carry objects but is itself not really an object. It is a higher degree of object. The others depend on it to be carried around, but in a sense it has no precise use. It is an incomparable object, a trans-object. That alone makes it worthy of attention from the objectologist – the person who specializes in things. The psychologist Pierre Janet held what he called "use of the basket" as the first manifestation, if not the origin, of intelligence. Not only does the basket allow us to carry several objects or goods from one place to another, it also makes this transportation permanent, easy and quick. "Small things discourage us", says Janet. "It takes too much time to move them around." By making it possible to carry small objects together, as if they were a single one, the basket resolves an acute contradiction. The same goes for the bag. It's a medium.

An intelligent object?

Yes, it gives concrete form to human ingenuity, the victory over objects. Think of the stick. It is the most elementary object that you could think of. The stick extends the fist because, by definition, the fist cannot reach further than the body. Moreover, it is relatively soft. The stick extends the body and, because its end is solid, hits harder. It's the same with bags. The human body cannot contain things, protect the things man needs, his treasures – for example, the farmer's seeds. These things that are important to him, well, in order both to transport and protect them, he gathers them together in a piece of cloth. And that, maybe, was the first bag.

The bundle?

That's it, the bundle!

Or, at the other end of the spectrum, the plastic bag?

The plastic bag warrants particular comment. It has contrasting properties. First of all, it would be hard to find anything finer, lighter and more flexible. But, at the same time, it can hold really heavy, bulky objects. That's why consumers appreciate it so much, because of its malleability, its capacity, its resistance to weight and its adaptability to the shape of what it holds. It is a meta-object *par excellence*. And, what's more, it doesn't wear out, even though it does reflect passing time. For it is an illusion to think that plastic bags don't age. They undergo a kind of slow oxidization, which means that they too are a part of time, a part of human lives. I'm not saying that they yellow, but that they become very slightly hazy – in a very subtle, infinitesimal, secret way. So much so, that one day, there might conceivably be a museum of plastic bags.

And the net bag?

Well, if the plastic bag can be said to have an ancestor, this is it, precisely because it is made with almost nothing, because it fits easily into a pocket; you can compress it without destroying it, because it is so light, fine and compressible. In this sense, it is like the plastic bag and unlike the great majority of other bags. And it has one other specificity. Through its holes you can see what it is carrying and protecting. You can see what's in it, and that makes it a kind of meta-object.

A moment ago you were talking about these "treasures," these things that are important to people and that the bag holds. It holds them but also, in most cases, it hides them.

There we are touching on all these actions of "hiding/showing" whose importance has been underscored by psychoanalysis. That's the other main function of the bag. The bag is at the heart of this powerful dialectic of the visible and the invisible, which is at work in human relations. By hiding things away in its depths, the bag preserves things, prevents them from being stolen and ensures that they will not deteriorate. But these same things are also going to be shown, made visible.

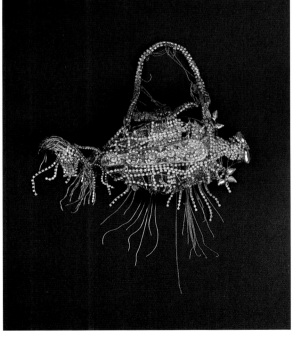

But, by carrying a bag, one is showing that one is hiding something that is kept hidden away in the bag. One is exhibiting, or at least making visible the existence, the form of a secret. This paradox does not arise with the pocket. There, invisibility is total. What distinction do you make between the pocket and the bag?

The pocket is the absolute hiding place. But I see no fundamental difference between the two.

And yet couldn't we say that in the invisibility of the pocket, in its extreme proximity, its interaction with the body, there is a kind of intimacy with the self that is very different from what occurs with the bag, which is completely outside the body, and visible?

I don't see it that way. True, the pocket is better than the bag at veiling, at not showing, but I don't think the pocket has any more "self-intimacy" or "interiority" than the bag. What is important is that both are external to the body (let's forget about the exception that are kangaroos!). As we said earlier, the human body can't contain things – it has no pockets! It is smooth, absolutely continuous; the body doesn't open, doesn't close – it makes a very poor bag.

Indeed, when we describe the body as a "bag" the metaphor is always degrading, in Western culture at least: bag of bones, old bag, scumbag… Still, it would seem that there was a time when medical vocabulary used the bag metaphor to describe certain bodily mechanisms. For example, there was the expression "lacrimal sac". As a philosopher, you too have studied medicine. What do you make of this use of the word?

When doctors talked about "bags", they were talking about the body's need to get rid of things. Its tears, its excrement, its dross – it put this in kinds of bags that it emptied as best it could. The body here was not so much a bag as a kind of cistern, or reservoir. If you think of the intestine as a bag, yes, it does use the conservation function before defecation. All that belongs to a very pestilential vision of the bag. We find traces of that in the French expression *vider son sac* [to empty one's bag], when the bag in question is full of bitterness, and bad moods. To empty one's bag is to empty the reservoir of what one has inside oneself, and usually it's pretty brackish. But the "bag-object" I am talking about here is not that. If you imagine a bag in the body, as the doctor metaphorically does, it's as if nature had preceded man and as if you took away from man the pleasure of having made something so cultural that it has no forerunner, no forebear. Yes, the body is a very poor bag.

You were talking about the smooth, irrevocably closed character of the body. Does that mean that interiority can exist only through external, intermediate objects like the pocket or bag?

Yes. If you have only interiority, you don't get anywhere, you are lost in an inert, heavy narcissism. Victory is not within, it is outside. Marx saw this very clearly, that what man makes is more important than what he is. Compared to a body that does not move, the bag is constantly changing, even only in terms of the systems for closing and opening it – the straps, buttons, zippers, press-studs, clasps and clips. Velcro, for example, is an advance that was inconceivable in the past. There are no strings to tie or untie, no time-consuming buttons, none of these systems that limited the bag to modest roles. At last, you can open it as easily as you close it – a real emancipation. That's why fashion is so important; it is the triumph of the outside and of change. Fashion bags are capable of the most subtle dialectics.

It is often said that the advent of the handbag, as we know it, is linked to the transformation of the status of woman, their newfound right to travel alone, their emancipation from the yoke of status, family and economics. Do you share this view?

Yes, I do think that the bag is linked to the development of the autonomous individual. One always gains something from throwing off obligatory inclusion in a group and dependency on that group. With my bag, I become autonomous.

From this point of view, one of the most extraordinary phenomena in fashion over the last twenty years has been the emergence and success of urban backpacks that millions of women (and men) have started wearing, like horizontal mountaineers or urban trekkers.

I can understand them! There is an element of servitude in a bag that occupies keeps your hand or arm busy. It's a further

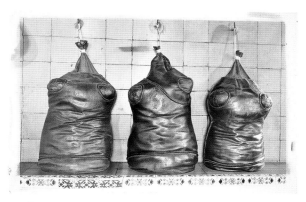

**Que le bese con los besos
de su boca mejor seran que el vino
sus amores**

Photograph
from the *Invraisemblance series*
by Ouka Lele, 1989

Alms purse

France, 1815-1830
tartan taffeta, steel frame
cut steel cabochons, taffeta ribbons
Paris, Musée de la Mode et du Textile
UCAD collection
Doisteau donation, 1925

Classic SkinBag

Olivier Goulet, latex, 2003

emancipation. Bags are getting lighter and lighter, with pouches and little compartments inside where you can put more and more things. They are that bit more conducive to movement, mobility, transport.

Like a little house on your back?

That's it! Once again, this frees us from fixity, from gravity. Where once I was stuck to the ground, tied to a place, closed in, dependent on those around me, who helped me. Now, with this bag, I can carry everything with me and move. And, with movement comes curiosity, responsiveness to the world. In this sense, the bag is more than a cultural object, it's a catalyst that transforms the culture.

Interview by Farid Chenoune, April 28 2004, Paris

1 *Rematérialiser : matières et matérialismes*, Paris: Vrin, "Problèmes et controverses" collection, 1985.

NIGERIAN CITY AND COUNTRY BAGS

○ "But where is the researcher's bag?" asked Hadiza recently, with her usual impishness. I answered my former schoolmate with a laugh and she responded in kind. "The *researcher's* bag": this clearly ironic attribution was not without importance. For we fathers in Niger, the term "bag" refers primarily to its contents: provisions of cereals such as rice, millet and corn.

As it happened, Hadiza was alluding to the bag that I had been carrying with me all through the last few months. After two long years of exile, I had come back with a diploma, a qualified "expert" in cultural heritage management, and was now applying to change ministries. I had to convince the authorities that the general education department, in which I had served for ten years, was unsuited to my new profile. The best proof of that was my freshly stamped diploma that I displayed in its container, a handsome bag, which was itself brand new – that couldn't do any harm! I had chosen it carefully, not long before I came home, and bought it for a price that, compared to my student grant, was no snip. It was a black bag with a double zip. As well as documents of every size, I could use it to keep pens, visiting cards and floppies, all in separate pouches. A real intellectual's bag!

Anyway, my efforts were successful and I was posted to the Ministry of Tourism and Trade. Now, though, carrying a bag, both morning and evening, seemed pointless; it was easier to do what everyone else did – well, all my male colleagues, anyway – and put the bag away until the next time I had the opportunity to impress someone. And there was nothing special about my situation. None of my colleagues, not even the director, came to the office with a bag, unless they had to. In most of the departments, male civil servants carry a bag only in particular circumstances; at a crucial turning point in their career. A positive turning point, mind. No one would dream of going to a job interview empty-handed. The right kind of bag is proof that its owner has class and an orderly mind. But once you've bagged the job, well...

ill. 1 ○ opposite
Officials' wives
during a ceremony

Niamey, Niger
photograph by Catherine
and Bernard Desjeux, 1978

In other professions the situation may be different: let's not lump all workers together here. Think of our poor dear teachers, for example, and their stressful working conditions: the rowdiness of the students, the draughty classrooms, the piles of work to correct. Unlike other civil servants, the teacher does not have a fixed office. Going from one class to another, how is he supposed to carry his documents, texts, chalk and other personal afflictions, without a bag? A real chore, the teacher's bag, sometimes so heavy it could dislocate your shoulder. Believe me, I've been there.

When I was a teacher, I had a leather bag. I bought it from the craftsmen's cooperative shop at the National Museum of Niger. It was new, impeccable. To go from the staff room to the classrooms you had to cross the playground, and I really enjoyed showing off in front of colleagues and students with that bag. With every hour of teaching, every school meeting, every Saturday afternoon spent in the library, my bag got a little bit heavier. But I still enjoyed carrying it. Then one day, I got caught in the rain on my way home and my treasure couldn't take it: "Soggy leather, dog's delight", murmured the students behind my back.

And the schoolchild's satchel? Torture, judging by some juvenile grimaces. And yet the kid surely picked it out from among a hundred others, admiring it on the shelves of a local bookstore or in the shops at Habou Bêné.[1] And yes, his dad dipped into his pocketbook. But let's not exaggerate. Education is for the masses, true, but some school bags are still filled with texts, learnt joyously by heart, and glowing reports.

BARBER AND CIRCUMCISER

Apart from the *mouchés*,[2] there are plenty of other socio-professional activities in which bags are carried, both in the city and in the bush. True, it's rare nowadays, to see a hunter leaving home at dawn, with his bag over his shoulder. You can fit a lot more game into the trunks of the 4WDs that belong to the new and richer race of hunters. But there is one bag you can still see on the streets of our towns; it belongs to the *wanzzam*,[3] the traditional barber whose job it is to do circumcisions.

I still have vivid memories from when I was a little boy. True, the trade is declining now, as more and more parents prefer to take their sons to medical centers for this delicate operation, but he is there at all the baptismal ceremonies and also to "make young boys pray",[4] at the express request of the family. Generally, the encounter between the young boy and the *wanzzam*, "the man with the knife", takes place in a corner of the concession. There, it is etched into the memory forever!

In the old days, the *wanzzam* did his work in the bush, well out of sight of the women, and the boys were, if I can put it like that, "delivered" to him in a bag by their own parents. Kunta Kinte, the ancestor of Alex Haley and hero of his novel *Roots*,[5] is taken to the *kintango* by his father, who first puts a hood over his head.

The *wanzzam* for the boys my age was called Houndouko. The mere mention of his name was enough to make even the rowdiest among us behave. We were terrified of Houndouko's bag. The sight of its contents (circumcision knives, dressings and accessories for initiation) was anything but a pleasure! A coarse bag, barely more refined than a cloth pouch, without the slightest decoration, and so covered in filth that you could hardly say what color it was. Whenever you met Houndouko in the street he would nearly always be carrying this lumpy "skin" that covered almost the whole left side of his body.

The *wanzzam*'s bag can still be seen in African towns today, notably among Muslims, for whom circumcision is a precondition for entry into society. However, the one used by his colleague, the excisor, seems to be reaching the end of its useful life. The campaign waged, in recent years, against female genital mutilation has borne fruit; official ceremonies for handing in knives continue to be held, at regular intervals, in a number of West African countries and they are backed up by professional retraining programs. The excisors empty their bag… but whatever new activity they choose to pursue in the future, they will not be deprived of the pleasure of carrying a bag. For women own cupboards full of the things. Of course, the excisor won't have as much choice as the models who work for Alphadi, the promoter of the International African Fashion Festival (FIMA), held every second year in Niamey. Well, come to think of it... It's true that the new range of bags carried by those gracious creatures are priced way beyond the reach of more modest pockets when they appear on the market after the festival, but the fakers soon get round to satisfying the rest of demand.

griots: all eyes on the Ladies' bags

Without a doubt, the bags you see in the streets are mainly women's, and one needs to know how to decode these visible signs of function, profession or social status, to identify the accessory used by the office worker, the shopkeeper or the housewife going to market. At baptisms or weddings, it is rare for a woman not to carry a bag, in her hand or over her forearm. Anyone wanting to show off a fine set of bracelets and rings, knows that the way to do this is to bend the arm daintily from the waist and hang one's bag from one's forearm. At smart social events, the handbag becomes the focus of a genuine wealth – and generosity – as ladies compete to see who will open her bag most often to cover the praise-singing *griots* with crisp new banknotes.

The handbag is a sign of elegance, and many models are made and sold with coordinated shoes. There is, of course, a concern to harmonize colors and forms in all this, but to match a bag with one's shoes is also to associate it with movement, with a necessarily elegant allure, a kind of chic and very temporary "nomadism".

The contents of a bag also contribute to female elegance. Here, women keep all those little things used for grooming. And, in that accursed Sahelian climate, in which dust storms alternate with crushing heat and the concomitant streams of sweat, you really do need to carry a small mirror in which to readjust your windswept hair, or a little bottle of perfume to freshen up with.

As for the materials from which the bags used in our cities are made, note that in Niger, like other countries of the Sahel,[6] which is cattle-rearing country, the most common one is leather, and the leather trades are booming. With the support of partners in development, crafts centers have been built in a number of towns

ill. 2 ◯ **Plastic bags
in front of the market**
Niamey, Niger, 2003
These bags (also called "Barbès bags"),
are taking over from traditional bags.

– Agadez, Dosso, Maradi, Tahoua, Tamaské. Drawing on ancestral skills, they make a host of accessories in leather,[7] including all kinds of bags: travel bags, satchels, briefcases, handbags, backpacks – you name it. Alongside these local products, the markets also offer imported bags, usually in man-made materials. These offer the advantage of standing up to weather (rain, for example) and above all, a low price.[8] This latter aspect is very important, bearing in mind that a "respectable" lady cannot constantly carry the same bag, and that, although made locally, leather bags are too expensive for many budgets.

Beyond the variety of materials, forms and uses, what meaning can we attribute to bags in African towns today? From an essentially materialist viewpoint, the bag is a sign of social status: to carry a bag is to show that you can afford one. *Griots* know this well: as they sing praises, their eyes are fixed on the ladies' bags. Clearly, it is the bag they are looking out for and following, once they have appraised its value. For a fine bag is a promise of riches. Also, and more importantly, it is a sign of economic independence and emancipation, for in African towns the status of women is changing.[9] Isn't the city dweller's flaunted fondness for her bag in some way an expression of the desire to break free of the rural model?

To a considerable extent, indeed, the authority of the male in traditional societies is a right earned by the duty to provide for the family. The Zarma expression *I na ay hiijandi aru kan sinda ziiba se* (literally, "They married me to a man without a pocket") describes what is an intolerable situation, for our traditions cannot admit of a man "without a pocket", that is to say, with no apparent means of giving. Conversely, it was considered perfectly normal for a woman to wear a pocketless garment. Today, especially in the countryside, you will still see what was long the traditional woman's garment: a single piece of cloth, loose and long enough to serve as dress, loincloth and baby-carrier. Further, this outfit may include a band-cum-belt called the *zeela*, which can serve as a kind of pocket.[10] Mounkaïla Fatimata notes that you can use it to wrap up any-

1   The big market in Niamey, the capital of Niger.

2   This term, a deformation of "Monsieur", is used for civil servants in general, and for teachers in particular. Note that its use, although common among speakers of most of the national languages of Niger, does have an ironic ring.

3   A term from Songhoy-Zarma, a language spoken mainly in Benin, Mali and Niger.

4   The literal meanings of the Songhoy-Zarma expressions for circumcision, *dan bangu* and *jingarandi*, are "to put in the pond" and "to make someone pray". No doubt these images can be explained by the idea of purification associated with the operation.

5   Alex Haley, *Roots*, 1976.

6   Burkina Faso, Mali, Mauritania, Chad, etc.

7   For aesthetic as well as functional reasons, these leather items are often made with fabric or rigid materials such as cardboard. The decoration is generally exquisitely fine.

8   The average price of a good handbag made by craftsman in Niger is about 50,000 CFA francs, as opposed to 10,000 for an imported bag (1 euro = 656.5 francs CFA).

9   *Les Femmes Nigerian's: le mythe et la réalité,* Department for Promotion of Women, NIN, Niamey: September 1995.

10   The names for this belt, in Niger's different national languages, are all pretty similar. For example, it is called *zeela* in Songhoy-Zarma, *jela* in Hausa, *jeelawol* in Peul, etc. Note also that to say a man is "*zeela* about his woman" is highly pejorative, indeed injurious. It means that the man is dominated by his wife, which, in societies like ours, where masculine authority counts for so much, is enough to write him off as a hopeless case.

11   Mounkaïla Fatimata, preface to Boubou Hama's book, *L'Essence du verbe*, Niamey: CELTHO, 1988.

12   A term used in Niamey, for youths who leave the country and stay in the city during the season when nothing grows.

thing from "banal gray lizard guano" (a suppository for children) to "a precious nugget of gold".[11] The *zeela* is also thought to be the place where women keep their secrets. Rightly or wrongly, it is seen as the womb of village gossip and rumors – hence the expression *I fo no ga kunsum ni zeela ga* ("What are you hiding in the band-belt of your loincloth?"), used when asking a woman for local news. Finally, typical of modern times, let's not forget the bright, parallelepipedic plastic bags "made in Hong Kong", with their red and blue stripes, dragged along by rich shopkeepers arriving at Niamey's Diori Hamani airport. You see these same bags on the road, too. After the cropping season, when the harvests are in, most youngsters leave the villages for the town, to work in modest trades as servants or polishers. Often empty and limp on the outward journey, stowed under the seat of the bush taxi, when homeward bound, this Chinese bag will have a roundness proportional to the *exodant*'s[12] efforts and sense of economy. The strong arms of apprentices are needed now to hoist it onto the vehicle's luggage rack. What is the young man bringing back to the village? Fashionable objects from the city: clothes, children's toys or cosmetics for wife or fiancée.

ill. 3 ◯ **Matali Crasset pouffe**
Digestion n°1

polyethylene bag, polyurethane foam
edited by EDRA, 1998
Matali Crasset collection

sylvie fleury's shopping bags

○ Did you know that Bernard Buffet committed suicide using a black plastic bag, emblazoned with the signature "Bernard Buffet", a kind a logo in gold letters? And do you remember those dramatized attacks on the performer Alberto Sorbelli, carried out with LV logo Vuitton bags? Where does this parallel lead? Perhaps to the simple idea of the violence contained in bags when artists get hold of them. A painter kills himself, a performer stages a massacre, and in both cases Exhibit A is a bag that sports a name: Bernard Buffet, LV.

Yes, but do we really need to explore the ins and outs, to track back for an explanation of these two actions? Can't we just leave it at that, not investigate, and limit our interpretation to the simple juxtaposition of the two events, contenting ourselves with the fable, namely, that here is danger, an act of violence, simulated or not, and that this action bears a signature: a bag is never anonymous because it always signs its crime. Here, we might acknowledge the existence of a riddle that can be answered by literally applying a standard verb: to sack. Meaning: to plunder, destroy, stuff in a bag. And to fire. Here, the sack of art becomes the sack of the artist, quite literally: Sorbelli gets a going-over, and Buffet sacks his life by sticking his head in a bag.

Sacking as performance art. Or, in our shopping culture, bagging. Isn't that what Sylvie Fleury was up to in 1990 when she first "deposited" her shopping bags in a Swiss gallery? What's so violent about that? Is it a distorted, terribly feminine and inevitably subversive echo of Duchamp's doings? An attempt to re-appropriate an oh-so-postmodern tradition of "appropriation"?[1] To bag Warhol? And so on and so forth. But I think we can leave these critical interpretations on the peg where they belong and concentrate instead on the nature of Fleury's action. And that includes the French verb used to describe it *déposer*: this can mean removing an object from where it hangs or is fixed (a painting, for example), sometimes in order to repair it (ask the plumber), or making a legal statement, or toppling a ruler (to depose). So: removing for repair, making a statement, stripping of power – that's a lot of destruction and affirmation that these bags were being asked to carry in Sylvie Fleury's first artistic gesture, her depositing of shopping bags.

So how did we reach this point? Maybe, first of all, we need to recall the context of Fleury's first show and the violent atmosphere in which she made her début. In 1990, star artists John Armleder and Olivier Mosset had been invited to exhibit together at the Rivolta gallery in Lausanne and, anxious as they were to avoid that

ill. 1 ◯ opposite
Sylvie Fleury
"C'est la vie !"
installation view, 1990, AM,
Rivolta gallery
shopping bags with contents
Tull collection

ill. 2 ◯ **Sylvie Fleury**
Brave

Sarah Cottier Gallery installation, 1994
shopping bags with contents

ill. 3 ○ **Alberto Sorbelli**
L'Agressé

performance at the Venice Biennale
photograph by Matthieu Deluc, 1999

industry standard, the two-man show, asked Christian Floquet to join them. He accepted, only to pull out a few days before the private view. With routine "duo-dom" staring them in the face, Mosset/Armleder got in touch with Sylvie Fleury. Then a virtual unknown in the official art world, Fleury had known Richard Avedon in the US and, under the name of Sylda Von Braun, had been a noted personality of Geneva's new wave nightlife in the 1980s. At the time she was living in an old clinic, wore white coats and white court shoes, and walked the fine line between Swiss swishness and the Helvetic underground, doing *events* but never losing her nail-varnished cool. Other snippets of biography: a wedding in Spain, a vampire movie with friends in New York, running a gallery, and artist friends of growing fame, including Armleder, in whose open, participative works she played an occasional role. In 1990, Sylvie Fleury was an unidentified fashion object on high heels. With us but not one of us. Exactly the sort of profile that got Alberto Sorbelli beaten up (*L'Agressé*, performance at the Venice Biennale, 1999). The art world being more conservative than one might think, it bridled at Sorbelli's "whorish" seducer persona, at this intruder, who once put on corset, high-heels and fishnet stockings and played the whore in a museum (*La Pute*, performance at the Hôtel des Arts, Hôtel Rothschild, Paris, 1992). So the person chosen by Mosset/Armleder was not so much an artist as a providential unknown. Her function was perfectly clear: to break up the unity of the artistic "couple". An iconoclastic mission, then. She was being used and came up with a reaction to match. Instrumentalized by her artist friends, who saw the presence of a third party as an alibi, a strategic addition helping them escape the pitfalls of the double solo, Fleury had to produce her own founding gesture, to "sign on" and register her presence as one does a trademark (*déposer* again). It was a matter of (art-world) life and death. And so here she was with her first *Shopping Bags with Contents*, labeled "Fleury" for art-historical eternity. Others would follow at other exhibitions, like spin-offs, franchises of the Fleury brand.

the art of survival

So what exactly is Fleury exhibiting, this woman who always turns up with generous supplies and leaves her full bags in galleries and museums, as at so many *après-shopping* parties? And what are we looking at here? Bags? Yes, but what else? Brand names? Symbols of luxury, going by the name of Chanel, Calvin Klein etc.? A feminist critical discourse on shopping, the Western world's favorite pastime? A literal application of Barbara Kruger's "I SHOP THEREFORE I AM"? The portrait of an over-consuming society full of fashion victims? Let's stay at floor level here, on this floor where the artist lays down her trophies. Trophies? Yes, if we allow that Fleury has been at war ever since day one of her first show, when she had to come up with a gesture that would assert her presence between the two heavy-hitters, a gesture that would both neutralize their own face-off, "depose" the two "Giants" and at the same time identify her as a full-fledged artist. "Having set herself the objective of making a perfectly personal work of art, after several sleepless nights, Sylvie Fleury decided to capitalize on the very thing for which she was getting stick from, in this art world in which she accompanied her friends: her look."[2] Her Gucci-Prada bags were an It-girl riposte, laid at the feet of Mosset/Armleder, a signature statement: these are the bags that she brings back from her travels around the globe, these shopping bags "with contents", as she always specifies. And what do these bags contain? Neither more nor less than what the bags display, that is to say, the title (or brand, maybe?) of each exhibition. This is systematically written on one of the bags presented in the series – just stick to the surface and read: *The Art of Survival* (1991); *Give Hope!* (1991); *Poison* (1992); *Brave* (1994); *Élite* (1997). As our vague impressions tell us, these titles are like bits of the narrative of Fleury's inaugural adventure in the art world, a commentary and account of the advent of a tragic but victorious heroine. Her mission was to depose the *Giants* (1990), and her first gesture therefore had to be *Spectacular* (1990), and rather *Égoïste* (1990), if not *Extrêmement Égoïste* (the title of a second show, in 1991), if she was to achieve *Victoire* (Victory, 1991) and attain *Vital Perfection* (1991), and so proclaim her own *Manifesto* (2000)… And so what are we looking at here? Answer, bag-statements, performance objects, objects-cum-processes that say what they do, and what Fleury does: prove herself.

1   This artistic gesture first appeared in the 1960s, and announced the crisis of representation in art, as well as the modern practice of quotation.
2   Éric Troncy, "The better you look", *Sylvie Fleury*, Paris: Réunion des Musées Nationaux; Dijon: Les Presses du Réel; Geneva: Mamco; Grenoble: Magasin, 2001.

the Destiny of a plastic bag

ill. 1 ○ **Hedya Klein**
Sun

IG Bildende Kunst Gallery
Vienna, 2003

○ Look at photos from 50 years ago. Look at the streets, the markets, and the people from that time coming and going; we won't see them: the plastic bag didn't exist. Today, the world is swarming with them: 18 billion plastic bags are distributed free of charge every year in France.[1] Plastic bags are everywhere, all over the streets, in the corridors of the subway, parked at bus stops, waiting in offices until someone needs one, bunched up in a corner, suspended from the back of a chair. The crumpling of the plastic bag has joined the other noises that form the soundtrack of the contemporary world. It's a light but precise rustling that emits a fragile, yet clearly distinct sound in the silence – and sometimes a silvery metallic crunching like that of a chocolate wrapper. Since the 1980s, this insidious audible presence – which is now an almost constant background noise – has even become a serious nuisance for sound engineers. Called the "all-purpose bag", in supermarket and department store vocabulary, the plastic bag is a sexless, classless bag, which travels constantly throughout the various strata of society, passing from one hand to another with total indifference, until it ends up hanging on the branches of a shrub in a public park, deposited as an improvised garbage sack on the sidewalk on early morning, abandoned to its fate everywhere and anywhere (122 million bags on the French coasts every year). Or – the ultimate consolation – it ends up as the overstuffed companion of bag ladies in large cities. Indeed, for these street women, these bags are the last bastion in defining a semblance of private territory around them; they sum up their existence and surround them like protective ramparts.

ill. 3 ○ *Shopping Center*
photograph by Martin Parr
Bristol, 2002

ill. 4 ○ *Bag Lady, Gare Saint-Lazare*
photograph by Farid Chenoune, 2004

We usually ask nothing special of this anonymous object at the bottom rung of the bag world. It knows nothing of the special privileges enjoyed by the handbag. It is not entitled to carry and protect the intimate, special objects that are part of a person's inner sphere, the special caretaker of primordial trinkets that are always on hand as reminders that we do exist and are indeed alive. The plastic bag knows nothing of the wallet, the central command unit for an identity, the guardian of photographs of friends and family, and a stronghold for money and credit cards. Unknown, too, is the address book, which when full of scrawled names, is a sign of the owner's social ease and dexterity. Or the cell phone, or the make-up, the mirror, the small tools of feminine beauty, cosmetics for the face, body, and mouth, and snacks as well as cosmetics for the inner person, the heart, the head, the soul – indeed, a prosaic Prozac.

As for the plastic sack, it carries everything and anything: a sweater for cold weather, a mini-umbrella, a thick, oversized book for the train, a bottle of water, CDs, and an apple for a snack. The plastic bag is not a storage device for the stable (or at least stabilized) self, but rather for the unstable self of the day, a more spontaneous, ephemeral and temporary self, limited

ill. 5 ○ **Women working
on the freeway, protected
from the monsoon by plastic bags**

photograph by Ian Berry
Bombay, 1999

to the fleeting necessities of the moment. It is also, as a carry-all, prepared for the unexpected events of the day, the gentle chaos of things that happen. It's something like the black box of daily ups and downs, minor accidents, micro-decisions taken spontaneously, which alter and add spice to events: a newspaper we buy, documentation we pick up, a thing we find – all the haphazard items we bring back home in the evening like some harmless loot. As an expression of nomadic behavior in the midst of a sedentary urban existence, the plastic bag has carved out a role as a second bag, the assistant of the first in some way, which does everything the other cannot or will not do. So goes the world today, with two bags.

The use of plastic bags for this purpose has become so commonplace that we have forgotten that it is an act of re-appropriation repeated by millions of people millions of times every day. No one ever buys a plastic bag. Garbage bags, yes; plastic bags, no. We bring them back from the market, the supermarket, the department store and shops. And we keep them: sometimes they are pilled up one atop another, stuffed like rags in a larger bag, and sometimes (in organized households) sorted by size or strength. They are hung on the kitchen door handle, stored in the broom closet and even placed in a bag for plastic bags that you can now find in stores. Claude Closky adapted the optimistic tone of supermarket and mail-order catalogs to the first person, and in his book entitled *Mon Catalogue*, paid tribute to this "bag for bags": "I hung my bag for bags in my kitchen, so that I would have the many plastic bags that I bring home and reuse within easy reach. I store them by adding them to the top and removing bags from the bottom as I need them."[2]

This storage technique also respects another boundary: that which separates
the ordinary, nameless plastic bag from the superior race of brand-name bags.
These luxury bags belong to the noble class of shopping bags. These are the
coat-of-arms bags, bearing the name and color of their label, it's the outer
skin of the gift. Above all, they are manufactured with thick, solid paper:
strong matt kraft paper (for the Muji label, for example), smooth, opulent,
or textured paper (Vuitton and Hermès, the Rolls Royce of shopping bags),
or lacquered or varnished papers (Chanel, Givenchy). These deserve care
and are long lasting. These bags and their distant plastic cousins co-exist
but do not mingle. Furthermore, when these shopping bags don't have
string, they have handles that do not tear, unlike the plastic bag that only
too often falls apart on the exit from a discount store like a heavy, badly
fed fish dangling off a hook above the water.

The advent of the plastic bag in the material culture of the past 50 years
created a revolution. It was obviously invented in response to changing
urban lifestyles. The carry-alls, net bags, baskets, and shopping bags that
were once carried to the market by the housewife and mother at a time
before women entered the job market in force have all but disappeared.
They have been replaced by the cheap plastic bag, provided by stores and
better suited to the choppy rhythms of contemporary existence, to its
urgencies, rushed purchases made during lunch breaks, and harried errands
at the end of the working day. But these bags were also a revolution in the
sense that they brought bags full circle, back to their original purpose, that
of a portable transportation device. This may be why a number of artists have
co-opted them in recent years, as a key argument in their criticism of

ill. 6 ○ **Salvation Army hostel**
Paris, Hôpital Bretonneau,
photograph by Olivier Coulanges, 1993

ill. 7 ○ opposite
Extracts from *Plastic Resistance*
video, Pierre Sportolaro, 2004

consumer society and waste (as, for example, the Austrian artists in the Viennese gallery, IG Bildende Kunst);[3] and as a new material recycled for alternative purposes (the clothing-bags in Pierre Sportolaro's video *Plastic Resistance*); but also – and especially – because as the latest innovation in the world of bags, it is both the most modern and the most archaic.

1   Concerning this mass of plastic bags, their ecological impact and alternatives under consideration by mass market stores, the primary supplier of plastic bags, see the study conducted by PriceWaterhouseCoopers for the Carrefour supermarkets, Assessment of the environmental impacts of Carrefour plastic bags, Paris, 2004.
2   Claude Closky, *Mon Catalogue*, Editions Frac Limousin, 1999, nonpaginated.
3   Exhibition *Plastic Bag*, organized by this gallery from November 20 2003 to January 16 2004, with artists Uwe Bressnik, Franck David, Johannes Domenig, Dietmar Franz, Hilde Fuchs, Robert F. Hammerstiel, Hildegard Jaekel, Hedya Klein, Andreas Kristof, Felix Malnig, Ulli Vonbank-Schedler and Lois Weinberger, as well as musicians Jacques Nobili, Paul Skrepek, Vincenz Wizlsperger and Martin Zrost.

venice 2003: biennale of fakes

○ "Everyone has an agnès b. bag marked UTOPIA", noted the artist Ben, rather curiously, in his "Notes from 1 to 10" at last summer's Venice Biennale. This is what one could read on www.ben-vautier.com: that the must-have bag in Venice in summer/fall 2003 bore a double signature: "agnès b." for fashion, and "Utopia", the name of the exhibition put together by Hans-Ulrich Obrist, for contemporary art. Never before had the frontiers between art and fashion been so permeable, and no doubt this breakdown of distinctions crystallized most clearly around the bag, with Ben playing the fashion-observer, and collector and designer agnès b. flirting, via her bag, with the curator Hans-Ulrich Obrist. At the same time, the post-Warholian Takashi Murakami invaded the town with customized Vuitton bags, covered with his trademark little flowers, which were on sale at the Vuitton store but also flooded the streets as fakes. You might even argue that this was the Biennale's finest spontaneous work: Venice "installed", or the site-specific installation of hundreds of Vuitton, Prada, and Gucci bags in the streets, under arcades, and on squares. While the official Biennale itself was considered the most disappointing of the decade, the off-Biennale – the *show-off* – took over the rest of the city in the form of an "environment" of bags so coherent that it had an almost conceptual rigor. At the Giardini, in the Arsenale, in all the pavilions, the contemporary art biennial was wilting in the solar and critical heat – the worst, zero, a failure, we were told – while in the streets a wildcat installation invaded the territory deserted by invited artists.

Just picture this historic city covered with white cotton. Martin Margiela had no hand in it, but he would have adored these sidewalks of white cotton, white cotton laid out by street vendors on the fly, usually Blacks, displaying with honorable regularity, like shop assistants at Colette, a whole *theory* of bags – fakes, of course: reproductions both clumsy and crude, and sometimes ironic ("XXL" replacing the LV logo on some). Imagine the sidewalks spread with white sheets on which stand simulacra of luxury bags. And the image would not have been complete without the finishing touch that gave it the perfection of a tableau vivant.

Sometimes, at prayer time, one would catch the most incredibly political mass performance: Blacks kneeling before their fake Vuitton-Gucci-Pradas, their heads pointing towards Mecca. Such was Venice in summer/fall 2003: one vast theme park with a single attraction: a museum-city exhibiting fake bags, or forgery as one of the fine arts.

The bag of the summer/fall, then, was Murakami's design for Vuitton with a colorful logo of ecstasy-infused flowers. This was his victory over all the Guccis and Pradas in the world. The Murakami bag bloomed along the canals. A bag maker called on an artist to perk up its image. Murakami struck the pose and treated Vuitton as a spin-off, one more license for the art that he puts everywhere, making the most of his images, his little © figures, the flowers and manga-eyed mushrooms that he has made his trademark and business. Thus the theme of the 2003 Venice Biennale was not "Dreams and Conflicts: the Dictatorship of the Spectator", as framed by Francesco Bonami, but "Mixing It Up" or "Identical Copy". Venice's handbag happening was all about the blurring of art into fashion and vice versa. It even contaminated the official selection. American artist Fred Wilson felt duty-bound to garnish the entrance to his pavilion with dull, logo-less bags guarded by a Black non-vendor. Yes, it could be read as an attack on the exploitation of these illegal immigrants, but it was hard not to see it as an opportune installation, a copy, even, of the spectacular fringe version that was coloring Venice with its intelligence: an official, sad copy with no logo or colors. Last summer/fall, art was something you carried on your shoulder. "Utopia, a true-faux LV on your arm", as Ben might have written if freelancing for *Vogue*.

12 movies, 12 bags

Michèle Morgan carries a bag. A small, dishearteningly plain clutch bag with no detail on the outside or bulge from the inside. The perfect incarnation of the paradox behind this kind of model: the bag that owes its shape to the emptiness inside. The clutch bag is merely the final punctuation, the signature of the silhouette. It actually requires the mastery of a special art, the art of negligence: held casually between the fingertips as if picked up without thinking, no heavier than the featherweight of its basic vacuity. Note that both partners here profess nonchalance: hands in pock-

Opposite her, Jean Gabin, full-face, jacket and shirt hanging loose, commands an open, frontal surface, casually exuding self-assurance. His hands are his sole means of attack, ready to strike. Michèle has her clutch bag, poised for a fearsome riposte: like a deadly boomerang, this "frisbee" will punish any man who gets too cocky.

But appearances are deceptive. The most loving couple of the 1940s are only bluffing. *In petto*, assured of success, you can almost hear Jean and Michèle murmur confidently: "It's in th

Julie Andrews carries a bag. A carpetbag with comfy sides, made from that unprepossessing cloth loved for its flowers by spinsters who were wallflowers in their youth. The owner of this carpetbag is a beautiful nanny, full of life, who breaks with the tradition of the evil governess, generally sporting a miserly reticule and a miserly bun, that we had become used to seeing in Anglo-American movies, from *Rebecca* to *Under Capricorn* (Hitchcock). Mary Poppins entered history from the sky. The bag helped her to land, an umbrella will help her take off; a well-balanced woman often needs two accessories, one to keep her feet on the ground, the other, her head in the clouds. Unleashing the powers of her bag of tricks, Mary Poppins pulls out a thousand and one stories, and leads the lonely children on a merry dance, that amazes and

educates them at the same time. Note the look of surprise on the face of the little girl, flabbergasted by the size of the objects coming out of the bag: she will learn that strength of imagination stretches the limits of daily life. Look at the little boy as he checks the bottom of the bag: he will understand that the secret of performance is not about imposture, it's about belief. If the bag does not have a false bottom, then everyday life will turn out to contain multiple worlds.

When Mary Poppins packs her bag, signaling her departure, she will say to the saddened children, a sober look on her face: "If I cried over all the children I leave…" And what if this bountiful bag full of colorful demonstrations was also a testament to Mary's modesty, concealing all the colorless tears she preferred to keep to herself?

Breathless (À bout de souffle)
Jean-Luc Godard, 1959

Jean Seberg carries a bag. A white, monastically austere purse, highlighted by the black Gothic letters of the *Herald Tribune*: a contrasting association, which reminds us that the actress entered the film world under the patronage of Saint Joan. Dressed in "probity and candid linen" (Victor Hugo), Jean Seberg looks like an innocent pageboy, an incarnation of the American frankness which delights Parisian film-lovers deterred by the "mouse-like French actresses" whom François Truffaut disparaged. While Jean is fundamentally honest, she is also very attractive: her bulging purse, curvy cheeks and round head ripe for amorous nuzzling. Beside her, Jean-Paul Belmondo plays it cool, cigarette dangling from his lips, hands in pockets, titillated by the forbidden fruit between her fingers. The purse makes Jean swing her arm gaily, its rhythm carrying the Champs Elysées back to bucolic days as Elysian fields where shepherds and shepherdesses strolled carefree across the grass. Jean and Jean-Paul look like they could almost fly away together.

But Jean's frankness is a double-edged sword. The purse strings will come undone in the intimacy of a hotel room as Jean ties her heart to Jean-Paul's in the whiteness of crumpled sheets. This happy but soon tragic bond will be Jean-Paul's downfall: he will die in the urban jungle of a Parisian street, betrayed by the little pageboy and her traitorous purse.

Tippi Hedren carries a bag. A large, stiff, patent-leather bag with sturdy handles. She holds it in the air, frozen in mid-motion: someone off camera has caught her by surprise. Why does she look hunted? Probably because she is making off with money stolen from her workplace. But what is shocking is not so much the theft, but the means of transportation: the honest secretary's bag now a lady-burglar's sack for swag. Such is the reversibility of respectability: secretary by day, thief by night. The bag marks the transition between the two worlds. Everything around her is uncompromising, even reproving: a grieving typewriter, erect penholders, sharpened pencils, etc. What is the point of all this? Is it about

straight lines of the blinds - everything is focus masculine viewpoint combined with the singula a woman red-handed. Witness* a villainous and between man and thief: I won't tell anyone wha bag, in exchange you will be all mine.

For Tippi, caught in the act, there is only one wa mail: unravel the web of memories, dredge up behind the neurosis, haul out all her emotion will do so at the end of the film. Will she be c will be eternally grateful to her savior, gratitude secret to keeping an masterful hold over wom

fluffy bag, reminiscent of the
y cuddles and tears and full of
le that brings calls of "Into the
nal object!" from psychiatrists.
famous transition, Shirley the
mastering the codes of adult
d rabbit ears, the doggy-rabbit
edient and occasionally affec-
efully with her fingertips and
rring to her touch. Who does
animal whose seductive urban
nk Sinatra. Frank pits a military
g, adult commitment against
anxious gait, scruffled orange

hair, wide eyes and freckles, Shirley imagines herself as a cute little squirrel easily coaxed with a gift of nuts. This young woman adopts the childhood ideal of domestication and comfort as a pose, annoying men with her tears and candor and suffering in return from a lack of esteem, shooed away like a begging dog. Shirley may not have understood that while the Rat Pack tough nuts (Sinatra, Martin and Co.) are annoyed by homebodies, they would no doubt be seduced by wilder hearts. To captivate them, she should have carried a panther-print bag like Ava Gardner – and isn't that kind of feline emancipation the implicit message of that leaping greyhound in the background?

A woman carries a bag. A square, stiff leather bag with an flaw-less surface, a sure sign of a 1950s bourgeois lady, well-off and a tad old-fashioned, with only one real concern: what is and isn't done. It's a faceless, bodiless bag, detached from its owner, emblematized by the cinema frame, which isolates it sharply from its context. This unnatural cut-out is where the genius of Robert Bresson lies, as a filmmaker who gave metaphysical dimension to the details of daily life: a hand opening a door, a hand resting on a shoulder, etc. The bag, floating in the air, hanging on the pick-pocket's sole desire, takes on the hypertrophied dimension of a terrible temptation.

There are many ways of slipping a hand into a lady's purse: vio-lently, softly, hesitantly, nimbly, from behind or from the front. Here, the hand enters the bag as it would a safe, feeling the mate-rial, undoing the clasp as though deciphering the coded secret of a lock. The thief, Martin Lassalle, displays a kind of wide-eyed indif-ference as he stares stubbornly off camera. Playing casual? Have you ever noticed how often pickpockets mime the attitudes of their victims in order to avoid being noticed? Good pickpockets are neutral, absorbed in the cares of daily life, pay no attention to their immediate entourage, basically know exactly what is and isn't done: they always look like a respectable lady carrying a handbag.

What motivates pickpockets? The lure of lucre? That's not all. The joy of trickery? That's not all either. The constant thrill of suspense triggered by a terrifying question: what do women's handbags conceal? Yes, indeed. Another movie about pickpockets portrayed how they can be left "holding the bag": in *Pick Up on South Street* (Samuel Fuller, 1953), Richard Widmark's life is made difficult by Jean Peters' bag and its contents – not as innocent as they might seem. Fuller's film inverses the Bressonian maxim: here, a respectable lady carrying a handbag always looks like a good pick-pocket.

Victoria Abril carries a bag. A red, quilted, leather bag with a gold chain, that comes from a major French fashion house. With her round-collared wool suit, daisy brooch and large pearl necklace, Victoria Abril is "Chanel" from head to toe. This adds her name to a string of actresses linking movies and fashion, in a pact born from sincere kinship and logical interests alike: Catherine Deneuve yvessaintlaurentified, Audrey Hepburn and Liv Tyler givenchycized, Sophie Marceau emmanuelungarocized, Carole Bouquet, Vanessa Paradis and Nicole Kidman chanelized, Sofia Coppola and Winona Ryder marcjacobized, and so on.

Jean-Paul Gaultier is the designer who usually wins the favors of Almodovar, with whom he shares the self-same eccentricity and radical sense of detail. In this scene, where the story of an unworthy mother and a suffering daughter comes together, Victoria Abril is tense and Marisa Paredes is casual. Inverting the hierarchy of generational styles, the daughter is ladylike and the mother dressed as a rebel. The reason Victoria is so ostensibly "chanelized" is because her character seeks refuge from maternal scandal in the respectable brand image. Dressing in Chanel, according to the little girls who play at dressing up as adults in front of their mother's mirror, clearly means you have a high-flying job. As always in family dramas, a problem of transmission is at play: in happy families, Chanel handbags are carefully handed down from mother to daughter. Here Victoria Abril holds nothing but shame in her hands – indeed her cheeks are constantly flushed with red, like the blood-red of her bag. Almodovar's iconoclastic energy is bound to ignite this wounded respectability and turn it into a passionate reunion between the two women. Chanel jeanpaulgaultierized at last?

Anna Karina carries a bag. A retro-style bag made of dark, pleated leather. It has a clasp that goes "click" when you open it, an essential noise that provides a snappy punctuation to the transactions and fixes the rules of the pleasure being sold: a bill for a fondle. The bag's broad aperture exhales the intimate scents of clients' sexual secrets, a suffocating smell that drives the passers-by wild. The strap enables the hand to twirl the bag, an essential gesture, when it comes to making the heads and bodies of the men you're touting spin. This twirling is reminiscent of a young rascal "hopping up" his catapult as he plots some dirty deed – no danger, no pleasure. Pinned to a colored backdrop of slogans and posters garishly highlighting her charms, Anna Karina is a prisoner of male law. The swinging of the bag – sometimes seconded by a swing of her legs as she roams up and down the street – seems to be the only movement she can allow herself.

Note Anna Karina's hairstyle, a kind of ascetic pudding-basin cut that hardly tallies with the sex appeal of a prostitute. In her spare time she goes to the movies to watch Dreyer's *The Passion of Joan of Arc*. If filming a prostitute character consists of inventing a path that disturbs the room-street, room-street monotony for her, Godard chooses to be a martyrologist here, with prostitution as a modern Way of the Cross and the bag an essential element of the liturgy of passion. The martyr-prostitute holds the straps of her bag in the same patient way that someone would hold their rosary beads, stoically waiting for the hours – and the suffering – to pass.

Sandrine Bonnaire carries a bag. In fact, it's a double bag: backpack behind, denim pouch at the front and, sandwiched between them, a woman. Not a sandwich woman touting a brand but a woman trying to survive. Never has the term "accessory" been so inappropriate. These bags are *necessaries*, the portable home invented by the vagrant Sandrine Bonnaire. They contain the objects that will keep her from dying: blanket, socks, scarves, bottles of water, heater, etc. You may be a beggar but that doesn't make you bagless. These sexless, anonymous bags assert a blankness that dedicates them to the purely utilitarian. Another itiner-nt, Barbara Loden's aptly named *Wanda*, will choose a different trategy and hang on to a handbag, that emblem of intact emininity.

Vhether for appearance or out of indifference, the bag attests the

is what you have left when you have forgotten everything else." Note here how the two bags hug the body, their soft materials bending to the shape of Sandrine Bonnaire, forming a carapace which protects her from aggression, and a cameleon-like surface that takes on the hues of the landscape and thus realizes the dream of every wanderer: to blend in with the scenery. Sandrine Bonnaire changes, abandons urban frippery in favor of natural defenses and thus finds the latest fashion: matching nature through the seasons – white in winter, green in spring, yellow in summer, russet in the fall. A determined arm sticks out from the mass of the body to indicate "Stop!" Sedentary types dip their hands into their bag; wanderers pull theirs out. We fear for this figure who has become a "bag-woman" and whose last remaining social gesture is to put out her hand. Who will find a worthy

and her friend each carry a bag. Two small
)e utterly insignificant if they weren't revitalized
s of their owners: eyebrows raised, eyes agog,
houettes thrown off balance by a surge of indig-
has just had a dig at the two women and they
back. We're at war here, a special kind of war,
women. In these circumstances, the accessory
h of these warring females to perfection is a bag.

detects an approaching enemy, the quiver, the
full of gossip, the casket containing the secret of
– but hush, it's a secret. In a film where the
ir time bandying insults, names, rumors, gossip,
abuse, the bag is the perfect tool: it's close to
) and ready to let fly. Does this movie provide an
orry sight of these harpies? A little girl and a
t untainted by the twisted thoughts of their eld-
the martial arts of language and fashion acces-
nly because they're young, and you can bet that
they will acquire a hard-edged bag and sharp

s den of enraged females there is a husband. He
ies. Another man is at the movie's helm: George
osent from the film, lurking in the wings, savor-
his hen-fight that rates only as a male fantasy.

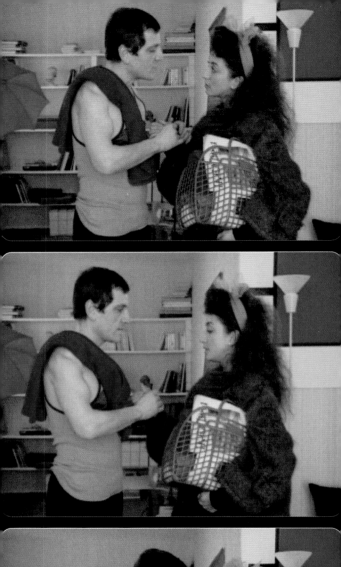

Jack Lemmon and Tony Curtis each carry a bag. One is a flat purse with a clasp, the other indulges in curves. Details about the models are irrelevant, the point is that they indicate that the person holding them is female. The stakes are high: these men have to pass themselves off as women. How can they succeed in defying nature? By displaying the emblems of feminine coquetry that signal the weaker sex, like the flickering beam of a lighthouse at night. At which point, we should note that a handbag is not all it takes to make a woman; it needs to be backed up with a multitude of other accessories that create a surface picture of feminine appearance: dress, false breasts, false eyelashes, make-up, high-heeled pumps, affected gestures, and so on. A man dressed up as a woman is a woman with too many accessories. But what, on the other hand, makes a woman into a man? The male transvestite's handbag is the female transvestite's moustache (Jeanne Moreau in François Truffaut's *Jules and Jim*), or greased-back hair (Julie Andrews in Blake Edwards' *Victor Victoria*). Economy is what makes the disguise credible. Femininity shows itself off, masculinity plays itself down.

Note that while the handbag is an essential element to achieve a successful travesty, it is also the element *par excellence* to debunk the hoax. Held close to the body it indicates a woman; held at a distance it indicates a man dressed as a woman. The only accessory that can be held at arm's length to express a degree of irony or even disgust, the handbag offers the option of a waiver, should commitment waver: "Hey, I'm a dame, but only up to a point!" Yuk! Dropped brutally on the ground, the handbag lends itself to a theatrical gesture, which expresses, with great pomp, an end to the alienation of a man who, at the end of the movie, will send dress, make-up, false lashes and bra flying. Liberated, the hand will recover its virile freedom of movement, free of the shackles – which "we women" find so attractive – of the handbag.

Nomads and Voyagers

route

expanse

migration

wandering

pilgrims

liberty

vagabonds

adventure

transhumance

caravan

ill. xi: **Shepherd**, photograph by V. Terebenine, undated, Tajikistan

ill. xiv **Spanish immigrants arriving at the Gare d'Austerlitz**, photograph by Pierre Blouzard, late 1950s

ill. xv **Young girl hitchhiking with her luggage** during the exodus of 1940, photograph by Harlingue

ill. XVI *Bécassine, Le Trésor viking,* Éditions Gautier Languereau, 2001

ill. XVII **Refugees' bundle,** refuguees driven out of Srebrenica (Bosnia) by the Serbian forces, photograph by Nadia Benchallal, 1995

ill. XVIII **Travel bag**, France, late 18th century, linen and wool, tapestry, steel clasp, metal lock, natural leather, siamese lining,
Paris, musée de la Mode et du Textile, UFAC collection, Boucher donation

ill. xix **Automobile bag,** Hermès, 1930, box calf, goatskin lining, collection of the Conservatoire des Créations Hermès

ill. xx **Steamer bag,** that belonged to Gaston-Louis Vuitton, personalized with his logo, France, cotton, natural cowhide and brass, Paris, Louis Vuitton collection

ill. xxi *The newlyweds on their honeymoon,* Anonymous, circa 1900

ill. XXII **Steamer bag,** Christian Astuguevielle for Nina Ricci, accessories collection Spring/Summer 1999, pink, red and orange suede kid cover on a resin and fiberglass structure, Musée de la Mode et du Textile, UCAD collection, gift of Christian Astuguevielle 2004 ill. 1 — opposite **Fur and leather pouch** from tumulus 2, Pazyryk (Russian Altai), 4th century BC, Saint Petersburg, Hermitage Museum

The Nomad Paradox

— Nomadic, the bag? How could it not be? For us, it is the instrument of mobility *par excellence*, the indispensable companion of our slightest displacements. And since the nomad is, in a sense, a perpetual traveler, surely he is bound to have a bag? Especially in the ancient world. In the fifth century BCE, Herodotus stated his surprise that "People who have constructed neither cities nor walls but who are all house-bearers and horseback archers, who do not live from tilling but from their cattle, who have their homes on chariots – how should such people not be safe from combat and impossible to catch?" And, we might be tempted to add, how could they not be carriers of bags?

But what of the reality of bags used by nomads, real ones? For the nomadism I am referring to is not today's variety, limited by the constraints imposed by the borders and existence of states, under siege from modernity and, at best, barely more than long-distance transhumance, usually motorized. I am talking here about the great historical variety of nomadism, the kind that constituted the long-obscure, other side of the ancient world, and that only really died out with the advent of firearms. For more than a thousand years, this kind of nomadism prevailed over much of Eurasia, from the Yellow River to the Danube, bequeathing us everything brought by the Great Invasions – which it would be more appropriate to call the Great Migrations. The nomadic world of cattle breeders on the Steppes generated, not a counter-culture to the great centers of civilization in the Orient and around the Mediterranean, but a powerfully original culture, a fertile alternative to the way of life of sedentary farmers, who were confined on a daily basis in the closed space of houses, villages, and, soon, cities.

In this economy of mobility, based on non-accumulation and strict necessity, there was no place for the bag. At least, not the bag held close to the body, as we think of it today. The idea of a necessary connection between the bag and nomadism is one more misunderstanding to be added to the long list of the misconceptions that we sedentary types cultivate with regard to nomads.

ill. 2 ── opposite **Leather flask pouch** from tumulus 2, Pazyryk (Russian Altai), 4th century BC, Saint Petersburg, Hermitage Museum

Nomads who don't walk

For the reality is that the nomad is not a walker. He is a rider, a horseman. In a society where everyone – men, women, and children – travels on horseback, those who cannot ride follow on in carts, amid the tools and other bundles. Ancient texts and images as well as 19th- and 20th-century photographs are formal on this point. Even today, when one crosses paths with a nomad traveling through the Kazakh Steppe, or the mountains of Kyrgyzstan, he may have binoculars slung over his shoulder, and sometimes a gun, but very rarely a bag. Nomads may have invented trousers, the saddle, and stirrups, and, for women, the crakow shoe and the hennin headdress, but they are not bag-carriers. However, one kind of bag that they have always used a great deal, and still do today, is the saddle bag. These are generally double, their colors and patterns truly worthy of interest, but outside our purview. In addition nomads have all kinds of packs and wrappings designed to facilitate transport – pouches, scabbards, sheaths, and cases used not so much to contain as to protect, to avoid breakage, to soften sharp corners.

Going back to antiquity, we know of the splendid scabbards used by the Scythians, and *gorytas*, the big cases, made of leather or wood with sumptuous gold covers, in which they kept both bow and arrows. Informing us of the way in which his nomadic contemporaries transformed skulls into drinking cups by cladding them carefully in leather and, if they were rich, lining them with gold, Herodotus tells us that they also used human skin to cover their quivers. The historian describes this as "thick and shiny, almost the most brilliantly white of all skins". But then are we ourselves any less barbaric? What about the – brilliant white – skin of a Chouan (French anti-Revolutionary) exhibited in a museum in Nantes?

The abundance and diversity of nomadic receptacles is eloquently illustrated by the second tomb at Pazyryk, in the Altai mountains of central Asia. A couple was buried in this tomb in the fourth century BCE: he was about 60, tall and brown-haired, of Mongoloid type, his body decorated with superb

tattoos; she was about 40, also brown-haired, of mixed race, her clothes and headdress extremely refined. The funerary chamber had been raided not long after the burial; pillagers had robbed the couple of their jewelry and weapons, taking all the metal objects. But the ice that soon formed around the bodies, clothes and furniture buried with them miraculously preserved these perishable objects through the centuries.

Even if we leave aside the material wrapped around the woman's locks and the grass-stuffed pouches that served as cushions, we can still number many bags, pouches, bottles, and cases among these finds. Some are in felt, the majority in leather and fur.

If pottery was a ubiquitous feature of the Greek world at this time, among nomads it was a rarity, with most bowls and platters being in wood, leather, or metal. This tomb contained a clay jug with the felt ring on which it rested, its neck surrounded by a band of leather and the belly with leather figures of cockerels, designed not so much to decorate it as to protect it from knocks. In the world of today's nomads, the indispensable teapot and precious porcelain tea bowls are also protected by suitable cases, which form a big, easily transportable bag.

Found – and this was certainly no coincidence – in the sepulcher for the horses of the deceased, a high rounded pouch with a narrow opening no doubt contained cheese. It is made of leather with, on one side, white and blue fur decoration forming complex motifs set in lozenge forms and, on the other, leopard skin (ill. 1).

Near to the deceased, small pieces of leather or felt were sewn together to hold human hair or nails, no doubt for magical purposes. A round bronze mirror was contained in a case made of leopard skin and fur, while a modest iron knife was in a wooden scabbard. There was small, simple, and very soft bag made of light and darker sable skins sewn together. Another, in thick leather, with a flap lined with leopard skin and, inside, a fine leather pocket, was decorated on the outside with small, sewn-on birds in copper with gold leaf.

A remarkably well preserved kind of flask, some twenty centimeters high, in the shape of a swollen-bellied bottle was

ill. 3 — **Lady's ankle boot** in leather and woolen cloth, gold and pewter embroidered leg, sole adorned with black pearls and pyrite crystals, from tumulus 2, Pazyryk (Russian Altai)
4th century BC, Saint Petersburg, Hermitage Museum

made of leather, with four salmon-colored strips of suede, the stitching emphasized by a fine strip of cushioning in the same dark color as the spiral and lotus-shaped appliqué work decorating the body (ill. 2). Did it hold coriander seeds? A liquid? In any case, the stitching is sufficiently dense for it to be a watertight. It was discovered at the same time as a small round silver mirror and a leather pouch. The rectangular pouch, made in suede finely decorated with appliqué work in smooth leather, has a side pocket. Was it a toilet bag? Either way, the bottle, pouch, and mirror had been slipped inside the only object found in the tomb that would fully warrant use of the term "bag" according to our modern criteria. This is a bag with a strap, or, more precisely, double bag. Its two pockets — rounded rectangles measuring 30 x 40 cm — hang athwart an elegant wooden rod, whose ends are decorated with open-jawed feline heads. But the most surprising feature is the strap that divides into three at the end so it can be fixed to the center and ends of the object, thus making it easy to carry. Does this mean that the bag was carried around by its owner when walking? One major argument against this idea of a woman on foot, bag slung over her shoulder, is to be found in the woman's footwear. Made in soft red leather, the uppers

of her boots are woven throughout with pewter thread (ill. 3). Above all, the decoration of the soles is particularly splendid, with dozens of pyrite crystals painstakingly sewn in a careful pattern: charming, but not very practical for trekking. We might therefore assume that the ladies of the Altai, when not on horseback, sat cross-legged, the soles of their feet in full view, and that when they rose it was only to take a few steps across the yurt's thick rug. Here antique depictions and modern practice concur: men, too, walk but little and often wear soft-soled boots.

A small round pouch with a narrow neck, knotted at the top, served to procure other transports. In leather appliqué work on leather, we see the image of a capercaillie killed by a griffin (ill. 4). Found with the vestiges of fumigation equipment (burner, stakes, a large leather blanket), it contained hemp grains – or hashish. Thus the presence of this pouch confirms Herodotus's words to the effect that "the Scythians took their hemp seeds,

ill. 4 — **Leather clutch bag** (with leather applications showing a griffon attacking a black grouse) which contained hemp seeds, from tumulus 2, Pazyryk (Russian Altai)
4th century BC, Saint Petersburg, Hermitage Museum

went under blankets and threw the seeds on to stones reddened by fire; as they threw them, they gave off a strong-smelling smoke and produced a vapor such that no Greek oven could be stronger: charmed to be thus smoked, the Scythians let out great cries." In modern times, too, the shamans of Siberia have special bags, sometimes in otter or fish skin, to carry their ecstasy equipment.

The second tomb at Pazyryk also yielded an object that, in both shape and size, looks identical to those round leather purses whose top fits exactly over the containing part. But of course, in a world where barter was the only form of exchange, and wealth was measured in head of steer – a nomad with his herd was never impecunious – this was no receptacle for change.

This set of "bags", which certainly constitutes the oldest find of such a kind and in such quantity, is very close to the kinds of objects found until very recently among the cattle-rearing nomads of central Asia and Mongolia, before they had access to tin, Chinese enameled bowls and plastic jerry cans.

Halfway between antiquity and modern times, we can refer to accounts by those who traveled to Tartaria and Mongolia in the 13th century: Giovanni Piano Carpini and William of Rubruck. They describe skins full of fermented mare's milk, the famous *kumis*, which greeted visitors at the entrance to the yurt, the animals with packs, and the enormous travel bags on wheels used by the nomads. The latter were trunks as big "as a little house", made of woven sticks with a convex top, waterproofed with soot or a coating of ewe's milk, and set on high wheels so that they would not be damaged when fording rivers.

Rubruck also describes how, when a sheep was killed, guests took away any leftovers in a doggy bag, "a square pouch that they carry for such purposes, in which they even put bones, when they do not have the time, so that they can gnaw on them later, so that nothing goes to waste". In his *Memoirs*, Jean de Joinville, who was a prisoner of the Mamelukes in the same century, complains bitterly of the pestilential odor emanating from his guard's provisions, explaining that "What they cannot eat [they] throw into a leather bag which, when they are hungry, they open and always eat what is oldest first".

There can be no doubt that, when on the move, the nomads took with them skins for thirst and bags of dried cheese tied to their harnesses or, when they had one, to their saddle. But it is equally clear that the nomads kept their hands and shoulders free. They did not carry bags.

Things were different for the sedentary folk of villages and towns. Even those who had remained closer to the nomads, the rearers and shepherds who moved with their herds to find fresh pastures, in that vertical form of nomadism known as transhumance.

This, apparently, was the case of the man found in 1991 in the Alto Adige, known as Ötzi. One day, more than five thousand years ago, when presumably on his way to be with his herds summering in the high pastures, he was struck down and his body was later buried under the snow. Warmly dressed in a fiber and goatskin coat, with a bearskin cap, he was equipped with a bow, an axe, and a knife in a scabbard of woven grass. In addition to a kind of backpack, this experienced trekker also had waist bags: carefully stitched calfskin pouches and boxes in birch bark hanging around his belt, which held by way of tools

pastures, the *armaillis* have a bag with a decorated flap slung over their shoulder. In these images, the shepherds of the miniatures and the shepherds of the Nativity, like *santon* crèche figures, usually have a bag, just like the shepherd David as depicted in frescoes and paintings, when he was making ready to kill the giant Goliath.

Portmanteau words?

In fact the most nomadic thing about bags are their names. The words used to designate many of them have done a lot of traveling. In French, this is the case for the words *sac* (*sako* in Esperanto), and also *sacoche*, *besace*, *bissac*, and *biasse*. This is also the case with *couffin*, which comes from Latin, but via Arab. And then what about *fardeau*, from the word for a half-load on an Arabian camel. As for the English *bag*, it seems to have come from northern Italy and Provence, where a purse was called *baga*, *bagues* being the possessions that one carried, before becoming, with or without associated weapons, *baggage*. In the Slav world, too, next to the words *sumka*, which designates the beast of burden and

packs (the Greek *sagma*) and *mechok*, which – perhaps in a distant echo of the nomads? – refers to fur, the vocabulary for what one takes away on a journey, a suitcase (*tchemodan*) or trunk (*sunduk*), came, as if by chance, from the Turko-Tartar world of the Steppes. Less nomadic, less rich is the name given to nets for provisions in the Soviet period, *avoska*, which refers to the container that one carried "in case" a providential truck happened to spill a few apples or water melons on the street corner. It contrasts with the very chic *sakvouaïaj* whose French root (*sac voyage*) as it is geographically distant.

Sailors, soldiers, and tradesmen: sedentary folk in antiquity

With the possible exception of Egypt and a few exceptional cases, such as the frozen tombs of the Altai or Ötzi in his snow drift, setting out to find the reality about bags in the ancient

such essentials as tinder to make a fire and small shards of flint, in other words, the traditional penknife and lighter, plus bits of a therapeutic mushroom, the birch polypore, used to treat the stomach aches caused by an unwelcome parasite. Had he collapsed in the snow a few thousand years later on the slopes of the Grand Saint Bernard, Ötzi would have been saved by those famous monks' dogs with their reviving flask of rum. But how many people know that these were not the only bearer-dogs, and that, up until the 1960s, the postal service between Montgenèvre and the mountain infantrymen stationed in the refuge at Gondrans was provided by a rather unusual postman, a Pyrenean sheepdog by the name of Barrabas, who brought the mail in two big leather satchels strapped fast to his bag.

As for what Ötzi was carrying up to the mountain pastures, it was pretty much the same as what modern shepherds take. Except that nowadays, after its popularity at hippie get-togethers in the 1960s and since, the traditional shepherd's scrip has been replaced by the backpack.

Pierre Tellène was a shepherd all his life. Every year, on foot, he led his herd between the Comtat Venaissin and the Vercors. Seeing him walking in front of his herd on the way down from Jonchères to Poyols was quite something, just as it was to witness the passion with which he talked about his work and the climb to summer pastures, about the packs carried by the mules, and the contents of his bag: a hunk of bread, cheese, the all-important Opinel knife, string, salt in a block or in grains, "which does the beasts most good", the anti-viper vaccine, the marker for the ewes, and the jute bag with a little hole for the head for carrying lambs born en route. To this can be added the versatile plastic bag, for mushrooms or edible plants, and, in the past, a miniature portable sundial, although, as Tellène said, pointing to the sun, "my watch is several thousand years old", and, finally, the only truly modern element, the newspaper "that you don't have time to read". If we are to believe Giono, in *Jean le Bleu*'s bag, fresh tomme cheese sat alongside a volume of the *Illiad*.

In the Swiss pastoral world, too, in the *poyas* of Gruyère country, paintings representing the *alpée*, the herd's ascension to its

world is an undertaking that is bound to lead to much disappointment. Whether in hide or in straw, the bag's archaeological posterity is often short. As they say, coffins have no pockets, and it is no more common today for a dead person to be buried with their purse. So true is this, indeed, that those who were to be ferried across the Styx and the Acheron held the payment for the ferryman Charon wedged in their mouth. So, for bags, we have only texts and images to refer to. Even then we must bear in mind that that the former and, even more, the latter, constitute a highly selective language, a system of signs that bears only a very distant relation to reality. Look at your family album: where are your grandmothers' or aunts' bags?

Still, people did travel a great deal in ancient times. The Greeks, especially, crisscrossed the Mediterranean in search of new lands in which to found new cities, keeping their modest baggage on the decks or in the holds of their ships. For let us not forget that the very foundation of Greek culture is the city, that is to say, a community tied to a territory. A person without a home anywhere was therefore excluded, asocial; and vagrancy was the greatest of ills. In total contrast to the practices of nomadism, the Greeks always traveled, however far and however permanently, for a precise purpose, with the image of the cherished fatherland, island, or city firmly in mind. One need only think of the tragedy expressed in the *planè*, Demeter's frantic travels to find her daughter, who had been abducted by Hades. Or Odysseus, that image of chronic nostalgia, who it is hard to imagine with a bag over his shoulder. It is the gentle Calypso who, taking care of him, "put on board a skin of black wine, a bigger one of water and, in a leather bag, provisions for the journey". In Greece, the worst curse one could call down on an enemy was that of homelessness. And, paradoxically, when a Greek made the journey to an oracular sanctuary, especially Delphi, it was often to find out if the journey he was planning would go well and if he would come back safe and sound.

If we set aside the boundless curiosity of the brilliant Herodotus, the idea of traveling for pleasure, of tourism, only began to emerge much later, when the rich, cultivated citizens

of imperial Rome went on pilgrimages to their cultural roots, in Greece. With them they – or, more probably, their servant – carried the Baedeker of the day, Pausanias's *Description of Greece*.

Major journeys were generally military or commercial in purpose. As is suggested by the image of the modest pack, no doubt a calabash, hanging from the lances of the footsoldiers on the Warrior Vase from Mycenae, the first campaigning armies probably traveled light. In the Classical period, we know that valets and equerries accompanied the hoplites (armed infantry) and cavalrymen, and carried their bags, leaving them only a light haversack. But things were very different in Alexander the Great's day, on his campaigns into India and those of his successors, the Diadochi. Behind them, the armies trailed a whole crowd, an enormous retinue of women and children, of mimes and musicians, of canteen keepers and *hetairas* (courtesans), of enslaved captives, not to mention professional marauders and the booty collected on the way, following in heavy carts. As the *Augustan History* informs us, the Roman emperor Heliogabalus never traveled with less than six hundred vehicles. More modestly, Roman comedy gives us the complaints of a valet trying to convince his master that when on cam-

paign one cannot expect to have all the conveniences of civil life, carried on men's backs. But all these accoutrements did not travel in bags so much as in rolled bundles that were tied and often sewn, as attested by the Latin word *sarcinae*, which designates the pack carried by soldiers on a pitchfork.

As for merchants, even on foot, they used soft bags as containers. When Odysseus disguises himself as a peddler and comes to the court of King Lycomedes looking for Achilles, whom Theta has disguised among the king's daughters so that he may be spared battle, he uses tied bolster-like bags to hold the women's trinkets and, hidden in their midst, the sword that will prompt the young warrior to reveal his true nature. Then there was long-distance trade, as on the Silk Road. The reliefs at Palmyra show whole caravans crossing the desert to go to the Euphrates, with loaded camels, men on foot or on horseback, in Parthian, Persian or Roman costumes, but without any other bags than those carried by the animals. Nor do the women in this relief

ill. 6 (opposite) et 7 — **Gold quiver cover** decorated with scenes from the life of Achilles, from tumulus 8 of the Five-brothers group 4th century BC, Rostov Museum

On the upper frieze on the left, Ulysses has disguised himself as a pedlar in order to enter the gynaeceum of the daughters of Lycomedes (King of Skyros). Achilles' mother Thetis has left her son there in the hope of saving him from the death at Troy that the seer Calchas has predicted for him. But the Greeks cannot win the war without Achilles – and the wily Ulysses has hidden a weapon among the trinkets he has for sale. So here is Achilles, full face, his warlike virility recovered. In the room full of goods, one of the women, sitting on a knotted bundle, is restraining her companion who is swirling like a maenad.

carry reticules, although the sculpture reveals every detail of their finery, embroideries and jewelry. But then were not the Parthians ultimately nomads?

Daily comings and goings

Baggage, though, is not the same thing as bags. What about everyday movements around the city – to the market, to the *palestra*? Let us leave aside the universal shoulder pieces from whose ends animals were hung, their legs tied together as they were carried to market, or on which buckets were taken to and from the fountain. We can also leave aside the vegetal containers of all kinds that survived unchanged through the centuries. Photographs taken when Tutankhamen's tomb was opened attest to the fact that in Egypt, the dominant receptacles were not leather bags but chests, baskets, woven panniers, back baskets, and other wicker items. These reflected the importance of the fertilizing river (crocodiles notwithstanding). Also, while we can certainly recognize the hollowed cucurbitaceae behind calabashes and pumpkins, few of us know that the ciborium used in churches comes from the dried cupule of the Nile waterlily.

Elsewhere, as in the forests of northern Europe, such functions were performed by woven bast and interlaced strips of birch bark, used as bags and even backpacks.

In Greece, too, we can be sure, when they went picnicking around the rural shrines of Attica, that Athenians took with them wicker baskets and pottery jugs. And when going to the *palestra*, young people carried their perfumed oil in a ceramic *aryballos* or alabaster, slipping their sponge and strigil and, in some cases, a game of dibs, in bags that were often made of net. On arrival, those who boxed could use a punching ball constituted by a big round leather bag filled with seeds.

As for the ladies, if perchance they came out on foot, and not in a litter, a follower would have been there to carry what they needed. In the gynaeceum, indeed, ceramic boxes known as *pyxis* served as toilet bags. As for Roman women, they sometimes went out with a *reticulum*, made of netting, which, with the advent of the woman's bag, would become the reticule, and as such, soon ridiculous. But what other kind of handbag would they have envisaged, since the law forbade that they traveled any longer than three days away from their husband, on pain of their marriage's legitimacy being called into question.

Carrying and being carried

The beginning of Aristophanes' *The Frogs* makes it clear that carrying was not a self-evident action for men. This play within a play parodies the traditional stage entrance of the master followed by his servant from Attic comedy. The master is Dionysos, ridiculously dressed in a saffron-yellow woman's tunic and leopard skin. As for the servant, he presents the equally grotesque spectacle of a man propped up on a donkey, carrying over his shoulder a stick with his master's heavy bundle. Dionysos complains that he is tiring himself out walking, leaving his slave the mount "so that he doesn't get tired and has no load to carry". There follows an aggressive exchange to determine whether it is the donkey or the slave riding it who is carrying the weight of the bundle. And

Dionysos, who is clearly in bad faith, replies thus to the slave who, for lack of any other arguments, exhibits his sore shoulder: "Well, since you claim that the donkey is no use, lift it up and carry it too."

It is true that the peplos and toga are not well suited to carrying bags over the shoulder. The holster of the day, the *zona*, a discreet belt-purse, was worn under the garment. This was the target of pickpockets, who were consequently called "cut-belts". This is where Lucullus' soldier must have kept the money before everything was stolen, "one night when he was snoring, shattered by fatigue".

On occasion, too, folds and pockets in the garment might also be used. Anticipating the later tradition of using hats, shoes, underwear, and puffed sleeves. Many a traveler carried more than hay in their boots and lined them with gold. Not to mention the other tricks familiar to customs men: fake pregnancies or recipients fitting the forms of the body, like the one used

be social rejects, outcasts. At the best, marginals, a *histrion* or low-class charlatan. Or the poor. Those who "go with the bag". They are the subject of the famous "Kyrie of the Beggars": "Hey! Walk, beggars/Wandering without hearth or home,/Double bag and empty belly,/To calamitous times".

And it was not until centuries later, with the triumph of Christianity, that the figure of the pilgrim appeared. Whether a *Romieu*, heading to Rome to see the tomb of Saint Peter, or a *Jacquet*, on the road to Santiago de Compostela, or a pilgrim walking to expiate his sins, his characteristic attribute, along with the cape (*pelèrine*) and *bourdon* (staff) to which his gourd was attached, is the scrip. Depicted in the images, and certainly used in practice, it was used mainly to hold bread – hence its other French name: *panetière*.

But for the land-loving, rather stay-at-home and somewhat xenophobic Romans, the *peregrinus* was little better than an enemy. Indeed, it would be easy to contrast the Roman, who, when he left home, filled a bag with his domestic gods, his *penates*, with the Phoenician or Greek, who traded what he had with foreigners. To contrast the bag that brings to the other the outside world and the one that cautiously carried one's own world.

The return of the nomad

People in ancient times would certainly have been surprised to see all the well-dressed people carrying superb bags in our modern cities. We rarely realize that this daily use of the bag is an extremely recent phenomenon. Not much more than a century ago, the Baronne Staffe, then considered the supreme arbiter of good manners, never mentions the things. In contrast, the use and gestures accompanying the hat, cane, and parasol, as well as gloves, handkerchiefs, and fans, were all strictly codified. Likewise, there is no trace of the bag in proverbs, sayings, and superstitions, except perhaps in the fairly rare but substantiated belief that to put a bag on a bed augurs poverty, since the money will sleep there.

Today, carrying a bag is no longer a sign of inferior status. If anything, it's the opposite. In a big city, in fact, going without a bag inspires mistrust, just as a traveler without luggage does

until recent times by smugglers taking alcohol through the Alpine passes between Italy and France. More innocently, anyone who has been to the markets in the Middle East or around the Mediterranean or elsewhere will remember that swift gesture made by men raising their jellabas. Or the Russian *baba* pulling up her skirt to get at the wad of notes stuffed into the top of her stocking. Hiding coins is hardly a problem for anyone except nudists, and even then...

Going "with a bag"

So, like the ladies of the Directoire in transparent dresses who, having no bag, used a kerchief-holding "protector", people of high station in ancient times carried nothing. They were accompanied by attendants, slaves, or bearers. Consequently, to carry was to be of low status. One had to be a philosopher like Seneca to praise the modesty of the elderly Cato who "rode a gelding loaded with a double saddle bag [*hippopera*] in which he could take what he needed", and then to boast, in a letter to his friend Lucilius, that he traveled "with nothing other than what our body is capable of carrying".

Only carriers and the poor – those who were obliged to travel on foot and could not afford attendants – carried a bag, usually a double bag carried over the shoulder. This is why an inscription on a cameo in the *Palatine Anthology* describes such bags as "the gracious panoply of poor folk". This is what Martial is referring to when he evokes "a procession of bags suited to the hoi polloi of the [Helles-] Pont" – that is to say, migrants from the Black Sea, whom Roman-born citizens, as one would expect, blamed for every ill and looked down on with a mixture of contempt and fear, much as gypsies are today. This made life hard for the Evangelists. In one letter, Saint Paul asks for his tablet bag, which he has been forced to leave on his way.

But to repeat a point, for the Greeks, who despised mule drivers, those whose profession meant being out on the road – unless they were doctors going to tend a patient, artists ready to carry out a commission, or, possibly, hawkers – could only

for the hotelier. Is it because contemporary life with its many changes of location is making us increasingly nomadic? Ever since the chest ceased to be the possession of the miser and ever since bugs went from beds to computers, along with the mouse, the self-theatricalization involved in carrying bags has changed radically. Today, the only people to carry short-handled handbags, or to place them primly on their knees, are women heads of state or the wives of heads of state. In the modern street, whether women or men, mature women or school children, the great majority of our contemporaries carry a bag over their shoulder, or even on their back. Thus, in these days of "doing it all oneself", when, as the poet says, "everyone is both the king and the camel", people increasingly tend to have the free gait and noble bearing of the walker with his hands free. Is the bag a symbol of liberation? It was, at least for those who wished to be freed of every constraint: philosophers.

The philosopher's bag: the Cynics

Philosophy seems ill at ease with comfort and confined spaces. Whether the Sophists who came from elsewhere in strange old clothes and had the cheek to deliver their teachings in the street, or the Peripatetics, walking with Aristotle through the porticoes of the Lyceum, walking and philosophizing have always gone well together.

The stories about Diogenes are well known. He was the "philosopher tramp", a man of no fixed abode who lived in a barrel, Diogenes the Cynic, the "dog" who lit his lantern in broad daylight and, when Alexander the Great came to visit him, waved him away and barked "Get out of my light!" It hardly matters whether or not the story is true. Or whether the anachronic barrel was not in fact a kind of kennel or, more likely, as ancient images show, a big jar. What is sure is that in Athens in the fourth century BCE, Diogenes and his disciples, such as Crates, Hipparchia, and Monimus, embodied not only a nonconformism, but a philosophy of total rejection, the wholesale rejection of established values in the name of the wisdom brought by self-mastery.

In a very amusing text, "Down with Sects", Lucian has Jupiter, helped by Mercury, deciding to auction off philosophers of every stripe and breed. After someone has come forward to purchase "the long-haired Ionian" Pythagoras, it is the turn of Diogenes, but the Cynic is pretty much unsaleable. This "filthy man born in the Pont", this "man with a bag and sleeveless tunic" preaches frugality, the renunciation of all things: home, family, homeland. Advocating impudence and insolence, the only compensation he promises, before his price is slashed to two oboluses, "a scrip full of lupins and books written on two pages".

This bag carried over the shoulder was the ordinary attribute of the Cynics, along with the bare feet they kept to all year round, their long hair, the coat they wore straight over the skin and their staff. The road was their home. Their philosophy made them hawkers and tramps, vagrants and raggedy loiterers, beggars of the truth. Citizens of the world and partisans of free love, their numbers included women such as Hipparchia, who left her rich parents to join the company of Crates the Cynic. Apparently little inclined to "mystical foolishness", she gave the lie to Bouvard and Pécuchet and had, according to the expression coined, curiously, by Flaubert, "serious intellectual baggage". One day, left speechless by her infallibly rigorous philosophical reasoning, her interlocutor lifted up her tunic to be sure that she was a woman. And, according to Antipater of Sidon, rather than take offence, she calmly replied that, "I, Hipparchia, did not choose the work of women with wide dresses, but the powerful life of the Cynics; I did not want the clipped tunic, the thick-soled clogs, the shining net, but the scrip." More than two thousand years later, the great traveler and mystic Isabelle Eberhardt, in an ardent encomium of itinerancy, wrote of one "Breaking all shackles [...] taking up the symbolic staff and scrip, and *leaving*".

What was there in Hipparchia's bag? In her vanity case? To list the contents is to play the game of "What do I put in my bag?" but backwards ("What do I remove from my bag?"). For a long time, the Cynic's bag contained a simple bowl, to draw water from fountains. But when, one day, he saw a child drinking from his cupped hand, Diogenes threw away the bowl. And the bag remained empty. Hipparchia's bag was empty too. Or rather, resolutely emptied – of face paints, deceptive mirrors, handkerchiefs unable to wipe away tears, books with the addresses of friends who are not friends, pens for unpleasant ink. Emptied of money that corrupts, goods that weigh down, accumulation that bogs down. Empty of everything that was renounced in the name of what Diogenes said was the most beautiful thing in the world: freedom of language and thought. Hipparchia's existential scrip represents the triumph of adventure over comfort, of uncertainty over certainty, of immediate being over accumulated possessions, of itinerant thought over rooted philosophy, of humor over irony. In this sense, yes, the Cynic's bag is indeed a nomad's bag. Empty, yes, but with what capacity!

The Secret Riches of Adelita

Ill. 1. — opposite **Soldadera, Pachuca, Mexico, 1911-1914, Casasola collection, Mexico, INAH, Pachuca photolibrary.

Should Adelita leave me for another,

I would follow her over land and sea,

Over the sea in a vessel of war,

Over the land in an army train.

— Banal and almost childlike, these four lines seem to be no more than a man's song about his love for a woman and his fear of seeing her leave. Wrong: for this is the refrain of one of the most famous *corridos* of the Mexican revolution of 1910. Naive ballads based on a simple, repetitive melody, the *corridos* first appeared in the early 19th century and enjoyed a steadily growing popularity that modern times and modern communications have done nothing to lessen. The *corrido* is a sung narrative, sometimes the product of the purest invention, sometimes founded on actual events as filtered through its author's emotions and musical abilities. The subject matter is varied and often tragic: everyday occurrences, crimes of passion, railroad accidents, wars, and revolutions. Inevitably the Mexican *soldadera* found her place in the *corrido*, immortalized as Adelita.

European travelers, a feature of the Mexican scene between the early days of independence and that famous revolution, were startled by a feature of the numerous local armies. Throughout a long and troubled national history these fighting bodies, as quick to break up as they were to form, were not composed solely of men. For rather than be separated from their families, the soldiers – poor peasants, landless laborers conscripted by force, hobos, and unemployed city-dwellers recruited in taverns – would bring their women and children with them.

Thus could Mexican troops be seen advancing towards some distant enemy: a long, colorful procession in which uniforms and guns mix with *rebozos* (native shawls) and long skirts, with clamoring, trotting children clinging to them. The enemy force, most likely, was very much the same. And even more than the valiant, ill-equipped soldier trailing willy-nilly behind his officer, another figure characterized these armies, and enriched them, both literally and figuratively: the *soldadera*.

Under the pens and the lenses of war correspondents from John Reed to Jack London, the revolution of 1910 brought her respectability and a fame immune to the passing of time. Out of the reality was born the myth of Adelita la Soldadera, the fighting woman of the armies of the North, a myth so potent that it still rivals those of the great revolutionary leaders, in all their maleness and violence: Francisco Madero, Pancho Villa, and Emiliano Zapata.

A veritable Madonna in arms, Adelita was the embodiment of devotion, fidelity, and courage. Famed for her readiness for combat, the *soldadera* was credited, often rightly, with acts of great valor: striding the battlefield when the fighting was at its fiercest, succoring the wounded, recovering arms and bullets from the dying, reloading rifles at her lover's side. Many are the photographs and newspaper articles testifying to her presence, her deeds of valor, and sometimes, even, her involvement in the fighting.

Yet these saints of the revolution were celebrated for other virtues too: for their sensuality, their beauty, and even an overt sexuality that would ultimately, in a typically potent Latino-Indian mix, transform fearsome warriors into objects of desire.

Loved by the troop was Adelita,
The woman the sergeant idolized,
Full of courage as well as of beauty,
And respected by the colonel himself.

Yet despite the military contribution of the *soldaderas* – many are the accounts of their admirable, fear-inspiring skill with a gun – the myth masked an often more unobtrusive and above all more humble role. Sometimes a fighter, and often present on the battlefield, Adelita was first and foremost a companion in war. The woman following her man. Sometimes wife, often mistress, she was also the servant who warmed his bed and bore his children.

Ill. 2. — opposite. **Jose Clemente Orozco**, *Las Soldaderas*, 1929, Mexico, Museum of Modern Art.

Her main duty was to keep her man fed so that he could fight. Supplies were crucial to these armies with no quartermaster and no health facilities; and Adelita had to compete with her sisters as, sometimes far from the main body of troops, they risked their lives roaming the countryside in search of food, clothing, shoes, and, even, money and bullets. Then, returning with what she had been able to find in villages already pillaged a dozen times, she would prepare the fighter's bed and his meal. Faithful to the man whose wounds she bound and whose sleep she protected, Adelita would be separated from him only when a bullet – or perhaps another woman – took him from her.

With massive use of the railroad allowing for rapid, large-scale troop transfers, the revolutionary armies of the North were constantly on the move, bringing thousands of people in their wake. From ruined barracks to railroad station, from desert bivouac to plundered palace, Adelita followed her soldier, setting up camp countless times and then, as soon as the order to march was given, gathering up her things in the piece of cloth that transported, protected, and hid them.

Made of wool or linen in the case of the wealthiest fighters or the most skilled looters, this item was most often no more than the broad *rebozo*, the simple square of cloth, sometimes ornamented, that has always fulfilled endless functions in rural Mexico. As a cover for the head and shoulders it protects the woman from the sun and the

eyes of others; tied around the waist or over the shoulder it is used to carry small children. And for Adelita, as for all uprooted people, it was also the *lío de ropa*, the universal bundle.

Heavy and bulging, capacious and inconvenient, it was dragged onto station platforms and open wagons, thrown into carts and transported on foot over long distances, sometimes for days on end: on the back, Indian-fashion, with a strap across the forehead to hold it in place. This traditional, pre-Columbian mode of carrying things is that of the peasantry; Adelita used it then, and it is still in use today.

While the 30-30 carbine she handled so well has become the media image of a certain violent and bloody form of emancipation, should we ignore the real symbol of Adelita's condition? Endlessly torn and patched, the bundle is the holder of her humble wealth. A nomad's sanctuary, the secret domain of a life offered to all, it shelters things we shall probably never see: a few holy images, her "war treasures", her poor clothing and, more importantly, that of the man for whom she is companion, nurse, and mourner.

And if I die on the battlefield
And the y bury my body there,
Adelita, I implore in God's name,
With your eyes you must weep for me.

ill. 2 — opposite **Travelling bag,** Paris, France, 19th century, tapestry bag, leather bellows, leather bottom, clasp in metal with leather sheath
round handles with leather sheaths, interior lined with cotton fabric, Emile Hermès collection

ill. 3 — opposite **Overnight case,** France, first half of 19th century, tapestry bag with leather padded bellows, clasp in metal, canvas sheath, interior lined in cotton
base lies on overnight case with wooden core and leather sheath, encircled with steel and pewter nails, Emile Hermès collection

The Carpetbag:
Packing the Essential

ill. 1 — **Abraham Solomon,** *The Mailcoach leaving Biarritz,* 19th century, London, Royal Holloway and Bedfort New College

— "But the trunks?" gasped Passepartout. "...We'll have no trunks; only a carpetbag, with two woollen shirts and three pairs of stockings for me, and the same for you."[1] Many generations of Western travelers, wealthy or not-so-wealthy followers of Diogenes, have made do with the simple sort of bag in which Phileas Fogg planned to store the garments for his 80-day journey round the world. This "useful furniture" for travelers, which contains those vital items for changing at night, is mentioned as far back as the Renaissance. Made in canvas or woven fabric, that modular, nomadic material supposedly copied from "the fabric of dreams", it began life with what would be its most enduring qualities: modest bulk, convenience, lightness. In the 16th century, we find a "carpet of night needs in orange damask with the fringe in orange-white and rosy-gray silk" alongside the "bag for combs and wool" in the inventory of Jeanne de Bourdeilles' possessions. Dating from 1599, Gabrielle d'Estrées' list describes "a small night chest, embroidered in gold and lined with satin, priced at XXX escus. In which was found garments, in cloth of gold, embroidered in same and a carpetbag in same with fringes and *crespines*".[2]

ill. 4 — page overleaf
Abraham Solomon
Travelling Third Class, 1854
Canberra, National Gallery of Australia

The carpetbag also plays a role in the literature of the Enlightenment. Diderot "throws it down" at his door as he "passes through", as if to hasten the end of his journey, with the vivacious spirit that so enlivens his letters to Sophie Volland.[3] The obscure author of the *Voyage de Saint-Cloud par mer et par terre,* published at The Hague in 1748, is more prudent, as we can see from his laborious preparations: "Having heard that when traveling one should encumber oneself with baggage only as little as possible, in this case: my striped calamanco dressing gown, two shirts with tails, two summer caps, a saffron-yellow velvet bonnet embroidered with silver, slippers, a powder bag, my recorder, my geographical map, my compass, my pencil, my writing desk, six packs of piquet, three games of Comet, a game of snakes and ladders, and my Hours."[4]

As a realistic touch, depicted as a supple pouch in carpet fabric or rep, closed with a cord drawn through eyelets, the carpetbag is a picturesque feature of the genre paintings evoking travel by followers of Boilly and Leprince, that were popularized in early 19th-century lithographs. Such bags were already competing with suitcases when, in 1826, a Parisian manufacturer, one Pierre Godillot, at the Bazar du Voyage, 55 rue Montorgueil, added some very persuasive improvements: a steel clasp with a padlock, known as the *feuillard*, and two handles. With the final touch of a bottom in leather and cardboard, the invention now took on the seductive allure of an *article de Paris*: practical, modern, and elegant. Hence the provincial Eugénie Grandet's doe-eyed fascination with her cousin Charles, who entered the dull life of Saumur haloed with the glamor of those handsome inventions of Parisian life – among them, carpetbags filled with fine linen.[5] Then, in 1836, the ever-smart Godillot had the idea of attaching beneath the carpetbag an independent leather suitcase with copper studs, closed by means of a clasp, and strengthened by buckled leather straps fixed to the carpetbag. Hawkers' catalogs of fancy goods presented shopkeepers in the provinces with pictures of attractive models, painted in gouache, offering a choice between canvas, carpet, and cotton, and with decoration running from multicolored stripes, to flowers, a galloping horse, or an eagle. This being the age of (the) steam (horse), the accessory was known as the "railway bag". Across the Channel, the carpetbag played

a comic role in many highly regrettable incidents that persuaded the English – among the world's greatest travelers – *never* to go abroad. A *frightful* place, indeed! Ideally combining the suppleness of the pouch and the rigidity of the box, the carpetbag epitomized the kind of light, who-dares-wins type of bag that Balzac recommended to his fortune-hunting heroes. An ideal companion for artistic hearts. In London one night, wandering along the tightrope of chance, fleeing the "limp bonds of habit",[6] Gérard de Nerval experienced the pleasure of being "master of the town [...] and all that thanks to the precaution of bringing only a very simple packet".[7] In tune with the bohemian spirit that sent a thousand Romantic writers out onto the road, the carpetbag contrasts with the unbearable clutter of trunks, packets, provisions, and itineraries with which the traveling bourgeois caparisoned himself, along with tons of certitudes and prejudices – and which made him a sitting duck for the sarcasm of Thackeray, George Sand, Hugo, and Flaubert. This bulging belly of baggage also irritated Stendhal, for whom the felicitous simplicity of the carpetbag made it essential to the tourist's happiness. "In France", he noted, "there is no more unpleasant moment than when the steamboat reaches its destination; everyone makes a grab for their trunk or packets, mercilessly toppling the mountain of sundry possessions piled up on the deck. Everyone is in a foul mood and everyone is rude. My poverty saved me from this predicament: I took up my carpetbag and was one of the first to walk the plank that took me to the cobblestones."[8] In the much more tragic Parisian mêlée described in the Goncourts' *Journal* for 18 April, the carpetbag holds the bare necessities called for by an emergency. It cancels out social differences. "At every street corner one came upon people, men and women, carrying the carpetbag, the travel bag, the little packet that was all they could take in their flight from Paris."[9]

Steeped in the charm and mystery of Romantic wandering, patinaed from the companionship of long coach journeys at night, pale in the moonlight, speckled with wax from the candles in inns, with the ink from fevered quills, the carpetbag disappeared from the world of rapid travel in the 20th century. Left in the oblivion of attics, over the years its faded carpeting sunk back into a faintly ridiculous silhouette over its wooden frame But this familiar form did not dis-

ill. 7 — **Overnight, travelling and hunting bags, hat box and trunks,** two sheets of a bound catalogue, France, beginning of 19th century, green suede, gouache and wash-paint watercolour on crayon outline, touches of arabic gum varnish, Paris, Emile Hermès collection

ill. 8 — opposite **"Railway bags..."**, sheet from a bound catalogue, France, beginning of 19th century, green suede, gouache and wash-paint watercolour on crayon outline, touches of arabic gum varnish, Paris, Emile Hermès collection

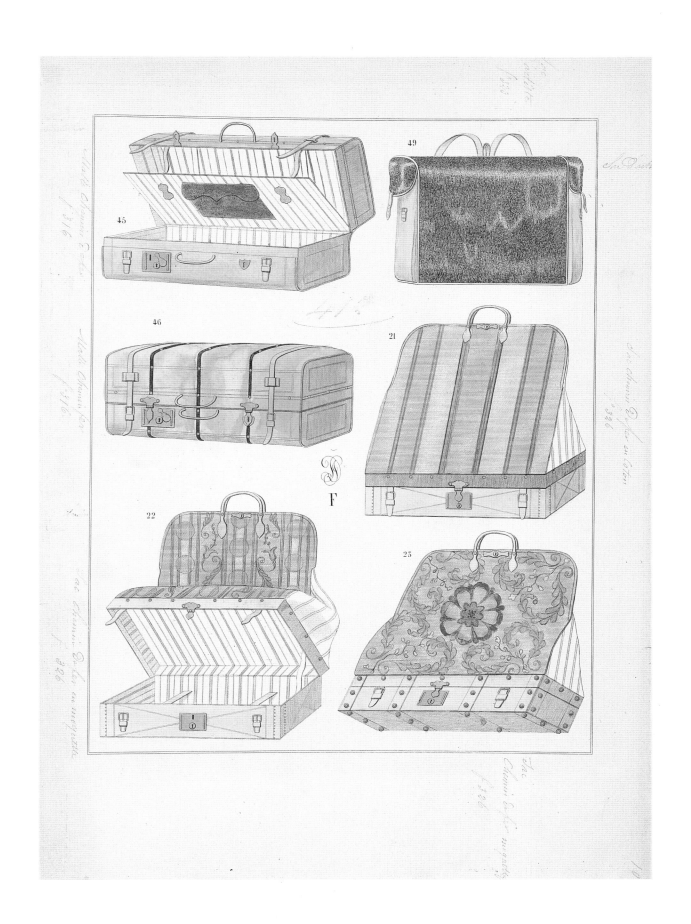

appear. Rather, it changed, thanks to visionaries and collectors, such as Emile Hermès, who loved to revive the soul of the days of the horse and carriage, a soul still alive among past objects and tastes. Calling it a *sac-mallette* (bag-suitcase), the Parisian saddler re-imagined the ancient invention, swapping canvas for the eternal youth of carefully stitched leather, adapting it to the age of "people in a hurry" by adding a zipper. The structure was organized so that it could exactly hold an outfit or a lady traveler's jewels. Later, a supermodel requested that it be made to hold her entire collection of make-up. Chosen from the Hermès catalogue for 1923, the bag-suitcase was acclaimed in the journal *L'Esprit nouveau* in 1924, where a series of anonymous articles set out to offer readers "preliminary thoughts on the big Exposition Universelle des Arts Décoratifs" to be held in Paris in 1925. Le Corbusier (who soon confessed to authorship) saw it as a response to the bold challenge that he himself had laid down to "decorative art today", which was to create tools suited to this new spirit, freed at last of the "dead end of deco-

ration" and the "fragility of sentimental design".[10] For the architect, the bags developed by Emile Hermès exemplified these "objects of perfect convenience, of perfect utility, whose elegant design, purity of execution, and efficiently rendered services exude a sense of true luxury, and boost our morale". Paul Valéry deemed the article remarkable. Was this homage from the pioneer of the "New Spirit" a prophecy that the travel bag, that essential companion of peregrinating poets, an item almost as old, useful, and reassuring as the night, would outlast fashion?

1 Jules Verne, *Around the World in Eighty Days*, Chap. 4 "In which Phileas Fogg astounds Passepartout, his servant," Paris: J. Hetzel, 1873, p. 18.

2 Henry Havard, *Dictionnaire de l'ameublement et de la décoration depuis le XIIIᵉ siècle jusqu'à nos jours*, Vol. 4, Paris: Ancienne Maison Quantin, 1887-1890, p. 865-866.

3 *Diderot's Letters to Sophie Volland*, Oxford: OUP, 1972.

4 *Voyage de Saint-Cloud par mer et par terre*, The Hague: 1748. Quoted by Henri d'Alméras, *Au bon vieux temps des diligences*, Paris: Albin Michel, 1931, p. 141: "The author is thought to be an obscure writer, Louis Balthazar Néel, born in Rouen, who died in 1754, or, according to de Jouy, Crébillon *fils* in collaboration with his friend Sallé."

5 Honoré de Balzac, *Scènes de la vie de province*, I, *Eugénie Grandet*, Paris: Furne, J.J. Dubochet et Cie, J. Hetzel, 1843, p. 230, 233.

6 Gérard de Nerval, *Oeuvres*, Vol. 2, *Notes de voyage*, Paris: NRF-Gallimard, Bibliothèque de la Pléiade, 1961: *Lettres d'Allemagne: I. Le Goût des voyages*, p. 886.

7 *Ibid., Un tour dans le Nord: II. Une nuit à Londres*, p. 859.

8 Stendhal, *Mémoires d'un touriste*, 2, Paris: A. Dupont, 1838, p. 1: "Nantes, le 25 juin 1837".

9 Goncourt Brothers, *Journal*, April 18 1871, Vol. 4, p. 211.

10 *L'Esprit nouveau, revue internationale illustrée de l'activité contemporaine […] Arts, lettres, sciences, Directeurs Ozenfant et Ch.-E. Jeanneret*, Paris: Editions de l'Esprit Nouveau, No. 24, 1924: "1925, Expo. Arts déco: L'art décoratif d'aujourd'hui," anonymous article included in Le Corbusier, *L'Art décoratif d'aujourd'hui*, Paris: Collection de l'Esprit nouveau, G. Grès, 1925, reprinted Paris: Vincent, Fréal et Cie, 1959, p. 91.

ill. 8 **Bag-suitcase**, Hermès, France, around 1925, *Crocodilus niloticus* in gold, lined in shagreen, nickel-plated brass, Conservatory of Hermès Creations collection

Among the Tuareg

ill.1 — opposite **Tuareg Chief**, photograph by A. Pérignon, 19th century, photograph album of Senegal, French Sudan and Dahomey Geography Society collection, small bags for various uses, money, amulets, tobacco, etc

Tanning hides and working leather

— For the Tuareg, a people of nomadic herders, leather is a material that is always available. On religious holidays (Eid al-Kabir, the end of Ramadan) and at social gatherings (marriages or feasts to welcome a distinguished guest), animals are sacrificed and their hides hold out the promise of the creation of new leather goods. In each family, it is the women who prepare the skins of the slaughtered animals. Leather is used in a wide range of objects.

Before tanning, hair is generally removed from the hides, using a process that involves sprinkling them with the ash of the bark and wood of certain trees.[1] Another method uses a decoction of *tezaq* leaves (*Salvadora persica*) that have been pounded and mixed with cow urine and a herb called *tazirt* (*Pergularia tomentos*), which is also dried and pounded. The skins are then scraped and washed before being steeped for several days in a wooden recipient containing various tanning agents like the bark of the *tamat* (*Acacia ehrenbergiana*) or *afagag* (*Acacia tortilis* subsp. *raddiana*) trees. This involves stripping off entire sections of bark and can cause considerable damage to the trees. *Tiggart* (*Acacia nilotica*) pods may also be used. Hides that are set aside for prayer rugs and occasionally for water skins are not stripped of their fur and hence are not treated in this tanning bath. The skins to be made into rugs are spread out in a hole in

the ground and only the inner surface is wet with a little water containing tanning agents. As for water skins, they are first sewn, then filled with the same tanning solution and regularly shaken over several days.

In Egypt, where the largest known piece of leather is the tent of Queen Isimkheb (21st dynasty, around 1050 BC), these tanning techniques, which are still employed by Sahelian herders, were already in use more than five thousand years ago:

"Egyptians were acquainted with two processes for tanning hides. One method, known as 'chamoisage,' uses only grease. In the other, the skins were steeped in a decoction of acacia (*Acacia nilotica*) pods. Both techniques were being used as early as 3500 BC, and certain depictions show the craftsman lifting the skin from its tanning bath in order to stretch it out on a trestle before working it... Leather was sometimes braided or cut into thin strips for decorative reasons."[2]

This reference does make clear the extraordinary continuity, with regard to time and place, of traditional leatherworking techniques.

While preparing skins is a domestic task, carried out by women across Tuareg society, dyeing, tooling, manufacturing (cutting and sewing), braiding or making trimmings is the exclusive domain of the wives of the *inadan*, who are specialized craftsmen. These women are never without their *elkeleb*, a small four-legged stool, on which they cut up the leather with a *wilred*, a knife, whose blade, like its handle, is flat, broad and rounded. Next to each woman stands a small pot of glue for assembling certain decorative elements on objects like wallets, sheaths or saddles.

Men's bags and women's bags

Vegetable dyes[3] are mainly used as coloring agents. The rusted husks of wild or domestic sorghum, for example, are dried and pounded to obtain the color red. Green, which is much used to decorate wallets, sheaths and camel saddles, is imported from Nigeria; Tuareg craftsmen use fragments of leather that has already been dyed, brought by merchants from Kano. The color green is obtained with a mixture of iron oxide, lemon, goat hair and peanut oil, to which a green powder, copper sulfate, is added.

Inside a Tuareg tent, bags can be seen hanging from poles. When a Tuareg travels by camel, his bag is almost always attached to the side of his mount. Names of bags sometimes vary from one region to another, even if certain models are found universally.

For the full picture of bags in Tuareg society, we can consult the dictionary written by Father Charles de Foucauld, which lists almost all the kinds of bags in use, with descriptions and often illustrations.[4] De Foucauld's work records fifteen different names, including the wallets that the Tuareg carry crosswise over the shoulder. Although we cannot go into all of them here, the list does clarify certain types of bags and their uses. This inventory excludes bags made from cloth or vegetable fiber.

First of all, there exists a generic name, *asamed* (plur. *isumad*), which refers to a bag of any shape, size and material — usually made of leather, although cloth bags also go by this name. Next, a distinction can be drawn between travel bags for women and those for men. Women's bags are quite wide, with an opening above, sporting a long fringe; men's bags are generally square-shaped and also open at the top. Both are ceremonial bags, which are elaborately decorated and designed to be carried on the side of a traveler's mount. There is likewise a series of bags, categorized by size, which can contain all sorts of things. Some, called *isumad*, (sing. *asamed*), contain grain, usually millet; these are kinds of mobile granaries that are stowed with the men's bags in the tent.

Over their clothes, men always wear a small leather bag with numerous pockets, hanging from their necks by a cord. Designed to hold written messages, most often it contains chewing tobacco, which the Tuareg are very fond of; they may also carry a supply of natron, which they mix in with each pinch of snuff. There also exist wallets in a range of sizes, although the most widespread type, meant for adults, measures 15 cm in length. Made of black leather, it sports a leather fringe along the bottom with colored wool embroidery on the side.

The ladies' travel bag goes by various names in the Ahaggar (also known as the Hoggar) Mountains and in the southern Sahara, where it is most frequently called *taseihat*. Meant to hold women's clothes, this wide bag has two straps on its upper part, so that it can hang beneath the saddle along the mount's flank. It also has a side flap and an abundant fringe of thin leather strips. It can be shut with a sliding fastener to which a lock can be attached. The Ahaggar[5] bag displays a decorative pattern of large crosses with colored diamond design in the corners and a series of fringes that have been dyed in harmonious shades of red and ocher.

An *eljebira* is a men's travel bag that is hung from a dromedary saddle:

"The *eljebira* is square; its sides measure from 10 to 65 cm in length. It is open above along its entire length; a flap made of scalloped skin covered with embroidery folds over the entire back part of the bag, reaching all the way to the bottom. The *eljibara* is used by male travelers to store all kinds of objects and belongings."[6]

Another model, the *abaun*, also used exclusively by men, is rectangular (from 70 cm to 1 m in length), with two straps that allow it to be hung from a dromedary saddle. It closes with a sliding fastener and a lock can be added if necessary.

The blacksmith possesses numerous tools that he transports to his work in the camps that he visits: hammers, chisels, bellows, anvil, burin, etc. He carries these implements in a leather toolbag. Finally, a special bag for tea things, *takabut,* is fitted with a stiff wicker basket to protect the tea glasses. Completely covered in leather, the *takabut* has a supple leather neck and a sliding slot fastener; the base is decorated with a fine leather fringe.

Ill. 6 — **Tuareg woman with an _eljebira_ leather salt bag,** Tamanrasset, Algeria, photograph by Catherine and Bernard Desjeux, 1991

From water skins to bags of tricks

"To the camel and the goat
To the vehicle and the recipient
To the two sole conquerors of the Sahara."

In 1937, Théodore Monod[7] dedicated his book _Méharées_ to these two animals: for what is a water skin, according to the dictionary, if not a "goatskin sewn in the form of a bag and serving as a recipient for storing and transporting liquids?" The most widely known and widely used water skin, the _abayogh_ (plur. _ibiyagh_), enables the Tuareg to transport well or seawater daily to the camp. Women attach the bulging water skin to the belly of a donkey, taking care to fit the ropes into the grooves in the wood protecting the animal's flanks. At the encampment, the full skin is suspended between two stakes;

the water naturally seeps through the sides of the skin, thus keeping the liquid inside cool.

Smaller goatskins, called _anwar_, are used for curd, sour milk, and other milk products, which are regularly shaken by a Tuareg woman in order to churn butter.

Bags are also mentioned as containers of impalpable things, things of the imagination. There are bags that can hold, or not hold, true or false words, i.e., language. One must indeed shut language fast inside a bag to have a chance of holding on to or taking account of it; as the Latin proverb puts it, _verba volant, scripta manent_, and we do get the impression that the spoken word quickly flies away while writing remains. The contents of the bag will be judged by the number of words, or its weight: a lie, as we shall see, weighs all the more inasmuch as it goes beyond the boundaries of the imagination.

l'eljebíra ·⊡Ɔ∐· ✳ sm. (pl. eljebíráten ⌐+⊙⊡Ɔ∐) sac de voyage en peau de forme carrée (fait pour être suspendu à la selle de méhari pour hom.) ‖ l'eljebíra est carré ; ses côtés ont de 0ᵐ,40ᶜ à 0ᵐ,65ᶜ de long. Il est ouvert, à sa partie supérieure, sur toute sa longueur αβ ; une porte en peau ABCD, festonnée et couverte de broderies, en ferme l'ouverture αβ et retombe sur la partie anté= =rieure du sac en la recou= =vrant jusqu'en bas. Deux oeillets en peau M et N servent à suspendre le sac à la selle du méhari ‖ l'eljebíra est employé en voyage par les hom. pour serrer toute espèce d'effets et d'objets. Les fem. ne s'en servent pas.

coupe   vue de face

1   Acacia (ehrenbergiana, seyal, senegalensis, raddiana),
as well as Balanites aegyptiaca, Ziziphus mauritiana, Commiphora africana.
2   J. Vercoutter, "Cuir" (leather), "Égypte" (Egypt), Dictionnaire archéologique des techniques, 2 Vol., (Paris: Éditions de l'Accueil, 1963), Vol. I, p. 344.
3   Jean Gabus, Au Sahara. Arts et symbols (Neuchâtel: Éditions à la Baconnière, 1958); Gironcourt, "L'art chez les Touareg," Missions de Gironcourt en Afrique occidentale. Documents scientifiques (Paris: Société de géographie, 1920), pp. 269-91; Francis Nicolas, Tamesna: les Ioullemmeden de l'Est ou Touâreg Kel Dinnîk, cercle de T'âwa, colonie du Niger, notes de linguistique et d'ethnographie berbères, dialectes de la Tamâzaq-Tavllamét (Paris: Imprimerie nationale, 1950).
4   Father Charles de Foucauld, Dictionnaire touareg-français. Dialecte de l'Ahaggar (Paris: Imprimerie nationale, 1951-52), 4 Vol., 2022 p.
5   The Bardo Museum of Ethnography and Prehistory (Algiers), Planches, album no. I, L. Balout, gen. ed.; preface by R. Capot-Rey; Marceau Gast, captions (Paris: Arts et Métiers graphiques, 1959); plates XXVIII.
6   De Foucauld, Dictionnaire, Vol. III, p. 1022; The Bardo Museum of Ethnography and Prehistory (Algiers), Planches, plate XXVI; Johannes Nicolaisen, Ecology and Culture of the Pastoral Tuareg, with Particular Reference to the Tuareg of Ahaggar and Ayr, (Copenhagen: National Museum of Copenhagen, the "Nationalmuseets Skrifter, Etnografisk Række" coll., 1963), p. 93, fig. 72, a.
7   Théodore Monod, Méharées. Explorations au vrai Sahara (Paris: Je sers; Geneva: Labor, 1937; reprinted by Actes Sud under the "Terres d'aventures" imprint, 1989).
8   Elkhah Ssoni, Petites Sœurs de Jésus, Contes touaregs de l'Aïr, L. Galand, introduction; G. Calame-Griaule, commentary (Paris: SELAF, CNRS, 1974), pp. 220-24.

ill. 7 — **Drawing of a bag** *eljebira*, illustration taken from the *Tuareg/French Dictionary* handwritten by Father Charles de Foucauld, around 1920
L'eljebira: a traditional Touareg travel bag

One tale told by the Aïr Tuareg is called "The Bag of Lies": "There once was a man... He set off on a walk and was drinking from a cleft in a rock when something leaped out and grabbed him by the beard. It was a genie... The man said to him, 'Let go of my beard'... The genie replied, 'I want a bag of lies. Otherwise, I shall put your entire family to death.'

The next day, the old man's little girl, who had remained alone in the camp with her little brother, welcomed the genie in and proceeded to tell him such lies (her father had gone off to shore up the sky that was collapsing in spots; her mother had left to sew up the earth that was beginning to tear; her older sister had gone to fetch one of her buttocks that had dropped off near the well) that the genie departed without carrying out his threats."[8]

The examples that I have touched on above clearly suggest the extreme diversity of Tuareg bags in terms of their purpose, form, capacity and decoration. The most richly decorated women's travel bags, for instance, with their elaborate patterns, displaying the most beautiful colors, make a notable contrast with the plainest bags, used to store millet and to serve as a unit of measure in the marketplace. It is most striking to find, among these herders, who spend their lives in tents, a number of objects, including bags, in which color and shape are lovingly combined with various decorative elements like fringes, pompoms, and so on. A regard for beauty is always present, and Tuareg craftsmen remain the keepers of this rich heritage.

Works and Days

ill. XXIII **The Limbourg brothers,** *Très Riches Heures du duc de Berry,* sowing in the month of October, Palais du Louvre, Chantilly, Musée Condé, late 15th century

ill. xxiv **Sower with a sickle in front of a team of oxen**, wall painting, Egypt, Tomb of Atet, Old Kingdom, Fourth dynasty

ill. xxv **Schoolbag** from Vallorcine, Haute-Savoie, France, 1930s, wood, Grenoble, collection of the Musée Dauphinois

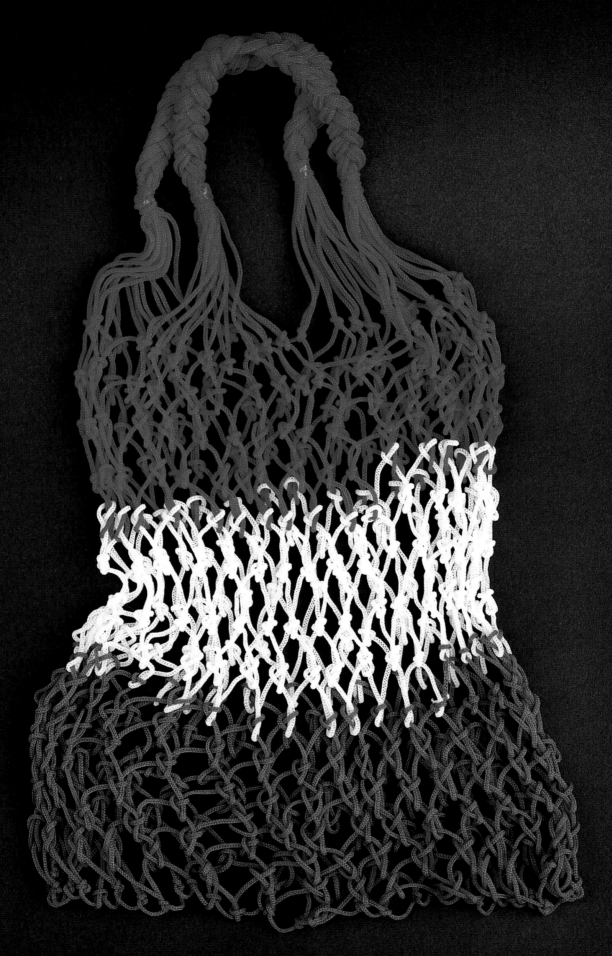

Ill. xxvi Red, white, and green string bag, Moschino, Spring/Summer 1988, red, white, and green nylon, Moschino Italie collection

ill. xxviii Extract from *Asterix, La Zizanie,* éditions Dargaud, 1970

ill. xxix **Women with their bilum bags on their foreheads,** photograph by Marie-José Guigues, Tari, Papua New Guinea, 1992

ill. xxx **Women going to Athens,** photograph by Charles Delius, Greece, circa 1930

Sewing Bags

ill. 1 | **Louis Carrogis, known as Carmontelle**
Madame Emangart, Intendant from Lille
1764, Chantilly, Musée Condé

| That sophisticated feminine accessory, the sewing bag, made its appearance in France in the 17th century, but its real popularity dates from the 18th century and the reign of Louis XV. A prized companion for milady, it had its own function among the diverse purses, pouches, and other containers that were part of her possessions. Its specific – and distinctive – character deserves particular attention: this was an everyday item whose use evolved subtly over the years and whose significance could never be grasped at first glance.

Sold by milliners, the sewing bag was defined in Diderot and d'Alembert's 18th-century *Encyclopédie* as "a kind of large, more or less decorated purse, with the same drawstring closure. Formerly used by ladies for holding their needlework".[1] While the basic shape was simple, the bag's appearance was enhanced by careful choice of materials. The *Dictionary of Furnishings and Decoration from the 13th Century to the Present Day*[2] quotes advertisements for lost sewing bags that appeared in the periodical *Annonces, affiches et avis divers* in the second half of the 17th century: sober descriptions with the primary element of identification – the bag's material – giving an idea of the range of fabrics utilized. *Marli*, a kind of gauze, was big for sewing bags, envelopes, and other useful items and decorative accessories, but plenty of other fabrics get a mention, too: taffeta and damask, for instance, and a lightweight mix of silk and

worsted known as challis; not to mention *raz de Saint-Maur*, a type of taffeta whose name, according to the *Dictionnaire universel de commerce*, refers to "Saint-Maur des Fossés, a large town near Paris, where Marcelin Charlier, the most skilled manufacturer of his time, set up the first factory in 1677".[3] Generally black, *raz de Saint-Maur* was especially favored for ceremonial and mourning wear.

These references to the actual material throw light on the close link between accessory and clothing: challis, taffeta, and *raz de Saint-Maur* (or *raz de Saint-Cyr*) were also standard items of the haberdashery and ladies fashion trades. In the Musée Condé in Chantilly, the portraits of ladies' by Louis Carrogis, known as Carmontelle (1717-1806), carefully stress the refinement of the sewing bag and the tastefulness of its match with their clothes. Take Madame la Vidame d'Amiens, for example: with a position to uphold – her husband was secular assistant (*vidame*) to the Bishop of Amiens – she chose a pink that went perfectly with her floral dress.[4] More daringly, maybe, the Countess of Beintheim went for a subtle association with the lace of her white negligée...[5] The sewing bag, then, was part of the simplicity and harmony of the outfit as a whole, although the quality of the material was no obstacle to a little ornamentation: "Lost in the Tuileries", reads one advertisement, "a white sewing bag embroidered with gold".[6]

Another intriguing aspect of the advertisements is the insight they offer into the missing bags' contents. These full-time ladies' companions held all sorts of items relating to sewing or what Madame de Genlis, governess of the Duke of Orleans' children and the author of a host of moralistic works for the young, termed "handiwork": scissors, fans, all sorts of little gold or shagreen containers for needles, thimbles, and shuttles, scraps of delicate fabric, and much, much more. The descriptions give us a glimpse of the level of sophistication: "Lost, on the first of August, in the rue de la Croix-des-Petits-Champs, a plain *raz de Saint-Maur* sewing bag containing a pair of gold scissors in a shagreen case, a gold guilloche-ornamented needle case, a gold thimble in its holder, two pairs of steel scissors and several strips of embroidered muslin."[7]

ill. 3 | **Small utility bag**
France, end 18th century
taffeta, lace trim, taffeta ribbon
Paris, UCAD collection

ill. 4 | opposite
Jean-Baptiste Siméon Chardin
The Bird-organ
1751, Louvre, Paris

ill. 5 | pages overleaf
Jacques Dumont
Madame Mercier
surrounded by her family
1731, Louvre, Paris

The art of avoiding idleness

One of the main items to be found in the sewing bag was the shuttle, that odd, oblong tool used for making knots, a form of handiwork much prized by the aristocracy and bourgeoisie of the second half of the 18th century – as indicated by the sheer number of shuttles acquired by Madame de Pompadour from jeweler Lazare Duvaux in the 1750s. Duvaux's daybook[8] waxes eloquent about the splendor of his shuttles, made of gold, tortoiseshell, mother of pearl, or porcelain – and rightly so: you only have to look at the French samples in the Wallace Collection in London, especially the gold shuttle with enameled floral decoration made by J. V. Huguet in 1757-58 and another with enameled pastoral scenes by J. J. Barrière of Paris, dating from 1769-70.

On display in the Musée Hermès in Paris are a host of items we can readily imagine snug inside a sewing bag: why not, for example, those silver-and-steel scissors in their chased silver case decorated with flowers and birds? One side of the upper part of the case bears a cupid with his quiver of arrows and in his left hand a long pair of tongs; and the tongs grip a double heart set on an anvil whose base bears the inscription, "I unite them". On the other side are two cupids, a double heart topped with a crown and a scroll that reads, "We are inseparable".

Then there are the "indiscreet" Rococo lorgnettes containing, on a minute scale, the wherewithal for jotting a quick love note; the red morocco perfume case in the shape of a book, delicately gilded and bearing the dedication "Love offers it to you"; and the openwork *pomponne* (imitation gold) shuttle with its repoussé flowers and green shagreen case. These highly personal items conjure up a warm, intimate portrait of a mysterious lady seen, as it were, in elusive patterns of light and shade.

As it happens, the sewing bag features regularly in portraits of 18th-century ladies, especially in France, along with those elaborate shuttles. As the symbol of needlework, embroidery, and knotwork, the bag gave the portrait an air of simplicity, modesty, and virtuousness, and it was perfectly natural for the daughters of the king to be shown engaged in these worthy occupations. Jean-Marc Nattier depicted Madame Adélaïde, third daughter of Louis XV, doing knotwork: the princess is holding a gold shuttle in her right hand while, with a graceful gesture of her left thumb and forefinger, she draws the thread from the sewing bag hanging from her arm.[9] Madame Emangart, born Marie-Juliette de Fresne and assistant governess to Mademoiselle d'Orléans, was captured for posterity by Carmontelle in a near-identical pose[10] (ill. 1).

Thus the sewing bag became the vector of a very precise image of 18th-century womanhood, as Madame de Genlis obliquely

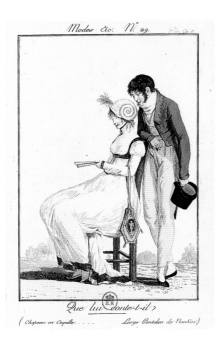

ill. 6 ▐ **Philibert-Louis Debucourt**
What is he trying to say?
1799, Fashion and Manners of the Day
engraving from *La Mésangère*
Paris, Bibliothèque nationale de France
Prints and Photography

ill. 7 ▐ **Anonymous**
Turban and spencer Algerian-style
1797, Parisien Costume
Paris, Bibliothèque nationale de France
Prints and Photography

ill. 8 ▐ **A woman's outfit**
1797, engraving from *La Mésangère*
Paris, Bibliothèque nationale de France

points out in her *Critical Dictionary of Court Etiquette, or The Spirit of Former Etiquette and Good Breeding as Compared to Modern Practise*: "The manual skill called for by this domestic work makes a true woman… A woman sitting idle assumes the posture of a man and loses the grace that characterizes her. This is why the shuttle was invented: so that women, even when in a large group, should appear occupied by some small task and thus maintain an appropriate bearing."[11]

The reticule: fashion goes immodest

The importance attached by Madame de Genlis to feminine handiwork makes it clear that the social role of the sewing bag went far beyond matters of everyday use: "In former times women, to remain seemly and composed in a group of visitors, would take from their sewing bags a handsome shuttle of gold, tortoiseshell, or ivory and make knots. As a rule this work served no purpose; but it was a kind of symbol of the aversion all women should feel for idleness… It fostered the graceful bearing that exemplified the true woman."

The portrait of *Madame Mercier and Her Daughters* by the 18th-century painter Jacques Dumont is a fine illustration of the social and moral dimension of the sewing bag and the objects that went with it (ill. 5). Set on a lady's knees or suspended grace-fully from her arm, it was the very definition of the demeanor, modesty, dignity, and elegance of gesture that she should assume in society, at Court, in a drawing room, or even in the intimacy of the family circle. Jean-Jacques Rousseau's *Confessions* (1782) likewise calls attention to the fact that the prime purpose of these feminine activities was to fend off idle-ness and boredom: "I maintain that for a circle to be truly agreeable, not only must each person be doing something, that something must require a little attention. Making knots is a form of doing nothing, and a woman making knots demands quite as much effort in the entertaining as one sitting there with her arms folded. Embroidery is another matter: it keeps her busy enough to fill the silences."[12]

However, the contents of the sewing bag and its cousin the workbasket – those mute confidants of feminine intimacy – were not limited to objects related to ladies' activity in society: "Lost: a workbasket of green taffeta with an enameled gold bot-tom. Inside are letters, family papers, and various other items."[13]

The second half of the 18th century brought changes in the sewing bag's use and function, and the *Encyclopédie* noted a clear shift that reinforced the already existing relationship with clothing and made the bag a full-blown fashion accessory: "Today they are part of women's finery; one no more goes out

ill. 9 | **String bag**

France, 19th century, silk taffeta embroidered in Beauvais needlework in polychromy silk, lapel and lining in satin
Fashion Museum Paris, UFAC collection, gift from Bisson-Prud'Homme, 1952

ill. 10 | **A handbag belonging to Pauline Bonaparte**

France, beginning of the 19th century, fine-grained Moroccan leather, gold embossed, outer layer decorated with fan motif
clasp in the shape of a lyre and small chain in polished steel, Emile Hermès collection

Little Old Women
To Victor Hugo

In the sinuous folds of the old capitals,
Where all, even horror, becomes pleasant,
I watch, obedient to my fatal whims,
For singular creatures, decrepit and charming.

These disjointed monsters were women long ago,
Eponine or Lais! Monsters, hunch-backed, broken
Or distorted, let us love them! they still have souls.
Clothed in tattered petticoats and flimsy dresses

They creep, lashed by the iniquitous wind,
Trembling at the clatter of the omnibuses,
Each pressing to her side, as if it were a relic,
A small purse embroidered with rebuses or flowers.

Charles Baudelaire, *Les Fleurs du mal*

without one's sewing bag than without one's shawl – and yet each is often as useless as the other." Seen in this light the sewing bag is a forerunner of the reticule, adopted by the *merveilleuses*, the feminine smart set of the last few years of the 18th century. The reticule complemented their flimsy attire and was to be seen in all shapes and sizes: flat or shaped like a purse with a drawstring, square, rectangular, irregular, polygonal, plain or embroidered with patterns, flowers or rebuses (ill. 6, 7, 8). One model – the reticule of steel filigree, lined with silk, and ornamented with rosettes and pendants – takes us straight back to the original Latin *reticulum*, a mesh bag.

Variously of fabric, leather, or metal and dangling from the wrist by a drawstring or a chain, the reticule was also taken up by kept women and courtesans – and respectable ladies – seen at the Palais-Royal and Paris' trendiest venues. Flaunted by women dressed in the latest fashion, it was not, like the sewing bag, the prime accessory of the virtuous.

1 *Encyclopédie ou Dictionnaire raisonné des sciences, des arts et des métiers*, Neufchâtel: Samuel Faulche & Compagnie, Libraires et Imprimeurs, 1765, Vol. XIV, p. 470.

2 Henri Havard, *Dictionnaire de l'ameublement et de la décoration depuis le XIIIᵉ siècle jusqu'à nos jours*, Paris: Librairies-Imprimeries Réunies, 1901, Vol. IV, pp. 866-867.

3 Jaques Savary Des Bruslons, *Dictionnaire universel de commerce, d'histoire naturelle et des arts et métiers*, Copenhagen: C. & A. Philibert, new edition, 1760, 3 vols.

4 Louis Carrogis ("Carmontelle"), *Madame la vidame d'Amiens*, pencil, red chalk, and watercolor on paper, 1759, Musée Condé, Chantilly.

5 Louis Carrogis ("Carmontelle"), *The Countess of Beintheim, a German princess*, pencil, red chalk, watercolor, and gouache on paper, 1767, Musée Condé, Chantilly.

6 *Annonces, affiches et avis divers*, June 29 1772.

7 *Ibid.*, August 7 1766.

8 *Livre-Journal de Lazare Duvaux, marchand-bijoutier ordinaire du Roy, 1748-1758*, Paris: Société des bibliophiles français, 1873, Vol. II; facsimile edition, Paris: F. de Nobele, 1965.

9 Jean-Marc Nattier, *Madame Adélaïde faisant des nœuds*, oil on canvas, 1756, Versailles, Musée national du Château.

10 Louis Carrogis ("Carmontelle"), *Madame Emangart, Intendante de Lille*, pencil, red chalk, watercolor, and gouache on paper, 1764, Musée Condé, Chantilly.

11 Caroline-Stéphanie-Félicité Du Crest, comtesse de Genlis, *Dictionnaire critique et raisonné des étiquettes de la cour... ou L'Esprit des étiquettes et des usages anciens, comparé aux modernes*, Paris: P. Mongie Aîné, 1818, 2 vols.

12 Jean-Jacques Rousseau, *Confessions*, Book V, 1731-1736.

13 *Annonces, affiches et avis divers*, January 10 1752.

❙ It was during the stifling summer in Kyoto in the 1960s and 1970s. My grandmother often went to visit friends or relations and before going out she would cover the tatamis in her room with kimonos, fabric, lengths of silk and multicolored cords.

My Grandmother's *Furoshikis*

ill. 1 ❙ **Fukusa symbolizing cranes**
18th century, silk and satin
Paris, Musée des Arts décoratifs

I remember her adjusting the *obi* – the broad silk belt – of her kimono in front of the mirror, and myself handing her a plaited silk cord that she would knot tightly around her waist.

Once ready she would carefully choose a *furoshiki* to match her kimono.

The *furoshiki* is a square of silk or cotton, plain or printed, which is knotted to form a bag. In the West, the result would be called a bundle, but no bundle has the aesthetic refinement of the *furoshiki*. The term comes from the *furoshiki*'s original function: before you went to the public bath (*furo*), as was long standard practice in Japan, the fabric was laid flat (*shiki*: to spread) and used to wrap your toiletries. Later, its function broadened and today, it is used to wrap the gift you take when you go visiting. Even if the gift is already wrapped, politeness demands another covering; as in the West, people often settle for a paper bag from a store, but my grandmother continued to use the *furoshiki*.

On that particular day she asked me to wrap the gift in the *furoshiki* she had chosen. Her *furoshikis* had our family name printed across one corner and I had tied the fabric up fairly approximately around the box with the name clearly visible. Amused by the difference between our cultures – I am half Japanese, half French – my grandmother made up the parcel again, explaining gently that more care had to be taken. You had to begin by folding two opposite corners smoothly over the box to be wrapped and then make a knot with the two other corners. And not just any old knot, but one that let the cloth fall neatly on each side. The name should not be seen. In this way, the package appears as a valuable item wrapped in precious fabric.

Then I accompanied my grandmother to the porch and she set off, with her clipped little step, carrying her *furoshiki* by its knot.

ill. 2 | **A young woman and her servant (left)**
photograph, Japan, 1875

Chinese Saying:
Never Trust a Bag

ill. 1 ▐ opposite

Woman holding a purse and a bag

China, Tang era, 7th century
polychromy terracotta
Paris, Musée Guimet

▌A bag, according to the dictionary, is a "container". Its function implies both a power over objects – which it may delimit, enclose or protect – and a mystery, one that is either disturbing or entertaining. In Eastern mythology, for example, the Wind God possesses a bag filled with whirlwinds that are endlessly replenished; this bag must be kept tightly shut. The popular God of Wealth also has a bag, which holds more gold than any man could count, but has any man ever been able to open it?

Moving away from the world of mythology, from the plain, wrapped package to the receptacle that you keep close at hand as if it contained some secret treasure or a kind of passport identifying the bearer, bags are as different from one another as their mythic counterparts. And in China, as elsewhere over the centuries, the simplest version of this container can be seen weighing down the backs of coalmen in the forest, crushing peddlers' shoulders, and hunching the spines of peasants on their way to sell their goods at market. These are utilitarian bags, used by laborers or paupers. The complex funerary iconography of ancient times (from the Tang to the Ming dynasties, i.e., from the 7th to the 17th century) bears witness to this: figurines bearing this accessory usually represent foreign merchants, identifiable by their Kyrgyz hats, or occasionally,

maids of elegant ladies whose own hands would never have been burdened by such things.

A familiar, even indispensable, object of our day and age, the little bag, holding personal objects that the owner wants to keep at hand, appears quite difficult to trace in China before the 20th century. We have to look for it on the arm or at the side of Buddhist monks and pilgrims. These bags contained the amulets and small traveling images that helped the faithful in their prayers and meditation. This is probably one of those rare occasions in which a Chinese bag, prior to the present day, is clearly associated with the idea of an inner life and intimate secrets. We shall never know whether these bags were also a familiar sight with intellectuals who claimed to be followers of Confucius or other traditions. The sage was usually represented standing among his followers, seated at a table before his books, paintings and musical instruments, or meditating amid mountains and bubbling springs. If the sage is traveling, a dutiful adolescent can be seen carrying his bags – a whole panoply of objects for serious diversion or study – but nothing that looks like a personal bag.

Apart from a few embroidered purses, which beauties of the period would hide in their skirts, along with potential secrets, the personal bag seems to have been entirely overlooked by both the political and bourgeois elite.

Bags as symbols of freedom

The "handbag" only became fashionable in China during the Republican era (1912-49). It then figures as one of the novelties of the New Life Movement, launched by Chiang Kai-shek in the 1930s to modernize Chinese society by proposing types of behavior and consumption that were better suited to a culture in the throes of industrialization. This was the age when advertising was instructing the Chinese in the use of unknown foreign products like fine cigarettes, delicately perfumed soaps, chocolate-flavored drinks, coffee, and so on, all of which were touted by beautiful young women whose appearance evoked a happy marriage of the past and the present. Clad in the Manchu dress worn by "banner" women (as they were known in the terminology of the deposed Qing dynasty), a kind of fashion that was reworked, Paris or Hollywood style, in order to draw attention to the body, these enticing young ladies were usually arrayed with luxury accessories. Borrowed from Western culture, such goods bespoke modernity, along with a seduction and a form of freedom that had only very recently been won. So we see swirling fur coats, high-heeled pumps, silk stockings and yes, bags – small, secret, charming bags – the kind that liberate a woman from the intrusive presence of servants. Certain talented craftsmen even devised astonishing creations fashioned from bamboo, imitating the designs of leather bags carried by elegant Europeans.

These bags came to epitomize the changes and refinements of a style of dress that was in the spirit of the times. For men, they presented a strange new form of female fetishization, in this case a painless one, unlike the terrible practice of binding women's feet, which had been widely observed from the 18th century onwards, except among the working classes and the Manchu. For the modern Chinese woman, handbags offered poise, by occupying her hands, now deprived of the brushes, fans and handkerchiefs of yore, whose mysteries she would have learned to master from childhood. Now, measuring up against the image of her Western counterparts, handbags enabled the modern Chinese woman to make a good impression in the new society in which she had to move, without a protector, and in keeping with an etiquette, about which she was still almost entirely in the dark. The eternal minor in earlier Chinese society, a woman would never have left her own home, for example, except to travel to the home of a friend, duly escorted and hidden behind the curtains of a sedan chair or palanquin.

Perhaps this is the crux of the problem then: bags lend one certain poise. Yet the Chinese of the Ancient order, both men and women, possessed a number of other accessories that perfectly fulfilled this role. The civil servant and man of letters, the paragon of the Renaissance man and administrator of the Empire, carried in his hands the insignia of his office, a long tablet, either lacquered or made of some precious material, that recalled the narrow slats or strips carved from wood or bamboo on which the lettered class used to write in the centuries prior to the Common era.

For her part, the lady of quality used graceful, coded gestures to express, in the appropriate circumstances, her attachment to belles-lettres and her privileged upbringing. It seems quite clear, however, that most of her belongings, even intimate ones, were kept at her disposal on trays or in cases borne by her handmaidens and other companions in her train.

As for those who, by chance, did not know what to do with their hands, we can rest assured. To express either their dignity or a polite attitude vis-à-vis others in those days, they only had to place their palms one over the other within the ample sleeves of their ceremonial attire.

If, however, we examine ancient paintings, the mystery deepens. In the different versions of the *Qingming shang he tu*, a long scroll whose lively play of ink and brush depicts the then Chinese capital of Bianjing (present-day Kaifeng) in the early 12th century, there are practically no bags to be seen. Is this because the narrative, as sociologists point out nowadays, practically never depicts a pauper? Were bags then an accessory that characterized only people of very modest means, those wretches who carried their homes on their backs because they had no roof to put over their heads?

Clothing, a rampart of the intimate

There remains a final refuge for the ego, which constitutes one of the essential roles of bags today. In pre-Republican China, it seems quite clear that one's clothing served that very function. The Chinese were in the habit of slipping into the folds of their clothes every secret, every indispensable object they might have occasion to use: from the negotiator's scale for weighing gold, which he would wedge into his belt, to the old person's snuffbox or medicine phials, to the dried openwork gourd that might contain a cricket (for singing or combat, according to its master's whim) or a grasshopper, or even a simple pet beetle. It is certainly an odd custom, to our way of thinking, to keep an insect close to one's heart as a bosom friend. It was, in fact, the ultimate freedom, in a subsistence society in which our modern "four-legged friends" often cost too much or were put to other uses, guarding one's property, for example, hunting, or keeping the home free of rats. Insects, on the other hand, attracted even the most gifted of men of letters, who were fascinated by these *chong*, little creeping, crawling creatures. They were tiny friends with wing cases that were worn over the heart and would never betray the secrets confided in them.

Given the lack of real privacy in traditional Chinese houses, which were always open to intrusions from the family group, clothing remained then both the last possible rampart of the intimate and the only true frontier of the self. To keep everything between one's bare skin and one's clothing was the best means of controlling access to and protecting the expression of one's self – a self that was, and is, so judiciously and effectively locked up that it has resisted every dictatorship to date, and still often defies modern attempts at psychoanalysis, according to some. Since they are so easily robbed or rifled through, did bags never really come into existence because they would have

too readily betrayed the self? Or perhaps because the self is too precious and too complex to be represented by any one object, whatever it might be?

Wrapping, vaults and death

Finally, should I refrain from mentioning yet another avenue that might be explored, however odd? It too begins with the intimate, the proximity to the body, of which bags are an extension. It is grounded, moreover, in the fact that in dictionaries from the first half of the 20th century, the definition of *bao* (i.e., everything that serves to contain something) refers first of all to funeral rituals.

Wouldn't it be possible then to draw a parallel between the form of the personal bag and the silk wrappings, in which, since Antiquity, the corpses of important figures were traditionally bound up with painstaking care? And wouldn't this link extend as well to the multiple lacquered wooden coffins in which the body was placed, before the deceased was finally laid to rest in a sarcophagus (an "outer coffin" as they say in Chinese), which held them all? Each of the wooden coffins was designed to fit as closely as possible into the next, so that no gap would allow even a few fragments of the heavy souls that the body still held to escape. For it was those souls, that enabled the deceased to survive "a bit," sustained as he was by the memory and the rites with which his descendents honored him.

The theme of wrapping and enveloping, however, does not end with our mortal remains. Tombs dating from the Warring States Period (around 475-221 BC) also contained series of baskets carefully lined up one against the other, like so many bags. Properly stored and intelligently arranged by category, these containers held all that the deceased needed for life underground, from provisions to clothes, to the texts that were absolutely essential afterlife reading. And what if this connection with the dead had eventually come to influence the use of bags in the world of the living – in an intellectual world, we should recall, shaped by a writing system based on characters, that is, one constantly playing off the resources of analogy? The idea may be something of a shock, yet there exists in fact a parallel, in this case to be found in choices made by Chinese culture concerning architecture.

Several recent studies have judiciously catalogued Chinese successes over the centuries in creating vaulted structures, elegantly fitted out in stone or brick. However, in practice, official buildings have always been designed and raised according to the primacy of wood and its use in construction, and architects would only resort to employing vaults in very particular cases that we might be tempted to characterize as beyond their control (absence of wood for structural work, for example, or the creation of cave dwellings). This nearly systematic exclusion of all vaulted forms from the world of the living arose during the Han dynasty, around the 1st century, precisely when vaulted structures were becoming a preponderant element in funerary architecture, eventually constituting one of the major indicators of the style. It is obvious to everyone, however, that the worlds of the living and the dead must always remain clearly separated. Is it possible then that bags, like the vault in architecture, were instinctively rejected by the world of the living because of their long association with the world of the dead?

The situation is changing radically. Today, in mainland China, by law, any person who dies must be incinerated, while the ancient burial practices are only tolerated – less and less so, by the way – in zones that are very largely rural. At the heart of transmutation by fire, neither container nor bag makes much sense, and even the urns of the great Buddhist monks of yore no longer meet with much success. Increasingly, people do their best to disperse the ashes of their loved ones at an auspicious hour and place. The idea of a return to the great Taoist One implicitly underlies these new practices. Henceforth, no reluctance or superstition inherited from a bygone era will clash with the current triumphant discovery of the personal bag.

❙ The variety of bags found in the different regions of Australia and Tasmania is considerable, in terms of both the materials used and the creative techniques applied. The anthropologist Howard Morphy describes some of these bags as complex forms based on simple principles, like projections of mathematical formulae endowed with both solidity and flexibility.[1] Western travelers were quick to start collecting these bags, admiring as they did their complex technique. These *curios* from distant peoples were then allotted their place in typologies of objects designed to demonstrate the evolution of human societies. Then came the work of the field anthropologists, who put the emphasis on the bags' deliberate aesthetic qualities and gradually changed the way we look at them.

The bags referred to here are known to us from the drawings by Nicolas-Martin Petit (1777-1804) and Charles-Alexandre Lesueur (1778-1846) kept at the Muséum d'Histoire Naturelle in Le Havre. These are the fruit of the "Voyage to the Southern Lands", the great scientific expedition instigated by Napoleon, which set out from Le Havre in October 1800, heading for New Holland (Australia) and Van Diemen's Land (Tasmania), and returned to a very politically turbulent France in 1804.[2]

Bags of New Holland and Van Diemen's Land

ill. 1 | **Nicolas-Martin Petit**
An Aborigine camp
from Dieman Land (Tasmania)

1802, watercolor and crayon on blue-tinted paper
Le Havre, Muséum d'Histoire Naturelle

A first watercolor, signed "Nm Petit", represents a native camp in Van Diemen's Land (ill. 1). Assembled strips of bark serve as windbreaks. In the foreground can be seen two spears and a bag, probably made of seaweed. On the left of the image a woven bag hangs from the branch of a tree. These bags also appear in one of Lesueur's compositions, alongside other local artifacts (ill. 2).

A nomadic people, the Aborigines followed the seasons and the resources offered by their environment, going from one camp to another and leaving certain objects behind them for the next time. Their bags, however, were nearly always carried with them. "We had only just reached shore when we saw a black-colored man carrying over his shoulder a kind of bag, holding a long stick in his right hand, and a flaming brand in his left."[3] The crews' logbooks offer little information about the use of these bags. They were of course useful for carrying personal possessions. Their forms were not always different from those of the bags used for hunting and gathering, which were filled with fruits, plants and small animals. A number of them are represented in paintings on bark.[4] Bags made in leather or sea-weed were used for carrying water, a rare commodity inland. "*Fucus pulmatus*, which they use to make their drinking vases […] is something I have seen only in one place."[5]

Other bags appear in the context of ritual, as repositories for sacred objects. They also play an important role in certain mythical narratives.

The bags are presented here in the form of images, made by artists who were external to the culture being described, and the two types of drawing reflect their intentions. Petit abided by the precepts of the young and short-lived *Société des Observateurs de l'Homme*[6] (1799-1805): he renders his own observation of men in their environment. The aim was to avoid the pitfalls of theoretical work that gets too far away from realities in the field. This Voyage to the Southern Lands was undoubtedly the first French expedition whose objectives expressly included ethnographic observation alongside the tra-ditional geographical, astronomical, zoological, botanical and geological missions. On top of their undeniable artistic merit, Petit's drawings constitute a unique ethnographic record: the members of the expedition were among the few Westerners to travel to Tasmania before the forced displacement and geno-cide of the indigenous population.

In addition to these studies, we have the drawings of Charles-Alexandre Lesueur. Whereas Petit studied with David, Lesueur seems to have been self-taught. Before starting on his meticu-

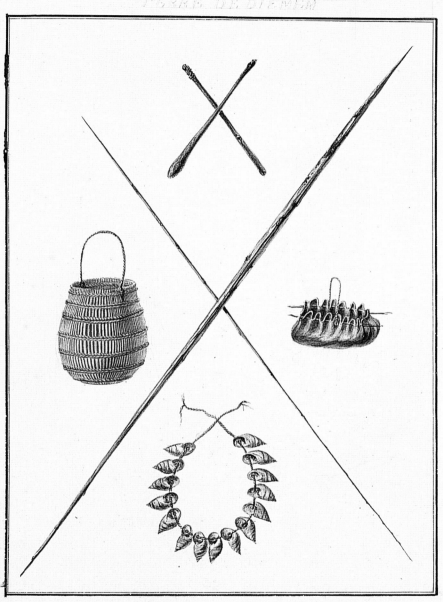

TERRE DE DIEMEM

Armes Vases Ornements

Coloré

ill. 2 | **Charles-Alexandre Lesueur**
Arms and ornaments
from Dieman Land (Tasmania)

1802, watercolor and crayon
Le Havre, Muséum d'Histoire Naturelle

Two spears, two clubs, a rush basket
a jar of water, a shell necklace

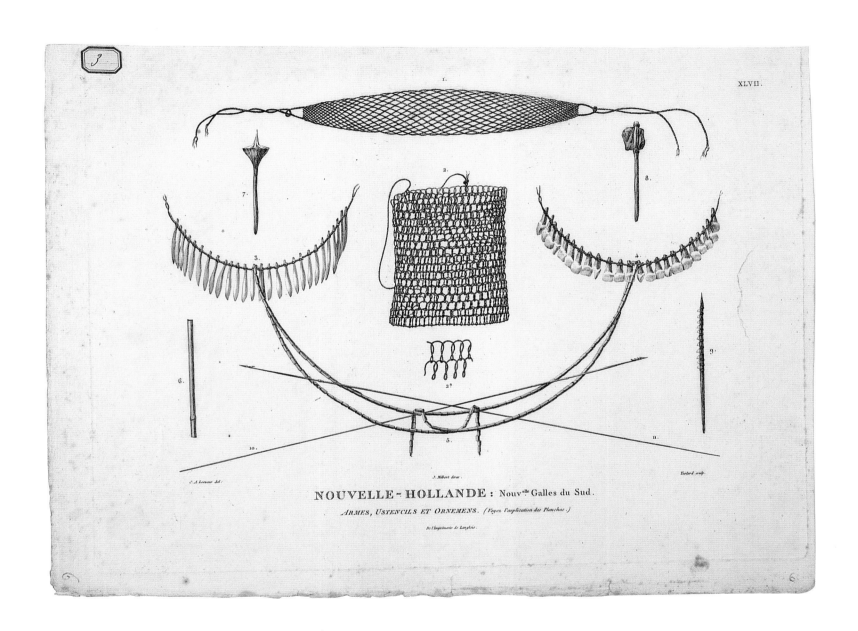

NOUVELLE - HOLLANDE : Nouv.ᵉˡˡᵉ Galles du Sud.

ARMES, USTENCILS ET ORNEMENS. (Voyez l'explication des Planches.)

De l'Imprimerie de Langlois.

ill. 3 ❙ opposite
Charles-Alexandre Lesueur
Arms and ornaments
from Dieman Land (Tasmania)

1801-1803, watercolor and crayon
Le Havre, Muséum d'Histoire Naturelle

Lesueur wrote the following description:

1 - a string headband which natives
    wear across the forehead
2 - a stringbag to store provisions
2a - detail of the preceding string mesh
3 and 4 - kangaroo teeth necklace
5 - a necklace made with pieces
    of reed
6 - a piece of reed, its natural thickness
7 - club, made from a single piece
    of gnarled wood
8 - a club made of stone attached to a
    piece of wood
9 - the extremity of a spear used
    for battle, barbed with shark teeth
10 and 11 - two barbed spears for battle

lous compositions, Lesueur drew each object individually, in the descriptive, naturalistic vein at which he became a specialist. The drawings of bags, for example, were accompanied by a scale in decimeters and details of the handles. The compositions show groups of cultural artifacts from the populations observed (ills. 2 and 3). These drawings are genuine "ethnographic plates" whose informative function is signaled by the scale at the bottom, but they also echo the presentational style of cabinets of curiosities, with lances punctuating the composition just as they did those sets of objects. Plates showing studies of this kind became increasingly common in the 19th century. One notable aspect is the emphasis on weapons – no doubt a subconscious reflection of Western thinking, which liked to see these men as fierce warriors. In the case of the Aborigines, the relatively small number of artifacts that they produced made the weapons that much more prominent. These are mainly throwing weapons used for hunting. A unique record of Australian and Tasmanian bags at this time, these drawings also bear witness to the discoverer's vision of the material artifacts made by the "natives".

1   Howard Morphy, *Aboriginal Art,* London: Phaidon, 1998.
2   See the account given by Captain Nicolas Baudin,
who led the expedition: Nicolas Baudin, *Mon Voyage aux Terres Australes.*
Journal personnel du commandant Baudin, transcription J. Bonnemains.
Paris: Imprimerie Nationale, 2000.
3   Pierre-Bernard Milius, *Voyage aux terres australes,*
eds. Jacqueline Bonnemains and Pascale Hauguel, Le Havre: Société Havraise
d'Etudes Diverses and Muséum d'Histoire Naturelle du Havre, 1987, p. 7.
Milius was second in command on the *Naturaliste.*
4   An image of the Waijara spirit carrying baskets to collect honey appears
on the cover of Howard Morphy's book, *op. cit.*
5   François Péron, "Île Maria – Suite des observations de phisique [sic]
et d'Histoire naturelle, ventôse an X," 1802, Le Havre: Muséum d'Histoire
Naturelle, manuscript no. 18 042, p. 22.
6   See Joseph-Marie de Gérando, *Considérations sur les diverses méthodes*
à suivre dans l'observation des peuples sauvages, 1799; Jean Jamin,
"Faibles sauvages… corps indigents: le désenchantement de François Péron,"
Le Corps en jeu, eds. Jacques Hainard and Roland Khaer, Neuchâtel: Musée
d'Ethnographie, 1983.

Bags:
the Archaeological Evidence

"With pouch and purse
And strong leather mittens"[1]

❚ Five thousand three hundred years ago, and a lone man is trying to cross the Hauslab Pass in the Tyrolean Alps. The weather is tricky and the wounded traveler finds himself forced to take refuge between two rocks. A few hours later, he dies in his improvised shelter and almost at once, a heavy fall of snow covers his body and everything he has with him.

Still locked in his tomb of ice, "Frozen Fritz" was found by chance in 1991. In addition to his hunting equipment, he had with him a calfskin belt with a sewn-on pouch containing small stone tools, another tool made of limewood and horn, a bone awl and scraps of tinder. Beside him lay a plant fibre backpack with a curved larch and hazelwood frame, and two cylindrical, quart-sized birch bark containers that he may have used for carrying embers.

What made this discovery all the more extraordinary is that leather and fabric, like all organic substances, usually break down when buried and so are rarely found on archaeological sites. Although sometimes preserved under specific circumstances – constant moisture and temperature levels are vital – this kind of protein-based material was, for many years, extremely ephemeral: lack of adequate preservation techniques meant that contact with the air set off chemical and biological processes inevitably leading to total decomposition.

Usually all we find are the metal parts – clasps, ornamental plaques, and so on – of what were probably oval or rectangular pouches attached to belts in graves dating from Merovingian times (6th century AD). Nothing remains of the pouches, but the small items they contained have been well preserved: thus we learn that the dead often went to their final resting place accompanied by firelighters – a piece of metal that produced sparks when rubbed with a flint – and needles, punches, small, precious or decorative objects like rings, and fragments of colored glass, knives, combs and shears (the ancestors of our scissors). The tweezers, found exclusively in men's graves, would seem to have had a more practical than esthetic function: removal of splinters left in the hands due to the use of weapons, for example. What we do not know is whether these were personal effects, dating from before death, or posthumous offerings, buried with the corpse. Daggers and sewing equipment are often found in the graves of young children; yet

ill. 1 ❚ opposite

Leather purse with circular design

England, 14th century
London, Museum of London

The London subsoil, humid due to the presence of former branches of the river Thames, is well suited to the preservation of organic materials such as leather. This purse, found during an archaeological dig in the city, was worn by a Londoner at the end of the Middle Ages. According to the illustration, it would appear that the purse, worn on a belt, was made from a piece of leather in the front (which is preserved) and another on the back separated by a colored bellows, maybe in cloth, from which small objects were hung.

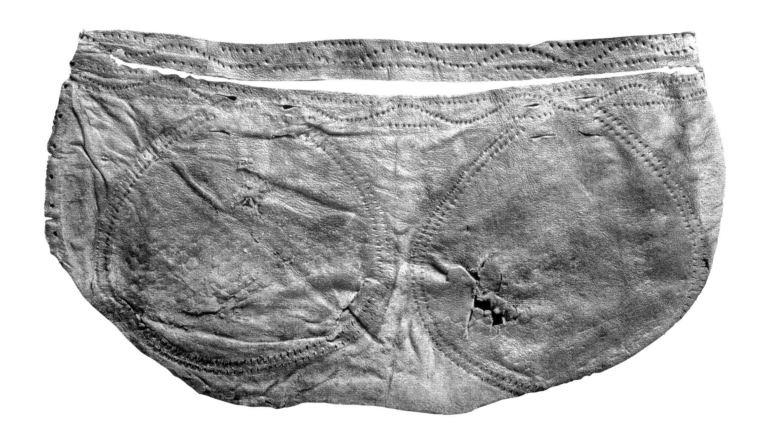

whatever the age of the dead person, the objects found are never new, which would seem to indicate that they were meant to be used.

Sometimes, urban digs on moist medieval sites – old riverbeds or latrine trenches, for example – yield a few scraps of leather: bits of shoes, belts and pouches of all kinds. A modern technique, that involves replacing the water in leather or wooden objects with polyethylene glycol, makes it possible to preserve, study and reconstruct these everyday items. Digs in London (ill. 1) (14th century), on the Place de la Comédie in Metz, France (15th century) and for the St Anne subway station in Rennes (ill. 2 and 3), France (16th century) have produced a number of pouches which, once restored, reveal real diversity of shape and decoration. Also designed to be hung from the waist, these specimens come in different sizes, some of them being ornamented with embossed parallel lines or embroidery: all that remains of the latter, in the Metz example, are perforations forming a lattice pattern. Some still have their fastener in the form of a hook or tie. Unfortunately, most of these pieces seem to have been thrown away, so they are generally empty and offer no clue as to what their original contents might have been: money, no doubt, but maybe also important or precious objects and documents.

The archaeological remains of bags and pouches offer indications of the everyday life of the men and women of the past. And unlike the luxury items to be found in museums, they cover all sections of the population, especially people living in cities.

1   *L'Outillement au Villain*, Paris, Bibliothèque nationale de France, ms. Fr. 837 and Fr. 1593.

ill. 2 ❚ opposite

Leather purse

an archaeological dig in the underground place Sainte-Anne, Rennes
16th century, Museum of Brittany

A rectangular envelope bag with a flap on which tiny pieces of leather are sewn to form a buttonhole. The front flap is decorated with vertical stripes embossed in the leather.

ill. 3 ❚ opposite

A piece of a leather belt

an archaeological dig in the underground place Sainte-Anne, Rennes
16th century, Museum of Brittany

This thin belt, which has a square metal tongue buckle, was perhaps attached to the rectangular purse which was found during the same dig.

ill. 1 ▌ **A woman with** *"haren sor"*
end of 15th century

An engraving by the anonymous
bourgeois, who, around 1393,
composed the famous
Ménagier de Paris, which included
a detailed treaty on cooking in which
the herring was a regular ingredient
in the dishes referred to.

Wicker Fish Baskets

ill. 2 ▌ An aerial view
of the top courtyard
of the Château-Thierry castle.

In the foreground is the ditch
where bags were hidden
in the 13th century
containing a thousand herrings.

▌ In 1991, an exceptional find was made on the archaeo-logical site of Château-Thierry, in a ditch dating back to the mid-13th century: pieces of wickerwork containing large quantities of fish skeletons, constituting a very rare example of wicker bags or baskets.[1] Analysis of these baskets and of the fish (herrings) that they contained[2] yielded striking, concrete evidence of one of the major medieval trades.

Red meat dominated the aristocratic diet in the Middle Ages, and nobles were also fond of fowl, which were among the most expensive meats. However, they ate a great deal of fish as well, not least because of the 150 days of abstinence ordained by the Church as part of the Christian year. Indeed, widespread adherence to these Christian rules led to overfishing of rivers, the development of fish farming, stocking of fishponds and creation of "water reservoirs." On a more luxurious note, it also spread the consumption of sea fish inland.

The trade in salt fish only really began in the 11th century, with the rise of the Hanseatic League, and herrings were the first sea fish to appear on the markets of Paris and Champagne. Their economic importance in the Middle Ages was considerable. In medieval texts, the herring is sometimes rather grandiosely described as the "prince of fish" or even the "king of fish." It was found in abundance in the northern seas, and its very name, *hering* (in Middle English), evoked its teeming shoals. In the 11th and 12th centuries, methods of conservation such as smoking, salting and drying meant that the major European cities could be supplied with sea fish. The Hanseatic towns of Germany, especially Hamburg, grew rich on this flourishing trade. The fish found at Château-Thierry, more than 300 km from the sea, are evidence of this medieval trade. No doubt they are connected to the fairs of Champagne. From 1180 to 1320, these played a vital role in the international economy.

The success of what were the biggest commercial events of medieval times was founded on the security of merchants traveling to these fairs, thanks to the safe-conducts provided by the counts and, later, the monarchy as of the 12th century, and, in the mid-13th century, to the guarantees underwriting contracts agreed in the trade association of fairs.

In 1254, Louis IX divided the sale of fish into fresh, salted and smoked (*saur*). This classification was maintained until 1345 by Philippe de Valois. The art of salting herrings in the modern manner was still unknown.[3] In spite of the growth in trade, these fish remained expensive throughout the late Middle Ages. A Parisian text, dated 1417, mentions "small herring *caqué* (in a basket): 6 Parisis deniers; fresh herring came to about the Saint-Denis *octaves* for three or four baskets, and was sold per piece three or four *blancs* [francs], all washed, and the *poudré*, two *blancs*, no less."[4] (*Poudré* or powdery is a less dry, salted herring of middling quality.) On the markets, the sale of herrings was a very singular proposition; it was carried out by women who were known by the sweet name of *harengères*. Writing in the 15th century, the poet Villon emphasized their unique talent for trading insults.

Apart from this major commercial activity, analysis of the container also tells us about the practical techniques of packing and transporting this kind of food in the 13th century, before the introduction of barrels, as attested in the 15th century. Curiously enough, these techniques were little known. This container bears witness to the form, the mode of assembly and the materials used to make it. The first hypothesis put forward here posited that the three elements discovered formed a single basket, with the two concave rectangles forming the upright parts and the circular form positioned at the bottom, in the manner of baskets represented in certain medieval illustrations. The relatively fine pieces of split wood (*éclisses*) and the uprights that were found here were, in themselves, not enough to validate or invalidate such a model. The only way to reach any conclusions was to experiment with full-scale reconstruction.[5]

This led us to reject the hypothesis of a single basket constituted by three elements, for the fact of dissociating the three elements implies the complete destruction of the forms, without finding the composition of the three archaeological forms found in the ditch. A second proposition was then considered, with three distinct bags or baskets, two identical ones and one with a round bottom. It was clear that basket-making techniques, which were generally considered ancient and immutable, had in fact changed between the Middle Ages and the Enlightenment, when they were laid down in the Encyclopedia by Diderot and D'Alembert.

In the end, we finally managed to recreate the mode of assembly. This came after much experimentation, combining fine pieces of split wicker threaded between uprights in hazel wood (*Corylus avellana*, known in the local dialect and in literature as *coudrier rouge*). The form of the basket thus obtained was similar to that of a *resse*,[6] a kind of large, open-topped basket without handles and with solidly woven sides.

1   In terms of archaeological context, the ditch in which these elements were found dates from the period when the castle was being reorganized after the construction of a new wall under the aegis of the Count of Champagne Thibaud IV, between 1220 and 1236. The ditch lies close to a small temporary masonry workshop. The materials used to fill the ditch indicate that this occurred not very long after it was dug. Three different ensembles were dumped here "rather quickly." These consisted of two concave rectangles stuck together, each 80 cm X 40 cm, and a circular piece with a diameter of 40 cm surmounting one of the rectangles. Only the two rectangles contained compact masses of fish skeletons. The extremely fragile and, given the difficulties of conserving vegetal matter in a dry environment, rare contents made prudence doubly necessary. The first step was to remove these three fragile elements and examine them in the laboratory. It was thus possible to conduct a rigorous and methodical archaeological study, extracting and separating, one by one, the bones of each fish in the containers constituted by uprights and fine wicker *éclisses*, while keeping a precise graphic and photographic record of each of these essential stages.

2   The ichthyological analysis entrusted to Benoît Clavel at the osteological laboratory in Compiègne (CRAVO) found and identified the remains of nearly a thousand fish. The fish were herrings *(Clupea harengus)* about 20-25 cm long. As was shown by the anatomical condition of the skeletons, the vast majority had not been eaten. The almost systematic ablation of one of the bones of the gills confirms that the fish had been prepared before being laid in the wicker receptacles where they were found. There are several ways of consuming these fish: fresh, salted (white herrings), or salted and smoked herrings *(harengs saurs)*. Unfortunately, analysis of the sodium levels in the sedimentological samples, taken in and around the ditch, yielded no conclusive evidence on this point.

3   Witness the many herring recipes in the famous *Mesnagier de Paris de 1393* (*Le Mesnagier de Paris,* edited by Georgina E. Breton and Jeanet M. Ferrier, translation and notes by Karin Ueltschi, Paris: Librairie Générale Française, coll. "Lettres gothiques," 1994). According to the tradition, salted herring was the invention of a man named Buckelz, who died at Biervliet, in Dutch Flanders, probably in 1447.

4   Excerpt from the *Journal d'un bourgeois de Paris*, Colette Beaune (ed.), year: 1417, No. 166, Paris: Librairie Générale Française, coll. "Lettres gothiques," 1989.

5   This archaeological experiment with strong ethnological overtones was carried out thanks to the great expertise of Jean-Claude Pernée, a master basket weaver and Meilleur Ouvrier de France, and with the advice   . of the teaching staff at the Ecole Nationale d'Osiériculture et Vannerie at Fayl-Billot (Haute-Marne), a current source of wicker *(Salix triandra)*.

6   Known in the 18th century as *resses bretonnes*.

The electrician's bag

The school bag or satchel

The plumber's bag

The guard's bag

The roundsman's clock bag

The bag for transporting money

The game bag

The Swiss army backpack

The fares bag

The artist's bag

The sailor's bag

Bags for Professionals

▎ The bag is an attribute of nomads, and that applies to the world of work, too. For some trades, itinerancy is part of the job. Soldiers, messengers, fitters, repairmen, etc. all carry what we can call professional bags. In this category of bags, practical criteria naturally outweigh aesthetic ones. What is expected is not beauty but solidity, appropriateness, and efficiency. Here, a good bag is a bag that is neither too soft (otherwise it is like a mechanic's bag) nor too rigid (in which case it's a chest, a box, or a suitcase).

The French term for the leather used to make these bags is of military origin: *cuirs d'équipement* (equipment leathers). It goes without saying that the fineness of the grain, color, feel, and smell hardly come into the equation here.

opposite, top and bottom rows, left to right

ill. 1 ▎ **Chiffonier**
photograph by D.R. Berrety

ill. 2 ▎ **Workers at the end of the day on the site of Haute-Seine de Villeneuve-le-Roi**
photograph around 1950

ill. 3 ▎ **The postman on his rounds**
photograph from French research department 1943, Bibliothèque nationale de France Engravings and Photographs

ill. 4 ▎ **Carrying hay**
photograph by Marc Paygnard

ill. 5 ▎ **The first French female billsticker**
ABF/BN

01 The electrician's bag

This fitter or technician's bag is virtually
a self-contained workshop, a bag that can be
transformed into a huge kit box. It enables
the electrician to be instantly operational
by providing a full range of tools. It is also like
a travel kit in which every inch of space is used.
In addition to its many features (a cut under
the rim, patch pockets, cartridge holders,
pull-out pockets, horse-flap pocket closed
by hasps and straps, moveable separation like
the moveable flap of a kit fixed to the base
by three pegs, straps and flaps of all kinds,
bottle-strap, etc.), the main innovation lies
in the double gusset that covers it. This structure
is held in place by a small leather strap fixed
to the lower part that fits onto three hasps,
which hold the other gusset that comes over
the top. This strap can be removed in an instant,
thus letting the front of the bag open to reveal
all its contents.

All the potentially weak parts are strengthened
by rivets or double stitching, yet all this
notwithstanding the bag is made with real
economy, even though it is unusually complex.
It has 15 pockets and some 30 compartments
for different tools (wrenches, tube wrenches,
pliers, screwdrivers, hammers, saw, etc.). Its base
is strengthened on the sides by aluminum bars
and its bottom with overstitched and riveted
strips of leather running crosswise. The bag
is closed by a pair of straps with roller buckles.
A median hasp allows the bag to be padlocked.
There is a nameplate on the upper side of the
bag.

The bag can be carried in three different ways:
on the back, at the belt, or over the shoulder
using a big, adjustable shoulder strap with
a very wide felt patch.

ill. 6 | **An electrician's bag**

Villeneuve de Berg for EDF
(National electricity utility)
private collection

02 The school bag or satchel

The sound economy of the satchel is based
on its simple, tried, and trusted form and solid
material: colored split hide.
The body and flap form a single piece
of material and the gussets are strengthened
by thick, stitched-on cardboard. The positioning
of the straps is very clever. They cross at
the front and thus perform two functions:
on the one hand, they help close the bag
and support the weight of dictionaries and hefty
textbooks; on the other, they ensure that
the weight of the bag is not concentrated on one
part of the back – corresponding to the position
of the metal tab joining them and which,
without this weight distribution, would give way
under the strain. One of the two straps can be
unhooked to facilitate putting the bag
on the back.

ill. 7 | **Robert Doisneau**
The jealous schoolboys
photograph, 1953

ill. 8 | **A boy's schoolbag**
private collection

03 The plumber's bag

Recognizable by its thick, elongated shape, it is
very similar to the roofer's zinc case (indeed, the
same tradesman can practice both professions).
Primitive forms of this bag sometimes turn up
in bric-a-brac shops: the sides or gussets are
made with pieces of wood cut into circles,
and the leather that forms the body of the bags
is nailed onto them. The drawback of this
cylindrical form was undoubtedly instability:
the bag must have rolled a bit when the tools
were put away.

This bag is used to carry not just very heavy
items – emergency tools – but also smaller
objects that always get lost in among the big
ones: pin spanners, adjustable wrenches,
pipe-cutters, joint compound, yarn, fiber joints,
torch, and grease were all kept together in this
bag with its flaring, rigid sides, rounded top,
and flat base. The sides are strengthened
by the bottom, which is folded over
onto the sides in order to make the envelope
more rigid and protect the stitches from rubbing.
A few studs on the bottom fixed in strips
of leather secure the underside. A strap with
a felt patch allows the workman to balance
the weight on his shoulder. The bag is
rudimentary, with the body and flap made
from a single piece. It is closed by passing
the two tongues through roller buckles.
The leather is vegetable-tanned equipment
or saddle leather and is fairly thick, so as to be
rigid enough to stand up to the deforming
pressure of its heavy contents.

The bag holds everything a plumber normally
needs, but this emergency equipment can be
complemented by cases or boxes of kilos
and kilos of other tools, screws, joins, bits
of piping, bobbins, and so on, like a moveable
hardware store.

ill. 9 | **A plumber's bag**
private collection

04 The guard's bag

The bag, with a flap covering the front, was part of the uniform for a guard on a horse-drawn public stagecoach. The guard's role was to ensure that the journey went smoothly, to ensure safety and punctuality, and to take payment for the tickets. The dress regulations stipulated that the bag be worn on the left, slung over the right shoulder.

The guard also had to announce departures with a trumpet. His bag therefore had a fob watch, hung upside down so that it could be read more easily, protected in a molded pigskin housing. Since the guard was responsible for possessions and valuables on unsafe roads, there are two slots in the front of the bag to hold the keys to the coach and the chests. The bag is in strong, vegetable-tanned calfskin and closes with a tab. On the top of the front we read "Paris 24 Faubourg St Honoré". Inside, the lining is in chamois leather and a small flap holds the watch in its housing.

The fob watch has a dial in white and black enamel, inscribed with Arabic numerals, and is equipped with a sweep second hand placed at the six o'clock position.

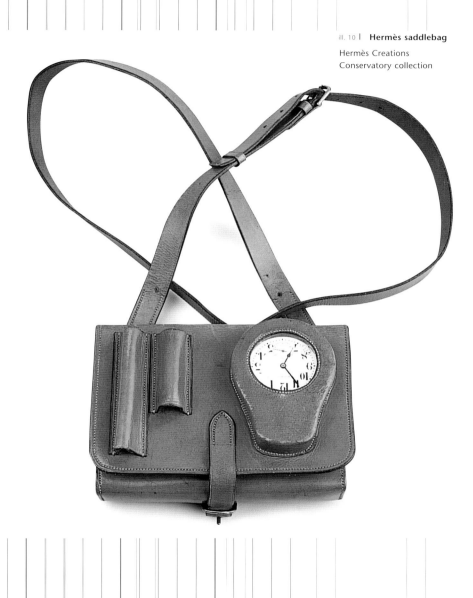

ill. 10 | **Hermès saddlebag**
Hermès Creations
Conservatory collection

05 The roundsman's clock bag

Commonly known as the *mouchard* (informer),
this bag, used by guards on their rounds
or personnel keeping a technical check
on certain installations, has one simple function:
to carry a clock.
It comprises two parts in molded leather that fit
together around the clock to protect it.
These two parts are joined by a pair of straps
on each side, fixed by tubular rivets. The front
allows a view of the dial, whose glass is
protected by an open grille. On the back, there is
a hole for the keys. Two hoops fixed in place
by rivets hold a simple shoulder strap.

ill. 11 | **Timekeeper's bag**

private collection

06 The bag for transporting money

This bag needs to reassure in a number of ways. It must carry heavy masses of coinage and other ingots that are as heavy as... gold. It must open wide in order to ensure that it has been completely emptied. And, lastly, it needs to close and lock with a key, and a key only!

This bag conflates several different traditions: it is opened and closed using a "frame" clasp with vertical movements. It is a "city" or "express" type of bag. The two brass locks are set onto the sides of the *battes* in the hunting style (the model is inspired by the English hunting bag). The gusseted lower part of the sides is strengthened by an added piece and held in place by rivets at the bottom. An original feature is the double pair of round handles, which are not only extended by the strips of leather around the bag, but are also held down with big strengthener studs, thus making it impossible to tear away the handles. Moreover, the strips of the bag's two side handles are at an oblique angle, so that it can be carried by two guards without damage. The overstitched strengthening strips are also at a slight angle. The bag is lined with hide. The clasp is covered with overstitched leather. The bag itself is assembled using battens.

Sales catalogues from the early 20th century show the standard model of this specialist's bag, but there was also a smaller model for a single guard, with only one pair of handles.

English-type bags were different from those in the French tradition. The French more or less made do with a big purse with a heavy lock made by Fichet, whereas the English developed a specific new kind of bag. This bag is generally made in vegetable-tanned leather with "long grain" finish on the body and smooth cowhide for the strips and handles. The locks are in brass.

ill. 12 | **Bag for transporting money**

private collection

07 The game bag

This kind of shoulder bag was originally used
to carry grenades. Its modern form – and name –
are characterized by an ample flap with rounded
corners. Its neck is narrow in order to leave
room to attach the shoulder strap. The flap,
in smooth, vegetable-tanned cowhide, is
decorated with a line following the edge
on the inside.

The bag comprises three juxtaposed pouches,
held together at the top by two pairs
of alternating leather buckles, overlapping
the sides. The first constitutes a rope net, used
to carry game, in alternating horizontal bands
of colors. The front is given rigidity by a strip
of perforated leather. An intermediary pocket
in brown tarpaulin is used to carry the hunter's
personal possessions. Finally, the last pocket,
in grained leather, with a straight, three-part
gusset, structures the whole bag.

A light shoulder strap is fitted using a square
buckle with a fixed bar. Its ends are held
by pieces of leather rolled in over themselves
and held in place by buttons. One of the ends
has a military snap hook.

ill. 13 | **Gamebag**
private collection

08 The Swiss army backpack

This complex bag is based on the principle that a "hair" leather is tougher than ordinary leather. The buckles are in black-lacquered steel and aluminum. The lining is in linen and cotton canvas. The rigid structure of this bag is built around a wooden frame. The edges in hair-side leather are flanked by goatskin.

The bag closes by means of two side flaps held by tabs and counter-tabs and protected by a canvas flap, strengthened at the fold by leather corners. A leather base protects the bag from dirt.

The covering flap is articulated around an ash rod, which forms a hinge. An external pocket at the bottom of the flap closes by means of a tongue. On it is a horizontal tab with a loop and a button at the end. Inside the flap, a deep canvas pocket with folded gussets is protected by a flap with cut corners and closed by a button formed by a roll of leather. At the base of the pocket, a middle flap is held in place by a riveted loop and is attached to a button. It is surrounded by two tabs, one with a roller buckle, the other with a hook. In addition to their basic closing function, these tabs can also be used to hang the bag when it is open (in the bivouac, for example).

Finally, a pair of straps, each divided in two, are fixed around the ash bar. One pair is attached to the base of the bag by an ingenious system with a buckle formed by a half-moon tongue that is fitted over a hook. The back curves inwards slightly and square pads further enhance the bearer's comfort.

An oval cartouche on the bag has the words:
G. GAMMA Sattler ERSTFEL 51
The flap, which gives form to the bag, is stamped: J.WINNIGER 50 HILDISRIEDEN

ill. 14 | **Swiss army backpack**
private collection

09 The fares bag

Derived from the English travel bag, or gipser, this bag has a number of names, depending on the person using it. It is also called the "collector's bag" or (train or bus) "inspector's bag". Its generic name clearly indicates its function. It is used only to carry money or forms, tickets, receipts, or fines. Its fastening consists of a nickel frame fixed by riveted studs. A central lock with a button makes it easy to close the bag, opening being facilitated by a triangular tab. A patch pocket with a flap closes with a small tuck blocked by a hasp. The bag is assembled using a cord (inside-out assembly) and has two inside pockets. Two large loops are placed on the gussets at each end and a third at the back to hold the shoulder strap. The system is completed by two D-rings with half-soles. Two leather buckles with "water drops" (vents) riveted on the clasp are fixed to the shoulder strap by a button. Other, more structured models were developed using a closing system with multiple *battes* in order to provide greater capacity.

ill. 15 | **Bag for day's takings**
private collection

10 The artist's bag

Following in the footsteps of English watercolor artists such as Bonington, Turner, and Constable, the landscape painters of the 19th century left the studio and set up their easels amid nature. They went out "by field and by shore", dressed like campaigning soldiers or those Romantic writers recorded by Flaubert: "bag on back, iron-soled shoes on the feet, water bottle in hand, smoke at the lips, and fantasy in the mind". These "hunters of the ephemeral" sought in their direct and assiduous contact with the countryside to capture the sweep and depth of nature – "or, if you prefer, of the spectacle that the Pater Omnipotens Aeterne Deus spreads out before our eyes", wrote Cézanne in a letter to Emile Bernard. By bringing rural landscapes closer to the city, the railway and the steamboat brought within the reach of artists a bit of pure sky, the curves of a river, a forest path, an expanse of heather and broom, and even the changing nuances of sweeping sandy beaches.

Replacing heavy vessels full of water, tubes of paint in pliable tin, which could be carried in a bag, were also conducive to visual sensation, as artists went outside to track the quivering of color and the movements of light. In the first half of the 19th century, hawkers' catalogues offered elegant, well-designed models of the "artist's bag," a kind of big leather satchel, sometimes in hair-side leather, hung from two straps, with two independent receptacles in the gussets. The *Nouveau Larousse illustré* offers an almost identical image in the second half of the 19th century. Many artists of modest means or disdainful of Parisian novelties simply kept their painters' materials in a versatile leather bag flanked by capacious pockets. But they often preferred the proven services of the indefatigable canvas and leather backpack made to hold all the footsoldier's packs. On the bottom or on the top of the flap, these peregrinating painters hung their easel and folding chairs. Now displayed in Cézanne's studio on the Lauves hill at Aix-en-Provence, the bag that we see on the artist's back in a photograph taken not long before his death brings out the lanky silhouette of the great painter, giving him an almost allegorical quality. Backpack, stick in hand, eyes veiled by the broad edges of his hat, mustering his final strength in the effort to experience the powerful sensation of Nature, the walker is like the legendary figure of the Wanderer found in German poetry.

ill. 16 | **Cézanne makes his way to his chosen spot, near Auvers**
photograph, 1875

11 The sailor's bag

This is the sailor's inseparable companion, neatly gathering in one large pouch and a small canvas one all the possessions and clothes needed for life on board. The contents of the sailor's bag are loosely evoked in 1786, but only specified after the French Revolution and finally fixed after World War I. The kit bag is like a large, high pouch closed at the top by a braided tie or a piece of leather pulled through eyelets. The bottom may be strengthened with leather. There is a strap for it to be carried over the shoulder, sometimes also a handle stitched on the side. It was stowed in the bag-locker, a small cupboard with padlocked and chained compartments. Regular inspection of bags was an integral part of the rules of life on ship. For a sailor, "going to the bag" meant checking his possessions and repairing those that needed it. Lighter than a chest, the bag was an essential and extremely versatile on-board accessory. It could also serve as a hammock, or be stuffed with wadding or wool and be used as a mattress for oarsmen in a galley. Sailors on the voyage to Newfoundland, recruited only to fish, were said to have "boarded in the bag". A French sailing manual explains that "a sail *bags* when it swells too much, when it is not flat". As for the topmast, it is "in the bag" when it breaks. In *Mon Frère Yves*, Pierre Loti evokes some moving images of this accessory synonymous with the sailor: "We were never bored. The days were sufficiently occupied with work or distractions. At certain times, on certain days set in advance by the sea service roster, the sailors were allowed to open the canvas bags where their kit was kept (this was called 'going to the bags'). They then spread out all their little possessions, which were folded up in there with comical care, and the deck of the *Primauguet* suddenly looked like a bazaar. They opened their sewing boxes, laid out the very artistically cut patches for mending their clothes, which the continual play and power of their muscles quickly wore through; some sailors stripped off and gravely patched up their shirt; others used extraordinary methods to iron their big collars (by sitting on them for a long time); others took from their writing boxes sorry little bits of faded yellow paper, with postmarks from different lost corners of the Breton or Basque country, and started reading: these were letters from their mothers, sisters, or fiancées who lived in the villages over there. And then, to the sound of a very special whistle, which meant 'pick up your bags,' all these things disappeared as if by magic: folded, packed down, taken into the hold, into the numbered lockers that the terrible sergeants-at-arms came to close with iron chains."[1]

In *Billy Budd* (1951), the fine opera that Britten based on the short novel of the same name by Melville, the sailor's kit bag becomes the object of a violent fight. The tense, dramatic atmosphere that prevails on board *HMS Bellipotent* even prefigures the final clash between the forces of good and evil.[2] At the beginning of the 20th century, renowned baggage makers conferred a chic elegance on this canvas bag which, by the name of linen bag or kit bag, was taken on steamers and liners for luxury cruises. Forgetting the hardship and toil of those for whom it was first designed, the sailor's kit bag conquered the world of leather, and invaded sports halls and beaches.

1 *Mon frère Yves,* Paris: Calmann-Lévy, 1889, chap. XCVI, p. 377-378.
2 *Billy Budd*, opera in two acts by Benjamin Britten, revised version, 1961, libretto by E.M. Forster and Eric Crozier, based on the novella by Herman Melville.

ill. 17 | **Guy Arnoux**
A 19th century sailor in the West Indies
1937, Musée national de la Marine

ill. 18 | **A French navy bag**
before 1914
Musée national de la Marine

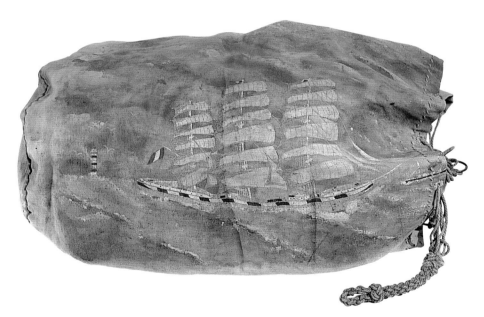

ill. 19 | **A sailor's bag**
first quarter of the 20th century
Musée national de la Marine

MONEY, POWER AND CEREMONY

fortune

alms

splendor

etiquette

robbery

denarii

munificence

cupidity

accounts

status

ill. xxxi **Vuitton bag,** sculpture of the Keepall bag, edition numbered 1/8, Sylvie Fleury, France, 2000, chrome bronze and silver, Paris, Louis Vuitton collection

ill. XXXII *The Homeless*, photograph by Olivier Coulange, Paris, 1991-92

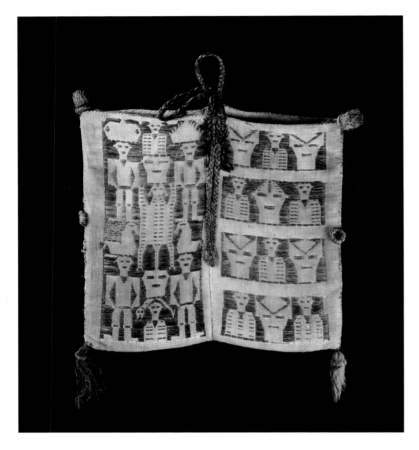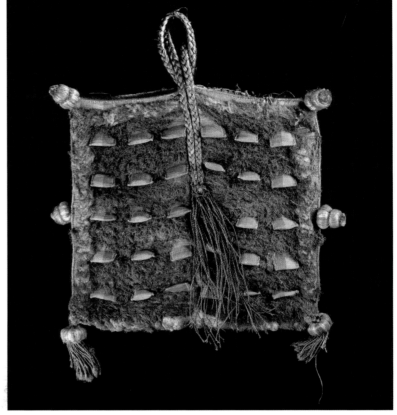

ill. xxxiii **Bamum or Bamiléké bags,** Grassland region, Cameroon, first half of the 20th century, vegetal fibers, wood, porcupine quills, Lyon, Muséum, gift of Denise and Michel Meynet

ill. xxxiv **Purse**, France, 1840-1870, knitted silk, steel beads, Paris, Musée de la Mode et du Textile, UCAD collection, Doistau donation, 1907

ill. xxxv **Purse**, France, first half of the 19th century, knitted silk, steel beads, bead lace, steel rings, Paris, Musée de la Mode et du Textile, UCAD collection, Palyart-Mancel bequest, 1911

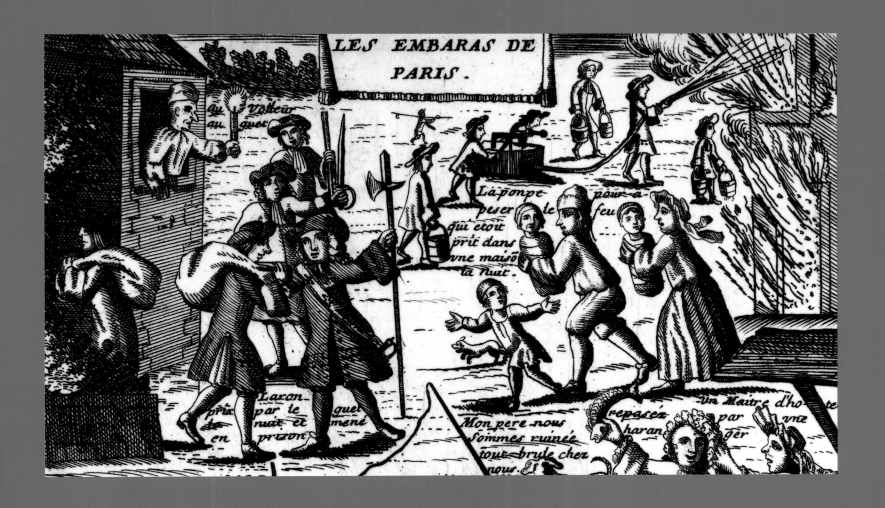

ill. xxxvii **François Guérard,** *Les Embarras de Paris,* circa 1680, Bibliothèque nationale de France (Prints and Photography)

CEREMONIAL BAGS

◻ The *aumônière*, or alms purse, originally used to collect alms, features in French inventories under the terms: *aumoisnière* (almoner's purse or pouch) *aloière; bourse* (purse), tasset or tasse, *gibecière* (gipser or game bag), *sac de fauconier* (falconer's bag) and *escarcelle* (moneybag or purse), to name but the principal terms. Any attempt to establish a rigorously chronological typology of these bags would be perilous. Viollet-le-Duc thought that a purse "with two drawstrings to close it and a cord with which to open it and hang it by the belt"[1] was the oldest form of bag (ill. 1). Victor Gay talks more cautiously of purses or *aumônière*s of all shapes where "small objects of all kinds were found, keys, jewelry, writing tablets and even medication, as seen on monuments from the Charlemagne era onwards".[2] In a collection of medical treatises from the Carolingian era,[3] Esculape can be seen discovering betony and wearing a purse with a double or even triple gusset and a flap; this type of very elaborate purse can be found on numerous monuments of the late Middle Ages. At approximately the same time, an ivory cover from Charles the Bald's Psalter shows Bathsheba holding a delightful round handbag, probably made of wicker, with a short handle. However, a journey back to the prehistory of humanity would show us that the bag was already indispensable to mankind, the container that enabled him to liberate his most precious tool: his hands.

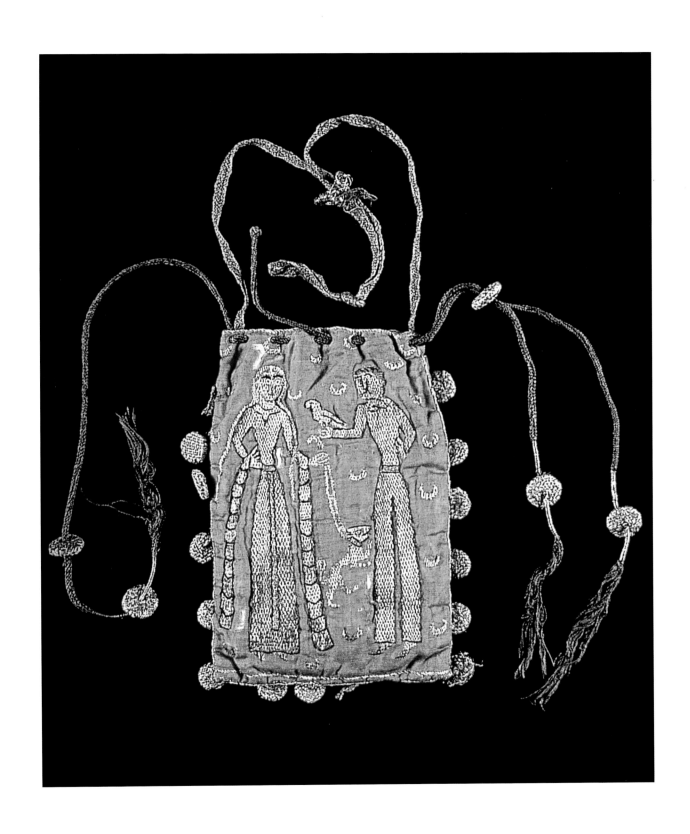

ill. 2 □ **A Roman relief**

1st century A.D.
Sankt Georgen
am Sanhof Church
Carinthie, Austria

On a 1st century Roman relief, a woman holds a rectangular handbag in her right hand and a mirror in her left, leading us to imagine that the bag contained personal effects (ill. 2). Two centuries later, a Roman sarcophagus shows a shepherd wearing a shoulder bag, like those seen on numerous sculptures of Saint Jacques the Major or Saint Roch (ill. 3). Over time, the shape and design of bags and clasps would evolve. We will therefore distinguish pre-14th century purses from 15th and 16th century purses in the history of ceremonial bags.

THE GIRDLE PURSE (10TH CENTURY – 14TH CENTURY)

If we restrict ourselves to the medieval era proper, the only pre-14th century bag that existed (apart from the pilgrim's bag and the messenger's box) was a purse made of a piece of square or round cloth or leather, sometimes with a string at the top to close it. Inventories and sculptures, especially funereal sculpture, provide the main iconographic sources, though inventories say little about the

ill. 3 □ *Saint Jacques the pilgrim from Compostella*

Burgundy, 15th century
Paris, Musée national du Moyen
Âge, thermes et hôtel de Cluny

The pilgrims usually wore their bags on their shoulders attached to a staff or carried like a sling. In the latter case, the bag was rectangular in shape with a flap and closed with a hook, probably a metal one. From the 12th century on, a bag with a rounded base decorated with a shell on the front appeared on the various sculptures which represented Saint Jacques.

different types of purses and their contents. Medieval literature is far more loquacious on the subject.

From the 10th and the 11th centuries, several documents show purses fixed to girdles with a double string hanging quite loosely down to the knees or even lower. This way of carrying purses did not really die out and could still be seen in Brueghel's day (ill. 4). Women's purses, invariably decorated with tassels on the bottom and the sides, were slim and elegant, like the purse which Mary carries in the 13th century *Crucifixion* group preserved at the Schnütgen Museum in Cologne. This is of course a *Buchbeutel*, a book holder containing Holy Scriptures. The shape of the book holder has scarcely evolved. The one in the Musée de Cluny, in stiff leather decorated with foliation, still has the round leather loops, which originally held straps that were tied to the belt, unless they were long enough to be worn over the shoulder.

In the Middle Ages and the Renaissance, clothes had no pockets. People therefore had to find somewhere to hang the objects needed in daily life: on their belts. Women's belts, which were generally made of a simple leather strap that was sometimes studded, could also be crafted by a gold or silversmith and considered veritable items of jewelry, estimated as such in dowry or inheritance inventories. On a splendid *Announcement to the shepherds* in a Book of Hours (ill. 5), very elegantly dressed shepherd couple wear accessories hanging from their belts: the shepherd's canvas bag, decorated with geometric motifs, is shaped like a crescent moon, running from the back to the stomach; it probably contained ointments to care for the flock. His wife, dressed in a beautiful red and blue dress with a square décolleté, has a white canvas rolled bag like her husband's, along with three other items attached to her belt: a small leather purse with three tassels, tied to her belt with two long straps, a voluminous pleated brown drawstring purse, and a scraper for the hoofs of the sheep she is feeding. Keeping your hands free seems to have been the golden rule throughout the

ill. 4 □ **Pieter Bruegel**
The Church Fête
or the peasants dance (detail)

1559
Vienna, Kunsthistorisches Museum

The reddish orange purse, perfectly proportioned, can carry several objects thanks to its main double pocket including a smaller one on the outside, closed with a cord.

ill. 5 □ **The Announcement to the shepherds**
Heures à l'usage de Rome

Paris, second quarter of the 15th century
manuscript 5145, folio 61v
Lyon, Bibliothèque municipale

ill. 6 ☐ **Meister Leonhard**
The Last Supper

1460, Bressanone, diocesan Museum

Judas, isolated from the other apostles
gathered at the end of the table,
carries "the purse with thirty denarii"
on his back. This is held by two straps
probably joined by a buckle situated on
the shirt on the upper part of the body.

The artist, Meister Leonhard, wanted
to underline the importance of the
symbolic aspect of the purse carried
by "God's traitor". Luke 22, 1-5

period we are looking at. All the necessary day-to-day objects were therefore hung from the belt: key ring, medication, beauty products, the money purse... When it comes to documenting the contents of purses, medieval literature is a much more precious source of information than inventories. In a collection of rather comical and facetious 12th and 13th century jugglers' texts, we read:

> And the priest reminds her
> Of all his sorrow and annoyance
> Concerning the matter from which he knows not how to extract himself.
> So the old woman promises him
> That he has nothing to fear
> And she will not fail to help him.
> The priest immediately takes ten sous
> From his alms purse and gives them to her.[4]

These purses, worn by men and women alike, were used to carry money. Two illuminations from the Luttrell Psalter bear witness to this: a man takes a few coins from a wide open purse and gives them to a crippled child, transported by its father in a barrow; another man hunts for a few coins in a purse hanging from his leather belt. An illumination in Aristotle's *Ethics, Politics and Economics* shows a man plunging his hand into his money purse to pay the cobbler. And then, of course, there was Judas' purse, filled with the thirty pieces of silver of betrayal. It is most often represented hanging from a ring on his belt, but in *The Last Supper*, a painting by Master Leonhard that dates from 1460, it appears hanging down his back, on two straps that were no doubt attached to his clothes at the chest and clasped together in a ring to avoid strangulation (ill. 6).[5] Literature of the 12th century already mentioned three clerics, who carried their books and linen in a bag, hanging from their necks,[6] and we can easily imagine that this "bundle" hung down their backs in the same manner as Judas' money purse.

In *The Romance of the Rose*, it is said that a woman should refrain from offering a gift of any value to a lover, regardless of how much she wants to cherish him; she can offer "a pillow or a towel, a kerchief or a purse, provided it is not too costly. Or she might give him a needle-case or some laces or a belt with a cheap buckle, or else a pretty little knife".[7] Wedding purses, a gift from groom to bride, were the object of a statute drawn up by the magistrates of the city of Zittau in 1353: "No one but the groom may give the bride a purse." In Brunswick, however, the groom, parents, brothers and sisters could all offer the bride "purses and linen clothing". Wedding purses did not die out until the 15th century: proof of this is found in the Château de Vincennes inventory (1418) which lists an embroidery and pearl bridal purse "with the arms of France and Burgundy on either side and in the middle the arms of Brittany". The purse was therefore part of the woman's wedding present (ill. 7). These drawstring wedding purses that hung from women's belts or dress girdles are identical to the purses embroidered with scenes of courtship. The Metropolitan Museum of Art in New York owns two delightful purses of this kind: one of them tells the tale of the virtuous Griselda, victim of her pitiless husband, according to the tale[8] taken from Boccaccio's *Decameron*. There has been speculation as to whether these purses were ever really carried or merely placed in safekeeping and used to store jewels or valuable personal effects. Few documents show them decorated with courtly scenes (ill. 9 and 10).

Another ceremonial purse was the *aumônière* known as a *sarrasinoise*, or Saracen purse. Some truly beautiful examples are preserved at the Troyes Cathedral treasury and the Musée de Cluny. Trapezium-shaped with a rounded tip, they were inspired by oriental products: "No haberdasher can make or buy Saracen purses where cotton is mixed with silk, it would disappoint the connoisseurs".[9] Saracen purses were subjected to harsh regulations: "[Saracen purse-makers] cannot and must not use threaded or twisted silk instead of fine golden thread from Luques, otherwise the work will be counterfeit".[10]

The *aumônière* said to have belonged to Henri I, Count of Champagne, is decorated with an embroidered scene of a unicorn hunt and a seated figure on the cover. These figures were embroidered separately and sewn onto a red velvet background. The hunter fighting the unicorn as it seeks refuge beside a virgin is an allegorical representation of unicorn hunting. The flap of another Saracen *aumônière* kept in Troyes shows a woman asleep, dreaming of a winged lady; the two women, probably rivals, also feature below, one dressed in beige and the other in green, sitting on either side of an altar and cutting a heart down the middle with a long saw. An arm protrudes from a cloud, armed with an ax: is

this an allegory of female adultery (ill. 8)? A third, even more astonishing Saracen purse, is lined with leather and has two pockets, front and back. As for the Saracen purse in the Musée de Cluny, decorated with three hybrid characters and especially remarkable for its raised appliqué embroidery, Henry Harvard calls it a *"tasse"*.[11] The falconer's bag, which also has a trapezoid shape, was made of cloth or leather attached to a round, iron clasp. Like the gipser, the *fauconnière*, or falconer's bag, was originally a hunter's bag which was then adopted by bourgeois and aristocratic circles and became a luxury bag: "No master saddler or furniture-maker must make falconer's bags without using high-quality sheepskin".[12] In the biblical episodes of the *Burial of Jesus*, Nicodemus and Joseph of Arimathea often wear this kind of bag, very similar in shape to the falconer's bags.

ill. 7 □ **The Sacrement of Marriage, the Glorious Hours of Notre-Dame**

circa 1380 (finished at the beginning of 15th century)
Paris, Bibliothèque nationale de France, Western manuscripts

This painting shows how many purses a woman could receive during the wedding ceremony: here there are four.

ill. 9 and 10 ☐ **Courting scene around a chestnut tree**
(front on left, back on right)
moneybag
France, middle of 14th century
silk on canvas and gold thread
drawstring tie
Sens, from Cathedral treasury

Purses were more than a luxury accessory to men's and women's outfits, they were also a sign of wealth and social recognition (ill. 11). Countess Margarette de Nassau thanked her aunt Mechtild von Geldern, Countess of Cleves, for the gifts she sent (14th century): hair combs and the little bag which she gave to her lover, another purse with two golden clasps. In 1375, a bag-makers' guild set the following regulations: "Moreover, bag-makers must make solid bags and not line them with linen or old leather. They must also not make the lining from untreated leather due to the odor that develops over time".[13] Despite the moral ban on all ostentatious forms of wealth, men wore very opulent purses or pouches. They would wear them against the stomach or slung slightly to one side. Some bags for men had a small slit to hold a dagger or sword and their initials could be engraved on them in gold or silver thread (ill. 12). These dagger purses weren't necessarily very big; they could be small, generally square-shaped and sometimes with a pointed or ecu-shaped tip. They were fixed firmly to the belt by loops inside the flap that were wound around the belt. These dagger and knife purses can be seen on numerous monuments from the 13th century onwards.

It is interesting to note that fashion had an effect on how purses were worn. An illumination in Boccaccio's *Decameron* is an eloquent example: the man wears a short doublet that forces him to hang his purse directly on his belt, while the woman beside him wears a long dress and a loosely strung drawstring purse that hangs down beyond her knees. Before 1330, long-string purses were hung from the belt and dangled down between the legs, but as soon as men started wearing shorter, close-fitting doublets, purses were worn close to the body, reducing the risk of theft and offering much more stability in the wearing. Older men, however, continued to wear long clothes. Dangling purses were therefore easy to steal: all you had to do was cut the strings.

In around 1400, women's dresses became close-fitting down to the waist, with a décolleté that showed off the upper bust. A belt would have been a superfluous and unsightly accessory. This change in fashion meant that, from as early as the 14th century, a new clothing accessory had to be invented: a "*demi-ceint*": a silver chain which various objects could be hung from (keys, purses, leather pouches, etc.). In 1316, the accounts of Geoffroi de Fleuri mention a velvet purse hanging from a silver chain.

It has often been said that the money purse was hidden in the main pocket of the *aumônière*, but we cannot be certain of this and numerous images of tiny purses carried on people's clothing tend to show the contrary. In an account of the King of Navarre's poisoned gift to his nephew, the Count of Foix's son,

ill. 11 ☐ **Peace Declaration
in Reims between Charles VII
and Philippe le Bon**

2 October 1435
Paris, Bibliothèque nationale de France

Froissart wrote that he gave him "a fine little purse full of such a powder that
no living thing could touch or eat without dying for want of a cure".[14] In her
account of a visit to the Poissy priory (1400), Christine de Pisan wrote that
before leaving, the people accompanying her bought "neither clasps nor rings
but purses embroidered with gold and silk birds"[15] from the nuns.

Charles V's inventory (1380) is quite precise about the contents of purses and
pouches: "a little purse with a gold chain inside, from which hang two stones of
bone, good remedies for venom, a little black snake strip called *lapis albazahar*
and another little square white bone"; "a little purse with a golden seal and a
square garnet hanging from a golden chain"; "a purse with five little buttons containing the cross which Emperor Constantine wore in battle, set on a gold jewel
with a large cameo bearing the image of Our Lord"; and finally "a gold object,

ill. 12 □ **Boccaccio**

The Decameron

1348-1353
Paris, Bibliothèque nationale de France
Bibliothèque de l'Arsenal

The man is carrying a purse
with two exterior pockets closed
with circular links. In the center
there is a space big enough for a dagger.

full of amber, in the shape of a small purse hanging from a vermilion braid".[16] Purse-makers formed a trade guild and made leather purses and then cases. In the journal of King John of England's expenditure (1359-1360), a reference is made to the purchase of "II purses and II black leather straps for Mgr Philippe"[17] from "Baudoin the purse-maker."

REFINEMENT AND SOPHISTICATION

At the turn of the 15th century, the size of a person's bag was a sign of opulence and wealth. It is noteworthy that, at this time, the increase in bag size coincided with an increase in the amount of money in circulation. Then everything started to go very fast: fashion changed constantly and purses became an indispensable complement to the outfits of gentlemen and ladies. The nobility and the bourgeoisie started off a veritable fashion competition. Despite the fact that knights were on the decline, the middle classes became aware that they did not hold pride of place within the State and discovered the ideal opportunity to flaunt their wealth. Bags became potent symbols, on the same level as helmets, coats of arms and knights' banners.

Olivier de La Marche, historian at the court of Burgundy in the 15th century, wrote a poem in which he described the accepted outfit of a noblewoman at court: he mentioned the accessories to this outfit, which included a purse, a small knife, a second belt for the paternoster, a necklace and gloves.

The purses we have already mentioned were still used over the next few centuries. However, new forms of bags with very elaborate clasps also came into use alongside traditional purses.

In the 1420s and 30s, bags with decorated iron clasps appeared on the scene. Shorter and wider at the bottom than falconers' bags, they were decorated with tassels, little ornamental buttons, pearls, gemstones and small outer pockets. The clasps were sometimes veritable masterpieces and often decorated with small towers, city architecture, castles etc. (ill. 13). This is where the opening mechanism was located. When this kind of purse had two pockets, front and back, a metal pivot enabled the back pocket to be placed in front for easy access to the belongings inside.

In Italy, where purses were less often worn at the belt than in France or northern countries in general, Master Venceslao's frescoes show a funny scene of a man and a woman carrying what look like white leather handbags on their wrists, in a thoroughly contemporary way (ill. 14). In Europe, purses continued to become increasingly diversified. The example of a purse fixed to the belt with a large knotted buckle was a very French fashion. At the turn of the 15th century, purses were still a symbol of wealth and would remain so in aristocratic circles. Purses adorned with illustrations (e.g. the wheel of fortune) belonged to wealthy people. The only inventory of Charlotte of Savoy (1483), Louis XI's second wife, records no less than twenty-three purses, more or less full: some were in white or red leather (Charles V's inventory already mentioned a purse in two-tone leather, white and red) and others were made of crimson velvet, satin or taffeta. One of them contained two hundred and seventy-five Saracen silver coins; another contained eighteen golden crowns; a third, "a small virgin with a sapphire stud; a gemstone set in gold; a small golden swine and a bell; a unicorn set in gold and two small gold virgins, all weighing one ounce".[18] Anne of Brittany's inventory (1498) informs us on the contents of two of her purses, one taffeta purse held a set of chess pieces and the other, a crimson velvet purse, held "a snake ring, a toadstone, a silver-gilt chain". A lady's toiletry bag, exhibited at the Musée des Beaux Arts in Dijon and made of embossed, chiseled golden leather with the words *Bonnes Nouvelles* inscribed on the side, is an extremely rare object in French collections. Loops on either edge of the bag prove that it was fixed to the belt by straps that have since been lost. This kind of bag contained combs, razors, scissors, mirrors and other toiletry essentials. Larger rectangular bags made of natural or dyed leather also appear in paintings and tapestries, where they can be seen attached to the belt by two leather straps, as in the *Anne and Joachim meet at the Porte Dorée* tapestry based on Albrecht Dürer's *Life of the Virgin* woodcut series. During archaeological digs at the Place de la Comédie in Metz, several kinds of leather alms purses were uncovered and recorded: from the simplest rectangular drawstring purse to one made of several compartments that closely resembles those seen on the Paris tapestry.

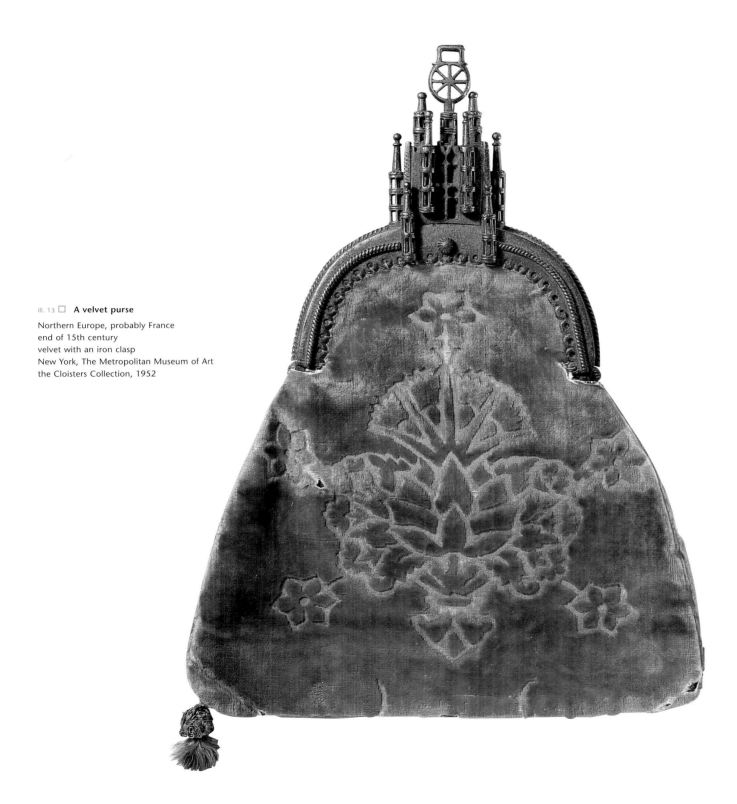

ill. 13 ☐ **A velvet purse**

Northern Europe, probably France
end of 15th century
velvet with an iron clasp
New York, The Metropolitan Museum of Art
the Cloisters Collection, 1952

EACH TO THEIR OWN PURSE

In the 15th century, bags were no longer the privilege of rich people and noble-men – they belonged to everyone. Servant girls, peasant women, servants, archers and shepherds all carried bags. A 15th century print, *Le Bain de Marie enfant*, riddled with details about everyday life, illustrates this better than words. A huge bunch of keys hangs from the servant girl's waist (this way of car-rying keys has not entirely disappeared today, with people sometimes also wear-ing them around their necks) along with a double-pocketed purse that appears to hold bath products: soap, soothing cream, anti-louse shampoo (ill. 15). An illu-mination in Aristotle's *Politics* shows a boy sitting reading his lesson aloud while the master, sitting on a Gothic bench, threatens him with a cane. The master is carrying an orange drawstring purse made of cloth at his belt; the purse is oval-shaped at the bottom and has numerous small tassels. On an illustration of the *Golden Legend* by Jacques de Voragine, the Nativity scene oddly takes place in the middle of the street, as though it was the scenography of a religious mys-tery. Joseph wears a splendid pleated purse made of light-colored leather; it seems very full and heavy as it hangs from his black leather belt. The leather flap of the purse is hooked over the belt and probably attached to it by a loop sewn inside the flap, like the system already seen in previous centuries. In numerous late 15th century Tournaisian tapestries representing bucolic scenes (Cleveland, London, Stockholm), men and women dance amid animals on car-pets of flowers; they have a very elegant way of wearing crescent-shaped purses made of white fabric (which would today be known as "banana bags"!) around their waists. This kind of purse was also seen in pastoral scenes, with shepherds using them to store ointment to heal their flocks. Much more surprising is this reference to purses in poor circles, made by the anonymous author of *Journal of a Parisian Bourgeois* (1427): "They were the poorest creatures you had ever seen in France. And they looked at people's hands and told them what happened or what would come to be, and created fights in many marriages, for they would say [to the husband] 'Your wife is cuckolding you' or to the woman 'Your hus-band is cheating on you'. And worse still, talking to [demon] creatures, by magic or other tricks, or even by skill, they would empty out the contents of the purse and put it in their own".

At the end of the 16th century, bigger purses with double pockets appeared. The clasps now portrayed the Italian iconographic repertory: arabesques, foliage, vases, birds or, as can be seen on a large light-beige velvet alms purse, clasps in the shape of dolphins' heads. This kind of alms purse, decorated with a finely carved square buckle that was fixed to the belt, can be seen on Brueghel's famous *Hunters in the Snow* painting.

ill. 14 □ opposite
Maestro Venceslao
The Cycle of Months: August
fresque (detail)
circa 1400, Torre Aquila
Bon-Conseil castle, Trente

ill. 15 ☐ **Israël Van Meckenem**
The Bathing of the Child Mary

engraving
second half of the 15th century
Paris, Bibliothèque nationale de France,
prints and photography department

While many words for "alms purse" have existed – like *aumônière*, falconer's bag, gipser, or money bag – their sumptuous outer clasps were humorously referred to by Viollet-le-Duc in 1874 as "strongly resembling the *ridicules* our mothers wore fifty years ago".[19] There is no need to go back that far, for these *ridicules* embroidered in gold or silver thread that people go mad over are very "hip" today, as we witness a comeback of bags carried close to the body in order to leave our hands free.

1   Eugène Viollet-Le-Duc, *Dictionnaire raisonné du mobilier français de l'époque carolingienne à la Renaissance*, Paris: 1874, Vol. III, p. 26-31.

2   Victor Gay, *Glossaire archéologique du Moyen Âge et de la Renaissance*, Paris, 1887-1928, Vol. I, p. 84-85, p. 196-197.

3   *Recueil de traités médicaux* (detail): Esculape discovering betony, pen and ink drawing on parchment, mid 9th century, pre-823, Hautvillers, Reims, lat. ms. 6862 f° 18 v°, Paris: Bibliothèque Nationale de France.

4   *Fabliaux érotiques, textes de jongleurs des XIIe et XIIIe siècles,* Paris: Lettres gothiques, 1992, p. 267-275.

5   It can be seen in another *Last Supper* by Conrad von Soest, dated 1403, at the Bad Wildungen parish church in Germany.

6   "La Bourgeoise d'Orléans", in *Fabliaux,* presented, chosen and translated by Gilbert Rouger, Paris: Gallimard, Folio coll., 1978, p. 164-168.

7   Guillaume de Lorris and Jean de Meun, *Le Roman de la rose,* Paris: Lettres gothiques, 1992, V. 14 410-14 422 ("un oreiller, un voile de tête, un couvre-chef ou une *aumônière* – à condition qu'elle ne soit pas trop chère –, un étui à aiguilles, un lacet ou une ceinture dont la ferrure sera bon marché, ou un beau petit couteau").

English translation: *The Romance of the Rose,* translated by Frances Horgan, Oxford: OUP, 1999, p. 222.

8   *The Tenth Day, Tenth Story*, X, *Physiology of marriage.*

9   *Réglemens sur les arts et métiers de Paris rédigés au XIIIe siècle et connus sous le nom du Livre des métiers d'Étienne Boileau,* Paris: Crapelet, 1837, article 75.

10   *Réglementation des faiseuses d'aumônières sarrasinoises,* 1290, chap. XVII.

11   Henry Havard, *Dictionnaire de l'ameublement et de la décoration depuis le XIIIe siècle jusqu'à nos jours,* Paris, 1887, t. I, p. 383-385 et t. IV, p. 1262.

12   Statute of Bordeaux saddle-makers, 14th century.

13   Otto Rüdiger, *Die ältesten hamburgischen Zumftrollen und Brüderschaftsstatuten,* Hamburg: 1874, p. 91.

14   Jean Froissart, *Chroniques,* Paris: Lettres gothiques, 2001, Vol. II.

15   Henry Havard, *op. cit.,* Vol. I, p. 386 ("pas de fermaux, pas d'anneaux / mais des boursettes brodées d'oiseaux en fil d'or et de soie").

16   Léon de Laborde, *Inventaire des meubles et joyaux de Charles V,* Paris, 1851, nos. 59, 70.

17   Victor Gay, *op. cit.,* "Tassetterie", Vol. II, p. 1263.

18   Alexandre Tuetey, *Inventaire des biens de Charlotte de Savoie, reine de France (1483), publié pour la première fois d'après le manuscrit original déposé à la Bibliothèque impériale,* Paris: De Lainé, 1865, p. 45-47.

19   Eugène Viollet-Le-Duc, *Dictionnaire raisonné..., op. cit.*

ill. 16 **Messenger box with the coat of arms of Du Guesclin**, an important lord from Beauvais (who died around 1310)
France, end of 13th century or beginning of 14th century, copper, champlevé enamels, Nantes, Musée Thomas-Dobrée de Nantes

The box is the most beautiful messenger box we have received to date. This kind of box is usually in the shape of a shield, and has two oblique metal straps on the back which are attached
to the belt. The position of the straps indicates that the box was carried crosswise, which allowed the messenger to walk freely. The flat part in the back was opened with a hinge, and the cover
was most probably closed with a lock with two keys, one for the messenger, the other to the person it was addressed to, in order to maintain secrecy. These boxes only had one lock and two keys,
one of which belonged to the lord, the other to the Lord's liegeman, the messenger. No one else had a key.

ill. 17 **A purse**, France, end of 13th century, polychromy silk embroidery, pearls, Paris, Musée de la Mode et du Textile, UCAD collection

ill. 18 **A purse**, France, end of 13th century, needlepoint, emblazoned badges, Paris, Musée de la Mode et du Textile, UCAD collection

MONEY BAGS

☐ In the inconstant course of their intimacy as container and contents, it is not surprising that the bag should have taken on some of money's rich imaginary associations. By metonymy, the bag can designate a measure of money and, in familiar usage, even become one of its countless synonyms: in the 17th century, Colbert, Intendant of France and, later, Controller General of the Kingdom's Finances, demonstrated his sense of imagery by describing some miserly character as "hunchbacked, obscure, living as a poor man, *loving the bag*".[1]

Thus, in the West, in the times and places where capitalism was beginning to triumph, the bag often compromised its native innocence through its murky contacts with gold, the all-powerful metal whose ambivalence contaminated this envelope of leather or velvet. The most passionate of the polemics to involve the bag was no doubt the one that occurred along the Rhine and in the former Low Countries, in that "time of Reforms"[2] that was torn so violently between the attraction of the abundance being discovered by an industrious

ill. 1 ☐ **Georges de La Tour**
Paid Money
1620, Lvov, Art Gallery

and prosperous Europe, and the belief in the Kingdom of Heaven that the rich man, as the Gospel said, would find it harder to enter than a camel to pass through the eye of a needle.[3] The Book of Tobias offers this advice to the rich man, so that his soul will not sink into the Shadows: "Give alms out of thy substance, and turn not away thy face from any poor person: for so it shall come to pass that the face of the Lord shall not be turned from thee. According to thy ability be merciful. If thou have much give abundantly: if thou have a little, take care even so to bestow a little willingly. For thus thou storest up to thyself a good reward for the day of necessity. For alms deliver from all sin, and from death, and will not suffer the soul to go into darkness. Alms shall be a great confidence before the most high God, to all them that give it".[4]

ill. 2 □ **Jan Galle according to Pieter Bruegel the Elder**
Battle Between Strongboxes and Moneybags
engraving
Boston, Historical Collections Department, Harvard Business School

MONEY BAGS AND ALMS PURSES

So now bags were judged in relation to the Bible. Purse, money bag (in Italian, *scarsella*, meaning "little miser"), the charitable purse or *aumônière* (almoner, from the Greek noun for compassion: *éleemosunê*), and other receptacles for money were sometimes vilified, sometimes justified, sometimes – more rarely – blessed, whether in the oratorical flights of preachers, by the pen of moralizing or satirical writers, or by the burins and brushes of artists in northern Europe. The vigorous curves of prosperity, daughter of judicious trade, the virtuous instrument of philanthropy, the black emblem of cupidity, of idolatry, of veniality, or corruption – the purse's associations are many and varied.

Certainly, it is rare for artists to omit this accessory, whose moral significance is essential to the scene represented: the purse held tight by Joseph's brothers during the culpable transaction that gives their younger brother up to the merchants, the one offered by the lustful old men to the chaste Suzanne, and, most accursed of all, the one taken by Judas at the price of his master's blood. More respectable is the purse of Matthew, the apostle and taxman. Bathed in nocturnal lighting of singular dramatic intensity, *Paid Money* by Georges de la Tour (ill. 1) casts a very disapproving gaze over the little bag of coins and notes, laid on the table with its neck wide open, stared at by the creased, greedy eyes of the protagonists. A money bag deformed by its protuberances in the left hand, big bags of which two gape open, revealing gold coins – these are the attributes of "Queen Money" in an emblem engraved by Adriaen Van de Venne and entitled *Gelt doet gewelt* (the violence of money).[5] Sometimes, even, in the visionary

ill. 3 □ pages overleaf
Pierre Mignard
The Fortune (detail)
1692
Lille, Musée des Beaux-Arts

imagination of Pieter Brueghel the Elder, the bag comes alive to allegorize the rapacity, chaos, and unreason of which lust for gold is the universal cause. Likewise those fantastical, swelling purses overcome with bellicose fury in the *Battle Between Strongboxes and Moneybags* (ill. 2), as popularized by Jan Galle's engraving. In the lampoons that were an effective weapon in the French Wars of Religion, woodcuts use the bag as a symbol to attack the corruption and simony for which the religious authorities were reproached. In the *Songes drolatiques de Pantagruel,*[6] spawned by the "invention de maître François Rabelais," the Church of Rome is represented in the grotesque, strange form of a disheveled woman, her eyes raised to the sky, as if in ecstasy. A big alms purse hangs from her belt, over a knife. The frontispiece of *Les Taxes des parties casuelles de la boutique du pape* (ill. 4),[7] a satire by the "Protestant gentleman" Antoine Du Pinet, launches a more precise attack in its caricature of the Pope, who is shown sitting on a high divan, in the middle of his "shop," holding out his hand to take the believers' money. Three of the latter are seen in the foreground, holding up bags of ecus. In the opposite (Catholic) camp, an engraving for *De tristibus Franciae* (1572) by Gabriel de Saconay, shows the "Huguenot monkeys"[8] taking over France, which is personified by a lion. One of them sits astride the animal's back and, laughing, lifts a heavy bag of silver.

In spite of these virulent attacks, the bag also had many fine opportunities to emblematically reconcile "the enjoyment of wealth and its contingent duties"[9] and to find its place at that point of equilibrium between two precepts brought together by Dutch culture in the golden century, inscribing "at the heart of civic legitimacy [...] The justification of wealth through charity".[10] The biblical decoration on a 17th-century Dutch alms purse kept in the Emile Hermès Collection (ill. 7) bears witness to the blessings scattered by the Most High on wealth, when this was shared with the least well-off. Oblong, in green silk-velvet with floral

ill. 4 □ **Caricatural frontispiece**
of *Taxes of commission money from the Pope's shop*

Antoine Du Pinet, Protestant gentleman
1564 (reprinted in Leyde in 1607), Lyon
wood engraving
Genève, Bibliothèque publique

Lay person putting offerings in a bag

14th century, manuscript 15274
London, British Library

ill. 6 ☐ **Marinus van Roymerswaele**
The Money Changer and His Wife

1539, Madrid, Prado Museum

motifs and a finishing touch of silver thread braiding, this purse has a chased silver clasp engraved with scenes from the Old and New Testaments. On the clip that was used to hang the richly decorated purse from the belt, Moses holds up the Tablets of the Law, the foundation of the prosperous but God-fearing Batavian Republic: a seated figure, quite possibly Noah, holding an anchor and a dove, evokes this "Christianized diluvian culture"[11] rooted in the minds of the Dutch, what with their constant battle with the seas, and consciousness that they owed the nourishing soil wrested from the waves to God's benevolence alone. Taken from Saint Paul, the anchor is an old symbol of hope and faith in the resurrection.[12] The patriarchs are followed by three scenes from the New Testament, engraved along the clasp. They show Christ on his donkey entering Jerusalem, Lazarus being raised from the dead, and the Agony in the Garden, illustrating the changes to which all earthly things are destined, a theme that was often expounded by Dutch preachers at the time: solitude and neglect could follow close on the heels of acclaim by the crowd, and death change into resurrection. The interior of the purse is lined with green leather and has a middle pocket with a silver clasp hidden between two side pockets, for, in addition to the coins required to fulfil charitable duties, the alms purse also held small valuables and enhancers of beauty.

Formerly in the collection of barons Nathaniel and Albert de Rothschild,[13] an alms purse dating from approximately 1550-70 is representative of the pieces made in Nuremberg in the 16th and 17th centuries. Probably commissioned by an important monastery or guild, it has a Latin inscription on its clasp, which translates literally as "The Lord has always given us all. May He thus never give

ill. 7 □ opposite
Alms purse
Holland, 17th century
silk velvet
Paris, Emile Hermès collection

less to anyone". The refined elegance of a model from the 18th century, in the Emile Hermès Collection, made of orange velvet lined with fine white leather, fitted with a silver clasp on which a flower-laden basket is engraved, would no longer have been justified under the – at least ornamental – pretext of charitable piety. We also find, finely engraved on the clip of an alms purse clasp from the same period, that in the century of the Enlightenment, a figure of Justice has replaced Charity.

In the Romantic period, alms purses survived only in the nostalgia of the Troubadour-style, in which charity was the gracious preserve of chatelaines. Like a provincial sister of Alfred de Dreux's amazons or the heroines of Walter Scott, the "young girl in the white dress" seen by Flaubert's Emma in her dreams, "behind the balustrade of a balcony, held in the arms of a young man in a short coat",[14] naturally wears, hanging from her virginal belt, the alms purse that was indispensable to medieval picturesque. The action of alms-giving was now left to Saint Julian the Hospitaller: "But in the evening, as he came out from the Angelus service and passed between the poor with heads bent low, he would dip into his purse with such modesty and such nobility that his mother fully expected to see him one day an archbishop".[15]

Om dat de werelt is soe ongetru
Daer om gha ic in den ru

STUDY OF MORALS: VENAL LOVE AND PANDER-BAGS

In the 19th century, the bag of *écus*, of *livres*, and rolls of gold was more an emblem of the egotistical, sometimes Faustian appetites of the triumphant bourgeoisie. Balzac's characters are constantly bringing the money bag into their dealings, big and small, not least their sentimental commerce. If there is no room here to dwell on the extraordinary collection of bags that teem in the Human Comedy, a few fleeting apparitions can convey the tone: for example, the character in *Illusions perdues* who, "out of all his splendors, saved his spotless love and a bag of twelve hundred francs",[16] those "twenty-three thousand *livres* in a bag"[17] that the land of Lanstrac brings in in rent, the illusion in *Le Contrat de mariage*, or that ambiguous scene in *La Vieille fille*: "Suzanne took the bag and went out, letting the old bachelor kiss her on the forehead".[18] There is more panache in the action by the Marquise de San-Réal at the end of *La Fille aux yeux d'or* as she goes to "get a bag of gold from the ebony sideboard and disdainfully [throws] it at the feet of the old woman". The Marquise has in fact recognized this "horrible figure" as the mother of Paquita, her lover, and understood that the avaricious mother had "emerged from her den" when she found her daughter's dying body, in the hope of "being paid a second time".[19]

Similarly, in those little scenes showing social mores by Henri Monnier or Forain, the mature and respectable woman is always holding a clearly visible and heavily meaningful bag (ill. 10), as she gives her daughter to a bourgeois with a protuberant belly. "It is with gold that I am made favorable,"[20] declares a cupid spreading a bag of gold pieces in the *Recueil d'emblèmes* by the engraver Verrien. The good La Fontaine is just as lucid but less sententious: "For his quiver, this land's/God of love uses a money bag".[21]

Nowadays, money is tending more than ever to take the place of the real, and is at the same time becoming dematerialized: fine and light, our magnetic cards no longer make money bags bulge. If we were to give alms, it would be via the impalpable flux of a bank transfer. Will we continue to remember those bygone times when the bag's bulging surface housed a thousand fantasmagorias? In this crucible, mixing golden legends and *roman noir*, the mythology of wealth grew rich.

ill. 9 ❑ opposite
Hendrick Goltzius
A Mismatched Couple
1615
London, Sotheby's

ill. 10 □ **Henri Monnier**
Récréations: 8, Promesse de mariage

color lithography, Bernard et Delarue
published by Giraldon Bovinet
Passage Vivienne, no 26 (Paris)
and (London) Frith Street, Soho Square, no 54
Paris, Emile Hermès collection

1   Quoted in the *Dictionnaire des dictionnaires. Encyclopédie universelle des lettres, des sciences et des arts,* Paul Guérin (ed.), Paris: A. Picard, 1884, p. 202.

2   Pierre Chaunu, *Le Temps des Réformes,* Paris: Fayard, "Le Monde sans frontière" collection, 1975.

3   Luke 18, 25.

4   Book of Tobias, IV, 7-12.

5   Adriaen Pietersz van de Venne, *Gelt doet gewelt,* in Jacob Cats, *Spiegel van den Ouden en de Nieuvven Tijdt, In's Graven-Hage; by Isaac Burchoorn,* 1632, Cambridge, Mass: Harvard University, Houghton Library.

6   François Rabelais, *Les Songes drolatiques de Pantagruel où sont contenues plusieurs figures de l'invention de maître François Rabelais,* Paris: R. Breton, 1545, n.p., Paris: Bibliothèque nationale de France.

7   Antoine Du Pinet, caricature as frontispiece to *Les Taxes des parties casuelles de la boutique du pape, rédigées par Jean XXII et publiées par Léon X,* woodcut, Lyon, chez Jean Saugrin, 1564.

8   Gabriel de Saconay, "Les Singes huguenots", *De tristibus Franciae,* 1572.

9   Simon Schama, *The Embarrassment of Riches: An Interpretation of Dutch Culture in the Golden Age,* New York: Vintage, 1997.

10   *ibid.,* p. 755.

11   *ibid.,* p. 71. "The tidal deluges of the late mediaeval period occupied the same place in the collective folk memory of south Hollanders and Zeelanders as the visitations of the Black Death in Flanders and Italy. [...] The calamities seemed to portend an apocalyptic end to a sinful world, a winnowing of souls, or – an image that meant a great deal to the Dutch – a wiping clean of the slate of iniquity. From that act of awesome retribution, a new and cleaner world was to be reborn, and the Noah analogy was here adapted to suit the Dutch self-image as a nation blessed with infant-like innocence." (*ibid.* p. 37).

12   "Which hope we have as an anchor of the soul, both sure and steadfast", (*Hebrews* 6, 19).

13   The brothers Nathaniel (1836-1905) and Albert (1844-1911) de Rothschild, members of the Austrian branch of the famous dynasty, put together prestigious collections of paintings, furniture, and art objects, which they displayed in two Viennese mansions. They were confiscated during the German Anschluss and kept until recently by Austrian museums, then finally restored to the collectors' heirs. A part of the collection was sold at Christie's, London, on July 8, 1999.

14   Gustave Flaubert, *Madame Bovary,* Paris: Librairie Générale Française, Le Livre de Poche, 1961, p. 56.

15   Gustave Flaubert, *Trois contes : La Légende de saint Julien l'Hospitalier,* Paris: Arthème Fayard, "Le livre de demain" collection, n.d., p. 59.

16   Honoré de Balzac, *Scènes de la vie de province,* IV, *Illusions perdues : Un grand homme de province à Paris,* Paris: Furne, Dubochet et Cie, Hetzel, 1843, p. 356.

17   Honoré de Balzac, *Scènes de la vie privée, Le Contrat de mariage,* Paris: Furne, Dubochet et Cie, Hetzel, 1842, p. 199.

18   Honoré de Balzac, *Etudes de mœurs, Scènes de la vie de province,* vol. III, *Les Rivalités : La Vieille Fille,* Paris: Furne, Dubochet et Cie, Hetzel, 1844, p. 25.

19   Honoré de Balzac, *Etudes de mœurs, Scènes de la vie parisienne,* Vol. I, *Histoire des Treize : La Fille aux yeux d'or,* Paris: Furne, Dubochet et Cie, Hetzel, 1843, p. 300, 301.

20   *Recueil d'emblèmes, devises, médailles et figures hiéroglyphiques,* by the Sieur Verrien, master printer, Paris: Claude Jombert, 1724, pl. 24, no. 10.

21   Jean de La Fontaine, *Contes et nouvelles en vers,* "Richard Minutolo," novella based on Boccaccio, "farmers general" edition, Amsterdam, 1762.

ROYAL BAGS

◻ In the past, various kinds of personal bags were found throughout the chiefdoms of western Cameroon. Most were in the form of sacks, woven from cotton or vegetable fiber, as well as rectangular bags decorated with figurative or geometric motifs. Among the Bamum, these bags, which were carried on the arm, were used to transport personal objects like pipes, tobacco or drinking horns for palm wine.

One such bag, the *pangu*, which signifies "Bag of the Country" or "Bag of State", was part of a sovereign's regalia, like the staff and bracelet given to him during his enthronement. The King's hair, beard and nail clippings were kept in the *pangu* to avoid their being misused by others in magic rites. For this reason, following the death of the King, the "Bag of State" was solemnly presented to his successor, who was the sole person allowed to reach inside.

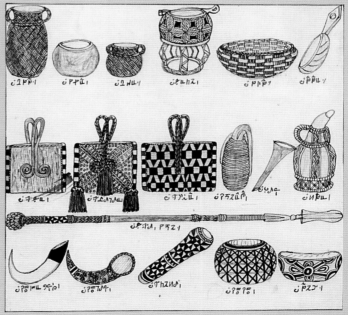

ill. 1 ☐ opposite, left
Ibrahim Njoya
Plate of king (detail)

drawing circa 1930
Geneva, Musée d'Ethnographie

Prince Nshare, founder of the Bamum
kingdom, with his "State bag".

ill. 2 ☐ opposite, right
Ibrahim Njoya
Plate showing objects from the palace
detail showing traditional Bamum bags

drawing, around 1930
Geneva, Musée d'Ethnographie

ill. 4 □ **Royal pakum bag**

Foubam, Cameroon
first half of 20th century
cotton fabric with black stripes
Geneva, Musée d'Ethnographie

ill. 6 □ opposite
Ibrahim Njoya
Prince crossing the river

drawing, around 1930
Geneva, Musée d'Ethnographie

According to *The History and Customs of the Bamum*, Prince Nsharö fled from Rifum to Tikar, following a family quarrel. Here he is shown crossing the Mbam river, on his way to create the kingdom of Bamum. Like all the Bamum kings, he is decked out with royal attributes, a spear and "the State bag".

ill. 5 □ **Bamum bag**

region of Grassfield, Cameroon
first half of 20th century
embroidered raffia fabric
cotton cloth border
Geneva, Musée d'Ethnographie

Secrets of the Gods

sacred

liturgy

spell

grigri

magic

cult

piety

shadows

prayer

initiation

Ill. xxxviii **Francesco Raibolini ("Il Francia"),** *Judith putting the head of Holophernes into the bag held by her maid,* middle of the 15th century, Paris, Musée du Louvre

ill. xxxix and xl **"Sorcerer's bags"**, Goroka, Papua New Guinea, 1993, photographs by Marie-José Guigues, small string bags of hibiscus bark cord; bamboo structure covered in cowrie shells and the vertebrae, teeth, and bones of various mammals, Marie-José Guigues collection

Hermès était le dieu des voyages, des voleurs et
des commerçants et aussi le messager de Zeus.
Il accepta de l'aider.

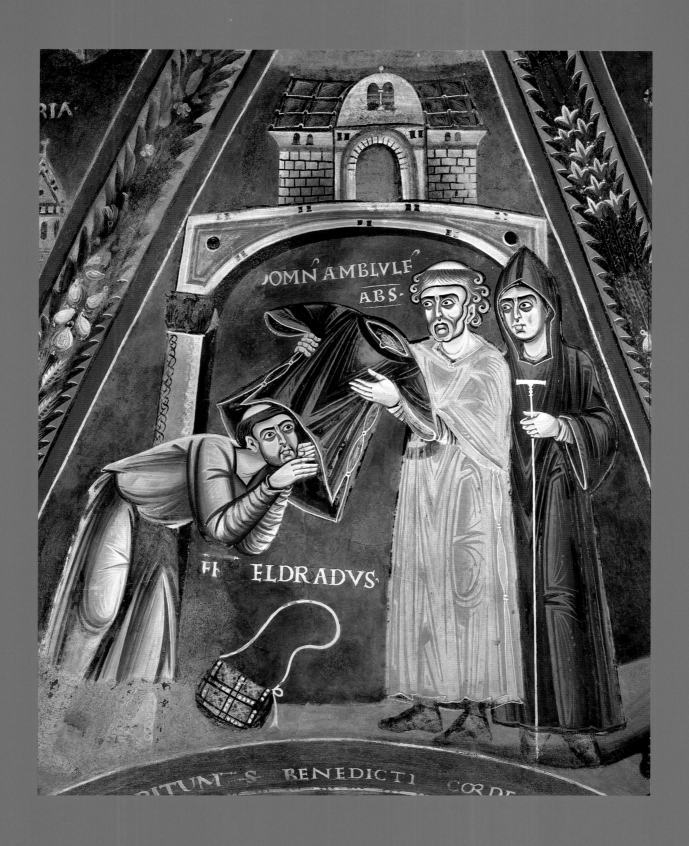

ill. XLII **The abbot of Novalesa giving Eldradus the monastic garb,** detail from the Byzantine-style Romanesque frescoes
in the chapel of St Eldradus and St Nicholas, late 11th century, Italy, Piemonte, Novalesa Abbey

ill. XLIII **Francisco de Zurbaràn,** *St Margaret of Antioch*, circa 1630, London, National Gallery

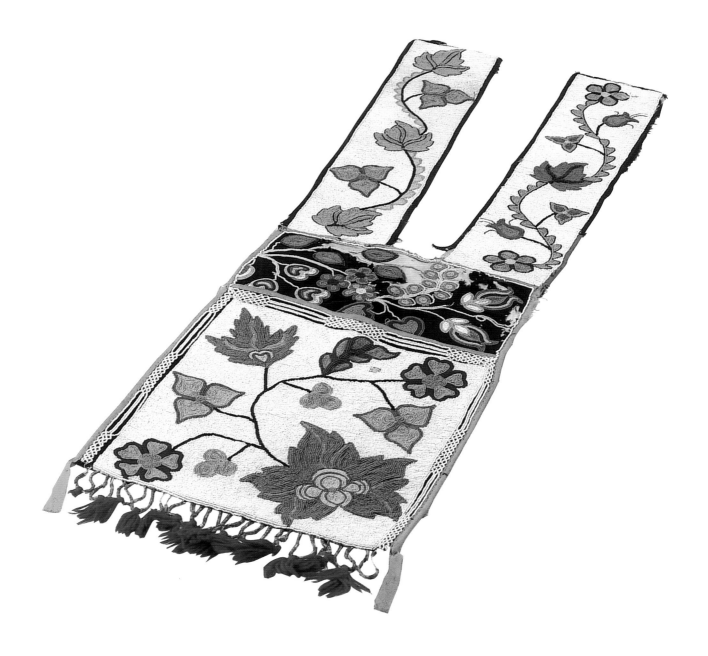

ill. XLIV **Shaman's bag with a shoulder strap,** Great Lakes region, Anishinabe, Canada, second half of the 19th century, beads, wool, cloth, Lyon, Muséum, Propagation de la Foi collection

A Few Wineskins
and Bags on Olympus

✳ If to be a carrier is to belong to the lower orders, then we would hardly expect to find any bags on Mount Olympus. And indeed, even if La Fontaine's fable has managed to make French readers associate Jupiter with a bag (*besace*), it is hard to imagine the dignified Juno carrying a handbag, or Venus hiding her nudity with a reticule. And yet there are exceptions, albeit marginal ones, since in such cases the bag is not so much an attribute as a tool, a vital instrument in a fine story or in an almost professional activity.

Aeolus' Bag of Winds

First of all, then, there is the bag where Aeolus kept the winds. The episode is familiar to us from *The Odyssey*. Taking pity on Ulysses, who, in his travails, has been driven onto his island, Aeolus decides to put the unfavorable winds in his bag for a while, leaving out only a little breeze, a zephyr, to carry his boat back to Ithaca. In order to give Ulysses this new kind of nautical bag, the god thus puts away his flying troops. Homer shows him using "the hide of a full-grown ox" to make a bag "tied with a glittering silver cord so that through that fastening not even a breath could stray". Aeolus no doubt "swelled" the hide beforehand – using an old butcher's technique in which the animal skin had air pumped under it so that it could be removed without damage. What he gave Ulysses was therefore an *askos*, made from the whole skin of an animal with all its openings but one tied up and the legs conveniently stiffened to form a four-handled jerry can from before the age of plastic, of the kind that can still be seen

ill. 1 ✳ opposite
Isaac Moillon
*Aeolus giving wind
to the sails of Ulysses*

17th century
Le Mans, Musée Tessé

in Africa and in those rare parts of the Mediterranean basin not yet to have become totally modern. But since this is a story of marvels, since Aeolus is a god and Ulysses a superman, the customary young goat has been replaced by an adult bull in the prime of life. But alas, just as Ulysses' native island is heaving into view, as they sight the fires lit by its shepherds, Ulysses sinks into slumber, and his companions, sensing there is treasure to be had, untie the knot and release the winds which, unleashed, drive the frail vessel inexorably back onto the high seas.

Clearly, in this story, the wineskin is a substitute for the swollen cheeks of the wind god, or for the cave in which, according to Virgil, he locked his zephyrs and aquilons. It is a surrogate who is there only so that the storm episode can happen later, at a distance. An accessory, then, as a bag should be, but a narrative one. A way of generating suspense and making the story even more thrilling. A time bomb. A bag for waiting, a bag full of pure time.

ill. 2 ✳ *A companion of Ulysses unties the goatskin containing wind*

Etruscan scarab, 5th century B.C. Paris, Bibliothèque nationale de France Medals and Antiques, Luynes collection

Overcome by curiosity, one of Ulysses' companions has untied the goatskin and the bearded head of one of the winds is emerging.

Hephaistos' Bellows

Less occasional and more frequently represented, another "airbag" has more positive virtues. It belongs to the bellows worked by the blacksmith god Hephaistos. Before the addition of the two wooden panels known today, bellows used to consist of a sealed skin or, rather, two, blowing and filling in turn. Greek vases and even sculptures – like the frieze of the treasure of Siphnos, Delphi – show two big leather pouches, one smooth and full to bursting, its twin collapsing into big, meaty folds indicative of thick and supple leather of the finest quality. The idea that Aeolus' bag of winds and Hephaistos' bellows are twins is confirmed by a later tradition in which the two gods are seen as so similar that a painting by someone like Piero di Cosimo can show Aeolus working the double bellows while Vulcan labors at the anvil. Indeed, if we are to believe Virgil, Hephaistos' smithy is located somewhere between Sicily and Lipari, one of the Aeolian islands. Clearly, Italy's reputation for fine leather goes back quite a way. Language, as is its wont, has once again played games here. From the Latin for bellows, *follis*, it has taken the image of the hollow bag that pumps out emptiness, stubbornly and repetitively, absurdly, too, but with the risk that it might fan the flames of tragedy. This is the root of the English word "foolish" and the French *folie* or "fols". Those designated by such words are fools whom we dismiss with a disapproving puff of wind from the cheeks.

Here is another count in the charges all too often leveled, if only verbally, at the bag. For does not this world of fools and buffoons with its underlying verbal link between bags and madness, combined with the bag's itinerant nature, explain the fact that in the tarot the fool or madman is shown carrying a bag. But thank God, if all madmen are "bags," not all bags are mad. Far from it. And if we ask Hermes to lead us from the world of gods to the world of heroes, we will meet one or two who are rich in meaning and very canny with it.

Hermes' bag

As the traditional intermediary between Mount Olympus and the world below, the god who guides mortals into Hades and the messenger of the gods, Hermes is the figure of movement par excellence, yet, oddly, he is rarely shown with a bag, even when accompanying souls towards the Elysian fields. Still, as the god of crossroads and outskirts, the protector of travelers and also of shepherds, the patron of thieves, Hermes has a thousand reasons to add the bag to the outward signs of mobility that are his cloak, winged boots, and feathered helmet, not to mention his caduceus which, over the years, has become a wand with two serpents wound around it in a figure eight, and which was originally a simple shepherd's crook in Arcadia or pilgrim's staff.

Now, what this god usually holds, at least in later depictions and under his Latin name of Mercury, is a purse, an attribute of his Roman function as a god who protects the market and trade. The purse in which people kept their money, in leather for the rich and in simple cloth for the poor, is closed at the top by a drawstring or a ring, and hangs from his belt, when not actually a part of it. This timeless purse is something that mortals prudently hide, whereas in the paintings Mercury is the first figure to actively display it, holding it out as a sign of divine prodigality. However, after that it recurs on many occasions. Among other things, it is the attribute of the apostle Saint Matthew, a publican and tax collector at Capharnaum, the patron saint of money changers, customs men and taxmen, and of many others usurers and skinflints.

In some cases, however, and for no obvious factual reason, Hermes is shown carrying a real handbag, its handle hanging neatly in the bend of his arm. This is the case, for example, when he is shown standing near Zeus, and presumably acting as his messenger. Should we therefore read it as the insignia of his function? His professional bag? His postman's bag? Perhaps. However, as our age knows only too well, the signifier is more potent than the signified. In other words, images are tenacious, more so than the stories they are meant to illustrate. Behind this image of Hermes with a bag there stands another, that of Perseus, slayer of the Gorgon.

Perseus' Gorgon Bag

Because Zeus impregnated the mortal Danae in the form a shower of gold, his offspring Perseus is only a demigod. Indeed, the life of this hero got off to an awkward start, since he and his mother were abandoned in the sea, not in a bag but in a chest. When forced to go and seek the head of Medusa, with its petrifying eyes, he kitted himself out in the proper fashion. The appropriate weapon, a sword or sickle, was supplied, as if by chance, by Hermes, himself an experienced beheader after he decapitated Argos, the thousand-eyed guardian of Io. The rest of his equipment – winged sandals from Hermes so he could reach the Gorgons in the air, and a helmet from Hades that made him invisible and thus able to approach the monster unseen, he obtained with the help of Athena, and through the intermediary of the horrible Graeae, three hags who share the same eye and tooth, and the three "young girls" and "fiancées" that are the Nymphs. However, from this list of the equipment of the perfect hunter of Gorgons, one essential item is missing. Or rather, an accessory. In a word, his bag; *kibisis* in Greek. Itself a nomadic word. Probably from Cyprus. Apollodorus tells us this pouch got its name because "it can hold food and clothes". This was where Perseus stored the bulky, petrifying severed head of the Gorgon. He removed it only now and again, to turn a few troublemakers to stone, then finally emptied the bag before Athena. Which is why, ever since, her shield has sported the wide-eyed monster's face.

You don't have to be a great psychoanalyst to grasp one possible meaning of this exploit and its eloquent details: a man and his blade, a feminine image all about holes and danger, a thing that cannot be looked upon, a chain of women without whom the hero could do nothing – including, in order, a virgin, three old women, and three nymphs. Without a doubt, Perseus has triumphed in a tough ordeal. Yes, he deserves to be called a hero. Most importantly, though, apart from the fact that it gives the bag the status it enjoys today, this story of the eye, of ocular impediments, of the visible and the invisible, of a container displayed and contents hidden, or vice versa, illustrates the very essence of the bag: the interplay of concealment and ostentation. That there is always something fearsome about the contents of a receptacle is what we learn from folklore, which is packed with stories about bags that must never be opened, and it also lingers in our own reluctance to rummage in another person's bag, even if we have good reason to do so.

Faced with this problem of the shown and the hidden, antique imagery took a bold approach. When, as was relatively rare, it showed Perseus, not accomplishing his exploit but just afterwards, the presentation was as follows: sometimes the Gorgon's head is on one side, held up by the hero, and the empty bag hangs on the other from the forearm or is worn on a strap over the back, as indeed Hesiod specifies; sometimes the hero is about to slip the head with its gaping mouth and lolling tongue into the deep bag; or sometimes the round face is half-way out of the bag, like a rising moon, peeping from the bag's crescent-shaped opening. One case is particularly disturbing, that of an archaic platter from Rhodes in which Perseus is shown on his own, running, with a small bag in his hand, which he is holding and swinging by the handle. The bag is a trapezoid with strengthened corners. It is much too small to hold a head. Above all, it seems to be crisscrossed by a net, rather like a reticule. Is this credible? And what would Perseus and his image-makers have done if they had known about the transparent bag, a monstrosity that is even more obscene than the Gorgon, a contradiction in terms, an unbearable oxymoron? For is it not the essence of the bag to be opaque?

Goat and *sakkos*

That, clearly, is what the history of the word tells us. For the Latin *saccus* comes directly from the Greek *sakkos*, a nomadic word of Semitic origin, probably brought by the Phoenicians and perhaps, at the very beginning, borrowed from the Egyptians. Now, this word refers primarily not to a use but to a material: a simply worked cloth, most often in horsehair or rough hair, or brown or black goathair. Thus, in fact, the bag is primarily bag material, and a *sakkos* is a garment made of this crude fabric. Sackcloth, hair shirt. That is why, as a faithful son of Byzantium, the Orthodox Church has continued to call the short cape worn by its bishops in place of a chasuble the *sakkos*. Indeed, when we come across the word in the Bible – and in Hebrew, it comes from the same root, *saq* –

ill. 4 ✳ opposite
Perseus carrying
the Medusa's head in a bag
Roman antiquity, circa 460 BC
London, British Museum

Assisted by Athena, Perseus has just killed the Gorgon, who is collapsing. The hero runs away, sickle in hand, carrying the petrifying head in the *kibisis* that he has slung across his shoulder like a game bag.

it nearly always designates the rough, dark material worn by those who have renounced ordinary clothes, be it in mourning or in mortification. Thus, when Jacob believed his son Joseph to be dead, he "rent his clothes and put sackcloth upon his loins". And it is not so much the form or even the texture of this material as its dark color that is to the fore when the prophet Isaiah voices Jehovah's threat, "I will cover the heavens with darkness and I will cover them with sackcloth". Or again, in the Apocalypse, when, "at the opening of the sixth seal, there was a great quaking of the earth and the sun became black like a horsehair sack".

In the Greek world, whenever the *sakkos* is a container, it is a big, crude, shapeless bag, a bag for sack races, or the kind in which the Megarian peasant in Aristophanes' *The Acharnians* hides his little girls so he can sell them on the market as young sows, exhorting them to grunt nice and loud to attract buyers. So, as we can see, in becoming a bag, and especially a lady's bag, the *sakkos* changed in a big way.

opposite

ill. 1 and 4 ✳ **A relic purse representing
a helmeted rider** (front, ill. 1)
and an eagle (back, ill. 4)

France, 12th century
silk on canvas, embroidery Byzantine style
Sens, Cathedral Treasury
(from the shrine of Saint Macaire)

ill. 2 and 3 ✳ **A relic purse decorated
with geometric designs** (front, ill. 3, back, ill. 2)

France, 13th century
silk on canvas, embroidery in chain stitch
gold thread braid
Sens, from Cathedral Treasury

Medieval
Relic Pouches

✳ Among the various kinds of purses known to have existed in the Middle Ages, the relic pouch is mentioned in historical texts, inventories and account books and also found in church treasuries. When relics had to be transferred or identified by the religious authorities, the precious remains of the first Christians were placed in pouches, small bags made out of already ancient fabric. Around the pouch was rolled and fastened a strip of parchment, bearing an inscription authenticating the sacred origin of the contents.

As each new transfer required a fresh identification of the relics in question, church treasuries boast a host of these priceless woven envelopes. One remarkable instance is the treasury of the cathedral of Sens – long the metropolitan church of northern France – described by Canon Chartraire in 1911 as containing ten examples made of Byzantine silk, or Hispano-Moorish or Sicilian samite (ill. 1 and 2). Among them are a "purse of gray silk with red stitching and red and green drawstrings", first mentioned in the inventory of 1540; and another of "yellow and vermilion silk decorated with chintz strips, inside which are several relics", described in the inventory of 1464 and found in 1896 in the shrine of St Paula. Both are still part of the

ill. 5 ✳ **A relic purse with the coat of arms of the Counts of Champagne**

France, 12th century
pleated bag with drawstring cord
tapestry technique
Troyes, from Cathedral Treasury

treasury. Douet d'Arcq's inventory of the royal silver, published in 1352, refers to "two relic pouches ornamented with embroidered images and large pearls…and with a good lace of Cyprus gold and silk for wearing them". Another royal inventory mentions the practice of wearing relics: in 1396 the Duke of Orleans owed "a Paris pursemaker 12 sousparisis, for two black velvet pouches to hold his relics, with another small pouch for the True Cross, which he hangs around his neck."

The princes of this world made a point of doing honor to the relics in their churches, commissioning sumptuous reliquaries and envelopes elaborately ornamented with embroidery and pearls and bearing their coat of arms. One particularly fine

ill. 6 ✳ **A pilgrimage phial**
(small bottle for blessed oils
holy water or relics)

Notre-Dame-de-Boulogne
second half of the 15th century
lead, pewter
found in Paris in the Seine in 1859
Paris, Musée national du Moyen Âge
former Forgeais collection

example, a pouch bearing the arms of the Count of Champagne, is part of the treasury of Troyes cathedral (ill. 5).
Other moving examples of a more profane kind suggest a similar practice. The shape and imagery of lead insignia found in the Seine testify to their use as a means of warding off evil or bad luck: reminiscent of pilgrims' ampullae, these little containers were worn, with their relics, on the pilgrim's chest. The relic pouch insignia of Notre-Dame-de-Boulogne bears a faithful reproduction of the purse decorated with the Holy Image to which people came to pray (ill. 6). Thus the insignia gave the wearer the protection of the Virgin Mary.

African Divination Bags

✳ In Africa, indeed, as throughout the world, men have always felt the need to know their fate and to attempt to improve it; there, however, the methods and world-view are very different. It is not simply a matter of discovering the future, but of bringing together two quite distant, antinomical worlds that are nonetheless related. These are the worlds of visible phenomena, which take material form in individuals' daily lives, and of invisible forces that act upon them. These forces, which represent ancestral spirits or local divinities, can be either benevolent or malevolent. The diviner's role, then, is to reveal the force that is making its influence felt and propose a "treatment" that either neutralizes its action or re-establishes a link that has been disrupted through neglect or oversight, in this way promoting a more productive relationship.

Diviners are therefore both priests and healers and must possess extensive knowledge of the social and cultural context in which they work. They are, in a way, practicing physicians attending to the health of both the body and the spirit, which often go hand in hand in Africa. Disease or serial deaths in a family, sterility of a spouse, failure or bad luck: all kinds of situations exist in which hidden causes are sought in the hope of finding a solution, an appropriate therapy in fact, that is in keeping with the diagnostic.

Several types of divination are found in sub-Saharan Africa, which, we hardly need to recall here, constitutes a vast continent that is home to numerous peoples

ill. 1 ✳ **A *vode* divinatory bag**
in white cotton containing
various symbolic objects

Fon, Bénin
Geneva, Musée d'Ethnographie

with a broad range of origins, languages and cultures. Thus, divination practices vary enormously from place to place. In some cases, very simple procedures are involved, in which yes and no answers are given to the questions put to one. For example, the Kuba (in the Democratic Republic of Congo) use wooden animal figurines, rubbing the back of the carving with a wooden button that has been moistened with oil. If the button sticks, the answer is positive. Elsewhere, animals are employed according to the mythical role ascribed to them. Among the Dogon in Mali, for instance, the jackal, the reincarnation of the "Pale Fox", comes during the night to eat a small offering left out for it and thus leaves its paw prints on a table carefully drawn in the sand by the diviner. In the Ivory Coast, the Guro place a mouse in the lower level of a small container with two compartments. They allow it to climb into the upper level and nibble grain set out on a plaque with small divining sticks, far from the prying eyes of humans! The Bamum of Cameroon, on the other hand, let a large hairy-legged trap-door spider move painted bamboo strips which are set out at the entrance to its burrow, each strip having its own significance.

In other cases, the diviner serves as a medium, entering into a trance in order to be "attuned to" the world of forces or spirits that are capable of providing answers to the problems put to them. Thus, among the Lobi of Burkina Faso, the diviner surrounds himself with wooden statuettes representing *thila* spirits, which are invoked when consulting the spirit world. To

ill. 2 ✳ **A bag of tihlolo divinatory ossicles**
Ronga, Mozambique
Geneva, Musée d'Ethnographie

ill. 3 ✳ **Kaltenrieder**
Divination with ossicles in the Thonga
tribe in Mozambique
photograph
Geneva, Musée d'Ethnographie

know what these spirits think, he takes his client's arm and strikes it against his thigh in an almost involuntary movement. With this gesture, he is now prepared to discover the answer provided by the spirits that have been called on to help.

The diviner may also make use of objects like the knucklebones that are tossed on a mat among the Ronga of Mozambique. The pattern they form indicates the individual's destiny. In Angola, the Chokwe and their neighbors, the Ovimbundu, practice a form of divination where a wide range of objects held in a basket symbolise a multitude of cases which the diviner attempts to decipher according to the questions he is asked.

Finally, there exist sophisticated systems of geomancy, practised by the Yoruba of Nigeria and the Fon of Benin. In this case, the diviner, called the "father of the secret", is in fact a kind of sage who "reads", in the 256 geomantic figures, the will of the gods making up their pantheon. He then indicates the necessary rites and personal actions to be undertaken to win their favor.

Ifa, Yoruba and Fon geomancy

To the Yoruba, who also introduced this god to their western neighbors, the Fon or Danhomenu, Ifa represents one of the important divinities of their pantheon, which comprises several hundred gods, called *orisha,* who are grouped in extended families according to their particularities and especially their role. As his name seems to suggest, Ifa is apparently a native of the holy city of Ile-Ife, which in the 9th century could already boast a royal court with a flourishing artistic output. Today, numerous bronze and terracotta figures bear witness to this rich history. Religious tradition places the first *orisha* in that city, including Oduduwa, who founded the *oni* dynasty of Ife; one of the dynasty's most celebrated descendents is Shango, the god of thunder and lightning.

The divination system of Ifa makes use of 256 signs, 16 main signs, or mother-signs, and their 240 combinations, or child-signs. Consisting of two series of four simple or double vertical marks, these signs are revealed by passing palm nuts from one hand to the other. They are then drawn in the clay or yellow wood powder that is spread over the diviner's tray. The diviner can also proceed by using a divining chain whose eight fruit-stone halves indicate two series of simple or double marks, according to whether they land on their convex or concave sides. Each sign has its own name and legend, and entails a whole series of sacrificial prescriptions.

A consultation is always accompanied by a propitiation rite, with a libation and spraying of lustral water on the divination objects, a sacrifice in the form of a small offering, and a greeting made to the first three diviners of Ifa. According to the problem he is presented with, the diviner will consult either the palm nuts or the divining chain. In the latter case, symbolic objects are also employed such as seeds, shells, stone fragments or animal relics, as well as potsherds, pearls and so on. These symbolic objects are usually held in a small cloth bag that is carried, whenever the diviner travels, in a leather bag along with the diviner's chain and other ritual objects used in consulting the spirits. Shaped like a large rounded pouch, the bag, especially among the Yoruba, is often decorated with beaded motifs like the model illustrated here, which boasts an enigmatic face, a frequent representation of Ifa.

Ifa divination does not only serve to discover the hidden reasons for a particular difficulty that an individual is trying to surmount. The practice also allows for individuals to organise their lives according to different parameters, to better adapt to the world of natural forces or ancestral spirits around them. In this case, the great Fa rite is performed in order to discover the sign that is to determine the future life of the new follower. Once the rite has been concluded, new followers are given a small cotton bag decorated with beads; this pouch contains the earth in which their sign was drawn and which they guard carefully until their death.

Knucklebone divination among the Ronga

Around the end of the 19th century, the Swiss missionary Henri A. Junod published a highly detailed study of the Ronga, a population living in Southern Mozambique, noting the important place that divination with knucklebones (*tihlolo*) was accorded in their culture. The Swiss missionary brought back with him a complete divination set, which is conserved today in Geneva's Musée d'Ethnographie. A precise description of the set is included in Junod's book *Les Ba-Ronga*, published in Neuchâtel in 1898.

In a small bag or sleeve made of wickerwork (ill. 2), the Ronga enclose 27 divination objects, including 14 knucklebones or vertebrae from different animals, both domestic creatures like goats and animals living in the brush. These kinds of knucklebones represent the different categories of people making up Ronga society, as well as the spirits of the surrounding natural environment. Thus, a vertebra from a kid she-goat stands for a young girl, another from a grown she-goat her mother, and one from a billy goat her father. A vertebra from a red antelope personifies criminals who spill blood and monkey vertebrae, the spirits of the bush. The other divination objects include shells (*Conus*, a male symbol, and *Cypraea*, a female one), fragments of tortoise shell and anteater nails, stones and oddly shaped fruit stones.

The diviner consults the spirits in front of his client or his client's family, generally for a serious problem such as an illness, accident or death. The diviner has his bag brought to him, which in some cases is a very elegant sheath of intricate wickerwork that is enlarged at both ends; the bag's sliding lid moves along the two straps used to carry it. Either the diviner or his

client, who is generally the head of the family, tosses the small bones and other objects onto a mat. Using a curved staff, the diviner then explains the arrangement of figures formed by the bones and other divination objects. Their interpretation varies according to the side they land on (either convex or concave), their orientation and their respective position. If the she-goat's knucklebone, for instance, falls on its convex side, it indicates that the family's mother is seriously ill. A *Conus* shell and a vertebra from the "threatening" red antelope signify that her illness is due to the actions of malevolent individuals. On the other hand, the presence of a *Cypraea* shell lying on its concave side and a well-positioned fruit stone reveal a possible treatment and a favorable outcome.

This divination practice enabled one not only to discover the problem, but also the profound reasons for this ill and the means for putting things to right. Difficult and occasionally contradictory, the interpretation represented the culture of the rural society of the day in a nutshell.

ill. 4 ✳ **Armband of Fang amulets**

Gabon, early 20th century
vegetal fibers, cotton, copper, brass
Geneva, Musée d'Ethnographie

Beaded Bags of Africa

✳ After what is often a superficial encounter with African art, Western aesthetes tend to associate it only with the wooden sculpture of masks and figures. The decorative arts, jewelry, costumes, furniture and other domestic objects are left to the ethnographers. Among these objects, bags are both little known and underestimated. And yet throughout Africa, or at least traditional Africa (this essay will not be concerned with modern, urban Africa), we find myriad examples: bags for porterage in fiber or hide, travel bags carried over the shoulder or on a stick, the more luxurious bags of notables, saddlebags and holsters for riders, hunters' game bags, professional bags holding the tools of the farmer, sculptor, blacksmith, jeweler or weaver, or the wares of the hawker, the bags that are water skins, air pouches used with the blacksmith's bellows, bags that housewives carry on their heads to and from market, bags in which mothers carry their children on their hips, and also bags of accessories used for initiation ceremonies for young boys, bags for masks and for fetishes, reliquary bags containing the revered bones of ancestors (ill. 1), bags of weights for weighing gold, medicine bags and, finally, "bags of words" (here I am thinking of the thousands of proverbs and fables that form the provisions of the storyteller, *griot* or simple traveler). Bags, then, are omnipresent in everyday life; their role is both functional and symbolical, as the embodiment of their owner's wealth, power and skill.

ill. 1 ✳ **Reliquary statuette, Pounou**

Gabon, beginning of 20th century
wood, skin, vegetal fibres
various organic materials
Musée du Quai-Branly
former collection
from Musée de l'Homme in Paris

With its fine-boned face covered with kaolin, the color of the next world, the small feminine statue is mounted on a package or bag, which holds the precious relics of an important ancestor of the clan.

ill. 2 ✳ opposite
**A *babalawo* beaded bag
with a mask**

Yoruba, Nigeria
middle of 20th century
cotton fabric, small molten glass pearls
Los Angeles, UCLA Fowler Museum
of Cultural History

Among the Yorubas, the soothsayer is called *babalawo* or father of mystery. Wandering from village to village, searching for the truth, the soothsayers carry a precious leather or beaded bag (*apo ileke*) which contains various accessories, a tray, rosary beads, a caryatid bowl and rattle, used to call upon Orunmila, the God of destiny, who inspired the geomancers' oracles (*Ifa*)

Made in a great variety of materials (leather, hide, vegetal fiber, raffia or cotton), African bags are often decorated with damascened or cut-out motifs (ill. 4), together with fringes, trimmings and embroidery. In addition, they may well be covered with appliquéd metal, shells (the famous cowry) or small, colored glass beads with a diameter of no more than two millimeters, sewed on using a special technique to form all-over geometrical or figurative motifs (ill. 2 and 3). Beadwork is also used on clothes, jewelry and even pieces of furniture; Cameroon, in particular, offers some interesting examples of this.

Large quantities of pearls from Venice and Bohemia were taken to Africa from the end of the 15th century and through to the beginning of the 20th century, to be used as a means of payment. But, as archaeology has discovered, beads made of polished stone, pottery and mother-of-pearl were in use well before the slave trade. Examples have been found dating back to the prehistoric and protohistoric eras. In fact, even today it is not uncommon to see people wearing jewelry containing ancient Egyptian, Phoenician, Greek, Roman or Indian beads from the trade routes that came across the Sahara from North Africa and Egypt, or inland from the shores of the Indian Ocean. Most of the time, though, it is difficult to date African beads because of their profusion, ubiquity and simple reproducibility.

The richest regions when it comes to beadwork are those of the Yoruba in Nigeria and Benin (royal clothes and sacerdotal accessories), of the Bamileke and their neighbors in the Grassland of Cameroon (masks and thrones), of the Kuba in Congo (clothes, headdresses and royal masks), of the Masai and their neighbors in Kenya (jewelry) and among the Zulus, Xhosa and Ndebele of South Africa (jewelry, aprons and small bags). In southern Africa, beadwork has been known from time immemorial; witness the white bead industry developed by the Kalahari Bushmen using the shells of ostrich eggs.

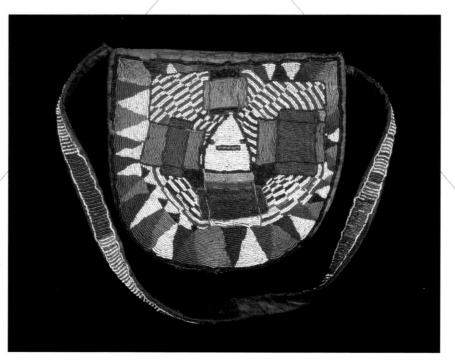

ill. 3 ✳ **Beaded *babalawo* bag with abstract design**

Yoruba, Nigeria
middle of 20th century
cotton fabric, small molten glass pearls
decorated with geometric triangular
designs, square patterns
and interlacing

The colors are symbolic: yellow and green represent the divinity Orunmila; red represents blood and life; white the afterlife and knowledge; black and blue are used as a buffer between red and white.

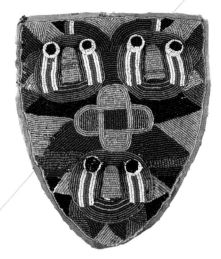

Without a doubt, though, the most spectacular beadwork bags are those made by the Yoruba in the extensive region that straddles Benin and Nigeria. This people, numbering some ten million men and women, has one of the richest and most deep-rooted cultures in this part of the continent.

In Nigeria, where they were introduced by Arab or Hausa traders, beads have always symbolized prosperity. We know of stone beads from the ancient Nok culture (5th century BCE), and glass beads were found in the royal tombs at Ife (12th to 15th century), the old religious capital of the Yoruba. They were no doubt made locally. Later on, in the Kingdom of Benin (15th to 19th century) coral beads from the Balearic Islands and glass ones made in Europe became omnipresent in royal finery. Nowadays, the main production area is in Bida, northern Nigeria, where the powerful corporation of Nupa craftsmen specializes in making beads from polished jasper and recycled glass.

According to Yoruba custom, beads were the preserve of the king, the *oba*. We find them sewn onto the crown, or *ade*, a kind of miter with long fringes designed to hide the King's face from his subjects, and also on neck and ankle jewelry. The beaded crown was instituted by Odudwa, the mythological founder of the Yoruba kingdom, who placed one on the head of each of his sixteen sons, from whom the current lineage of kings is descended. Prohibited to women, these crowns often have a bird on the top as a symbol of communication with the gods and the spirits of former kings.

The beaded bags that interest us here belong to the world of divination. The *babalawo*, or "father of mystery", as Yoruba seers are known, travels from village to village in a constant search for truth, carrying a precious leather bag, or *apo iléké*, which has a flap often decorated with cowry shells and beads in shimmering colors. It is Orunmila, the Yoruba god of destiny, who addresses

ill. 4 ✳ left
Bag in embroidered leather

Fon d'Abomey, Benin, formerly Dahomey, end 19th century
leather, cloth
Musée du Quai-Branly
former collection
from Musée de l'Homme in Paris

Acquired during the conquest of Dahomey (1894) this richly decorated leather bag is thought to have belonged to Behanzin, King of Dahomey (1844-1906) and carries the following inscription in ink under the flap: "King Dahomey's tobacco pouch during his expeditions".

ill. 5 ✳ right
The bottom
of the soothsayer's bag

Yoruba, Nigeria, first half of the 20th century
cotton cloth, molten glass pearls
Angoulême, Musée des Beaux-Arts

This piece of beaded cloth in the shape of a shield forms the flap of a double bag in which the babalawo stored the accessories required to exercise his art. In the centre are three small masks but it is more usual to use a bird, a python or another allegorical figure linked to the Yoruba religion.

his oracles (*Ifa*) to the geomancer through the accessories kept in the latter's bag: a wooden tray *(opon Ifa)*, generally circular; a rosary for divination *(opèlé Ifa)* made with half-stones from a certain variety of wild mango; a caryatid bowl *(agere Ifa)* containing thirty-six palm nuts *(ikin Ifa)* which are thrown successively from one hand to another, causing signs referring to one of the thousand divinatory verses *(odu)* to be written in white powder that has been scattered across a divination tray, and to thus reveal the truth; a small ivory head representing Eshu, the other tutelary divinity of the Yoruba pantheon; various objects, curiously shaped stones, shells and bones, each of which plays an almost semantic role in the delicate process of augury.

The flap of the bag would be covered with beads forming a geometrical pattern of triangles, squares and symbolical interlacing (ill. 5). In the central position we find the bird (*okin*), the python, small masks and other allegorical motifs related to Yoruba religion. Yellow and green are the signature colors for Orunmila. The other colors are also significant, revealing as they do the nature of all things and the personality of each type of being, in accordance with a complex theory of colors. Thus, white symbolizes cold, age and knowledge, red, heat and blood, and black serves a medium term between these two colors.

In addition to his precious bag, the *babalawo* carried other beaded insignia of his function, including a long necklace *(odigba Ifa)* with one or two pouches (ill. 6), worn around the neck or over the shoulder, and, finally, a hat, a fly swat and a cane, redolent of the insignia of chiefs or kings.

Beaded bags are synonymous with the seers, so much so that the latter are known as *akapo*, "bag carriers." These bags, which are inseparable from their contents, are a concentrate of a whole system of thought, whose roots go deep into the mists of time, and whose ramifications are evident today from Brazil to the Caribbean. In spite of the fascinating decoration of the flaps, two-dimensional artwork with consummate mastery of color, these bags are sadly absent from French public collections. However, there are some very fine examples at the British Museum and in the Ethnologisches Museum in Berlin, as well as in several American collections.

ill. 6 ✳ opposite

A *babalawo* necklace with a pouch

Yoruba, Nigeria
middle of 20th century
cotton cloth, small molten glass pearls
Los Angeles, UCLA Fowler Museum
of Cultural History

As well as his precious bag,
the *babalawo* carried other beaded
emblems referring to his position,
including a long necklace (*odigba Ifa*)
with one or two pouches, carried
around the neck or on his shoulder,
a tall hat, a fly swatter, and a walking
stick reminiscent of heads of state
or kings.

ill. 1 ✳ opposite
**Preparing the blowpipe darts
before storing them in the quiver**
Photograph by Bonnie Chaumeil

Bags of Health and Illness

✳ Like many other peoples of the Amazonian rainforest, the Yagua use blowpipes to hunt birds and monkeys. This tribe, which now has some four thousand members, has long been renowned for the quality of its blowpipes and curare, that famous hunting poison, in which there was once a flourishing trade along the Amazon and its tributaries. In Peru, notably, tourist agencies now tout the cynegetic prowess of the Yagua "blowpipe men" to customers fascinated by the Amazon, talking up these dyed-in-the-wool hunters, whose weapon is as deadly as it is silent, and can fell big game with a single dart from a considerable distance. Chapters on the subject can be found in countless books, from the most colorful adventure stories to the most rigorous scientific studies. The fact is that the prestige and symbolic power of the blowpipe in Yagua society goes well beyond its function as a hunting weapon. Indeed, Yagua blowpipes are such magnificent objects, and the technique for making them is so precise, that it would be no

exaggeration to consider them as works of art. This weapon comprises several elements. First of all, there is a straight, fine barrel, up to three meters long, cut from the trunk of a carefully chosen tree (often a palm), and a "mouth" (the mouthpiece), in hardwood. The most delicate operation, the one that makes the weapon so effective and powerful, is the preparation of the barrel, which needs to be as smooth as a gun's. The projectiles are darts, which are made by meticulously polishing the stems of palm leaves. They are then tipped with curare. These are kept in a quiver, a perfect container, which can hold hundreds of poisonous darts. This conical pouch, made from palm leaves, pleated like a skirt, is hung from the blowpipe when this is standing idle, or worn over the shoulder on hunting expeditions.

Carried with the quiver, the third and final item is a bag for kapok (a kind of cotton which is wrapped around the darts). About the size of a purse, knitted from vegetable fiber, this bag comes complete with piranha jaws, which are needed to sharpen the poison-bearing tip of the dart, so that it will remain lodged in the wounded animal's body.

The Yagua look upon this weapon and its accessories as a private, even intimate, personal possession, and are loath to lend it without a very good reason. Like many other objects in these Indian cultures, the blowpipe is thought to have its own indwelling spirit. It is therefore treated with the same respect as a human being, and such is the hunter's identification with it that he names it after himself, cares for it as he would a member of his own family, and has it with him at the moment of his dying breath (the barrel is placed beside the corpse in the grave). The quiver is of particular interest to us here because, as a holder of darts, it evokes another important aspect of Amazonian cultures, i.e., shamanism and its relation to illness. In the Amazon, as in other parts of the world, illness is not seen as a natural phenomenon, but as the consequence of malevolent intentions on the part of other beings, whether human (hostile shamans) or non-human (animals, forest spirits). These illnesses which, we might say, are "blown in" from outside, are often imagined as invisible projectiles, identical in every other respect to the very visible hunting dart. In this shamanistic view of things, we can already see a marked parallel between the act of hunting game (with hunting darts seen as "illnesses" fired off at the animals) and the shamanistic idea of "hunting" humans. Indeed, if a shaman is to stand a chance of curing illnesses and protecting himself against enemy attacks, he must store up as much ammunition as pos-

sible – in this case, invisible darts – and the only way of doing so is to introduce them into his own body or, to be more precise, into the waterproof sac of his stomach. The process is one of symbolically ingurgitating invisible darts. Once inside the organism, these are thought to slide along the digestive tube to the stomach, where they form rows like arrows in a quiver. They are then kept there and "fed" with the shaman's own blood.

Instead of inert objects, the darts are thus seen as living beings (illnesses) capable of growing and reproducing inside the body. The stomach (connected to the digestive tube), in which the shaman stores up "illnesses" in the form of invisible darts, clearly recalls the quiver that hangs from the blowpipe, and in which the hunter stores his own projectiles. The association becomes even more striking when we bear in mind that, in order to be effective (as both cure and aggression), the darts lodged in the shaman's stomach must be shot out from the top

ill. 2 ✳ opposite
Yagua hunter with his blowpipe
which is inhabited by a spirit,
treated like a person, and buried
with the hunter.

photograph by Jean-Pierre Chaumeil

(the mouth), passing along the digestive tube as if through a blowpipe, and not from below (the anus), like excrement. The hunter's quiver and shaman's stomach are both bags that contain personal objects, and these empower their owners in similar ways. Likewise, just as the shaman "blows" the illnesses kept in his stomach along his digestive tube, so the hunter sends the poison-tipped darts that he keeps in his quiver along the barrel of his blowpipe. We can therefore say that, for the Yagua, the hunter's quiver is to his blowpipe what the shaman's stomach is to his body-blowpipe – a bag of ailments. Here once again, we see that in such cultures the object is not self-contained, but exists in relation to a set of practices and representations in which the model of the human body plays a central role.

Native American Bags

✳ "It's not my bag", in other words, "it's not my kind of thing". And then there's the old-fashioned kids' expression for a woman they dislike: "an old bag". For us Westerners, bags are vital, quite literally, because our civilization is all about possessions – the best proof of which is the fact that, unlike all others, it claims to distinguish between the spiritual and the material. And it is the material side that constitutes the most tangible foundation of our existence, socially speaking at least. It enables us both to define individuals and to sort them hierarchically. One can see why it is important to have what one owns, with or on one's person. And that is why a woman would never go out without her handbag and that men's clothes are literally loaded with pockets, like so many small bags patched onto the body.

For a phenomenology of predation

The bag would appear to be just as vital for the Native Americans, but not at all in the same way as it is for us. The bag is a container, and among the indigenous peoples of America, all containers evoke the notion of the body. Life is synonymous with substance, a substance that is contained and maintained in a corporal envelope – a bag – that endows it with both an appearance and limits. Appearance enables identification, in that each individual is assigned a corresponding animal species (here, humanity is put on the same level as the other animals), while the limits of the body circumscribe an individual as an element existing in the registers of the sensorial – that is to say, as a discrete element that can be removed from its environment, seized and captured, to be perhaps adopted, or killed or sometimes even tortured. According to this founding paradox of Native American thought, appearance is creative, in that it implies the exercise of a positive mental faculty, that of classifying the entities of the world. At the same time, however, sensorial apprehension can be destructive, acting as a force of hindrance and death. For hunters – and the Native Americans we are concerned with here are essentially that – the crucial actions, in man's everyday relation to the world, are those of killing an animal and, even more, skinning it. For the latter act is what strips it of its appearance which allows it to be identified, and of taking its contents, its flesh, which is destined to become food. This end of the hunted animal should not be written off as banal, for it marks the beginning of a process synonymous with the breaking down and annihilation of this flesh, by cooking, chewing and ingestion. Nothing is left of the flesh, the substantial part of the animal; it is transformed into vital energy for those who eat it. The process produces two residues: the body's envelope and armature, in others words, its skin and skeleton – both the outermost and the innermost parts, but also the most visible and rigid ones.

Four bags in perspective

I propose to take this phenomenology of predation as the starting point for an interpretation of Native American bags, focusing on the great stretch of land that runs across the heart of North America from the Saint Lawrence Valley to the Plains, via the Great Lakes. There are two reasons for this choice of region: there is a fairly coherent corpus of pieces and, looking beyond their differences, these do not seem to have been shaped so much by practical needs as by symbolic concerns. These bags, which I have divided into four types, are in fact all fairly flat, without volume, as if designed to contain nothing, or rather, as if they had been emptied of their original life content. There is something of death in these bags, in the way the skin is used as a simple envelope, in their rigidity, in their transfiguration of the skeleton and, less obvious on one's first approach, in the fringes found on some of them.

The first of these types of bags, the ones belonging to the Midewiwin, the "Grand Medicine Society", are made using a

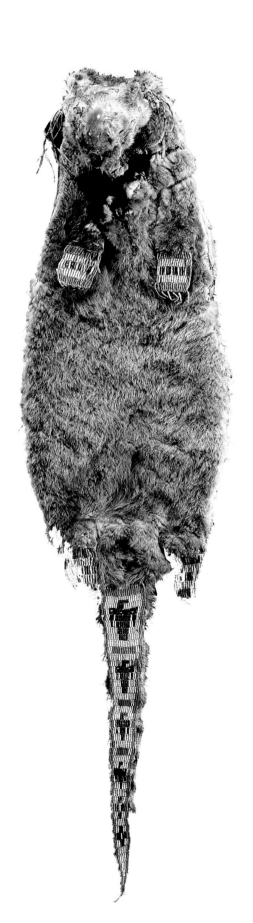

ill. 1 ✳ **Midé Bag (otterskin bag)**

Pinjiigosaun, circa 1850
Founders Society Purchase
The Detroit Institute of Arts

The otter is an amphibious animal
and a symbol of the passage
from the land of the living
to the land of the dead. This is
a ritual bag and made of the otter's
remains, holding elements
with which the initiated was
"killed" among the Midewiwin
brotherhood, before being reborn
in the animal's breast.

whole otter skin, of which only the extremities (legs and tail) or orifices (eyes, mouth, sometimes the ears) are embroidered. The members of the Midewiwin enjoyed considerable prestige among the Ojibwa Indians. Admission to the brotherhood, or promotion to a higher rank (there were four), required that the candidate be put to death (not for real, of course) and then come back to life. The small shells, with which the initiate was ritually "sprayed" and "killed", were kept in the otter skin bags, and it was by rubbing his body with these same bags that he was subsequently brought back to life.

In fact there was nothing arbitrary about the animal chosen here. If we look to ethology, we see that otters are as much at home on land as they are in water. Outstanding divers and swimmers, they can also run well on land – better, for example, than beavers. Above all, though, in winter, when the lakes and watercourses ice over, otters are particularly adept at maintaining passageways, in the thickets along the banks, between the snowy surface of the landscape and the water beneath it. This gives them the status of cosmological mediators, for in the myths, the layer of snow and ice over the land and water is clearly seen as a kind of separating stratum, between two opposing but complementary zones of the cosmological order, the celestial and the chthonic (ill. 1).

Let us look now at the second type of bags. These are the quiver-bags, in semi-rigid skin, used by the Iroquois and Hurons. Their elongated form evokes that of a human body, as indeed does the otter skin. These bags are decorated in a two-colored (black and red) spear pattern, and have a fine fringe along their lower edge. The red and black, as the colors of spilt blood and charcoal, and therefore fire, designate killing and its direct consequence: cooking. The motif has a figurative value: it represents the spear or arrow, the penetrative element that pierces the body and thus breaks into its wholeness. This first reading does not exclude a second, more immaterial one, which has the advantage of taking into account the very abstract treatment of the motif. The Native Americans in these regions adhere to what is, in fact, a very widespread belief in North America, concerning the fearsome weapon possessed by the shaman: invisible darts that can lodge inside the enemy's body and make him ill. Therapeutic action, the work of breaking the spell, will therefore consist in removing these exogenous elements. That the shaman's bag may be an emblem both of aggression and therapy matters little here (although the ambiguity is significant in itself): what is striking is the almost "radiographic" quality of the motif. For the design on the bag also images its contents: those darts, which in fact are invisible in the ordinary realm of the senses. And if the general shape of this kind of bag evokes a body, it also makes it something of a supernatural quiver. The bag becomes a fusion of the weapon and its target, doing away with distance and shrinking time – the time between aggression and cure – within its own material (ill. 2).

The third kind of bag we need to consider here is found among the Sauk, Fox, Potawatomi and, a little further west, on the other shore of Lake Michigan, the Menomini. Generally catalogued as shamanic, these rectangular bags, in woven vegetal fiber, have figurative decoration that is different on each of the two sides. On one, we find the motif of the thunderbird and, on the other, that of the "water panther". These two mythical creatures belong, respectively, to the empyrean and chthonic worlds. In addition to the great skill with which the elements are distributed around the iconographic space, tending towards harmonious saturation – which is why they are called *panelbags* – the figurative handling of these two entities reflects a twofold objective: on the one hand, a concern to stylize the lines, in a way that verges on the abstract; on the other, a "radiographic" approach, insofar as the contours and the internal lines of the body are equivalent, meaning that the latter are automatically thrown into relief. For the Native Americans in this region, thunderbirds and water panthers really exist. They are considered as creatures that hunger for death, and seen as responsible for death by lightning and drowning. As a pair, however, they also embody cosmological duality: the celestial versus the chthonic domains, whose meeting point, the real world, is the home of man. The human condition resides in this intermediary space, like the possible contents of the panel bag, held in by the double representation of the thunderbird and panther – in other words, by the representation of two contrary, but ultimately equivalent, dire deaths.

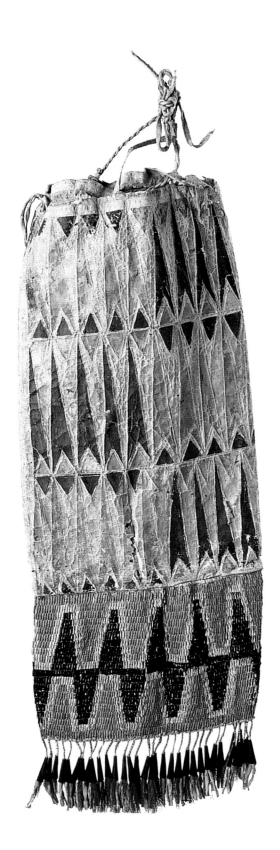

ill. 2 ✳ **A large bag with Huron geometric design**
18th century
Angers, Musée Turpin-de-Crissé

The "parfleches," which come from the Plains, constitute the fourth and final type. Some people, myself included, see them as one of the greatest artistic achievements of the North American Indians. The bags are fairly large (on average, about 70 x 50 cm), rectangular, and made in almost raw bison hide. A single hide is folded in on itself, rather like a pocketbook (ill. 5). These bags are similar to all the others mentioned here in that they are relatively flat. The object's rigidity, size and thinness no doubt explain the fact that the first French travelers to adventure out into the Plains in the 18th century mistakenly took them to be shields (hence the name "pare-flèche": arrow-stopper). Their real function was more domestic. They were used to keep and carry food, mainly the famous "pemmican", made with dried meat. The charm of the parfleche lies in its decoration. This is boldly geometrical and, stylistic variations apart, is characterized by the all-over treatment of the surface (as with the panelbag) using a graphic composition in which isosceles triangles are dominant, and with a variety of pastel colors playing on full and empty forms. Ethnographic studies of the Plains Indians tell us that figurative art was masculine

ill. 3 and 4 ✳ **Panel bag**
(front ill.3, back, ill.4)

Tama, Iowa, circa 1860
Founders Society Purchase
The Detroit Institute of Arts

and connected with the narration of warlike exploits (ill. 6), whereas abstraction was the preserve of women. It was thought that the latter first saw the patterns they painted on the parfleches in their dreams. These abstract representations do not refer to any kind of sight in the sensory world, but rather to their femininity, which lies in their capacity to bear children. Just as the somewhat naive figuration practiced by men excels at relating past events that always have to do with death (with which all war is synonymous), the feminine language of this very bold abstraction makes visible what will be; the child that may come. This future possibility is conceived not only as virtuality, but also as an absolute singularity, and therefore an entity that has no model in the world of the senses. Note that, unlike our own, Native American thought sets little store by biological heredity. It is not interested in the physical resemblance between an individual and his or her genitors but, on the contrary, on the uniqueness that makes each person unlike anyone else. Ultimately, as all young parents can attest, until the coming child is born, it remains a pure abstraction. We can therefore understand why the parfleches contained pemmican,

ill. 5 ✳ opposite
Parfleche
folding bag for dried buffalo meat

American-Indian Art, Prairie Indians
Arapahos or Cheyennes
non-curried leather with painted
geometric design
Berlin, Museum für Volkerkunde

In the Plains the bag was sewn
and decorated by women, and carries
a highly abstract design. This form
of art refers to the procreativity
of the woman, her pure potentiality,
regardless of her biological make-up.

tangular panel bags and parfleches on the other. These different kinds of bags describe a sequence that goes from *in natura* representation, the animal's whole skin, to the absolute abstraction of the parfleche, via a form of figuration tending towards abstraction (the kinds of glyphs representing thunderbirds and panthers) and an attempt to balance abstraction and figuration (the spear- and arrow-tip patterns). We can observe a similar chromatic development, from the two-colored panel bags (black motifs on a white ground), to the three-color spear-pattern quivers (red and black on a light ground), the polychrome parfleches and, finally, the otter skin bag with the many forms of decoration around its edges and their broad palette of colors, both natural (the gray-blue-brown shimmer of fur) and artificial (the many embroideries covering the legs and the tail and the decorated "stitches" sealing the eyeholes and other holes in the skin.) Finally, we could note a progression from soft to rigid, going once again from the otter skin to the parfleche, via the quiver-bag with its spear-pattern decoration and the panel bag.

Lévi-Strauss tells us that the ideal permutation group forms a quadrant. That is what we have here. The group generates a meaning and impacts on all the elements together. What all these bags announce, with the same voice, is that if human life can, *in fine*, overcome death, it is because of a twofold disposition in our mind. First of all, there is the fundamental intuition that a life will never be equivalent to a death (or reciprocally), in the sense that every individual is unique. Then, there is the determination to maintain ways of access, however indirect, to the regions inhabited by the dead. These dispositions come from a refusal to let ourselves be imprisoned by the many screens successively held up to us and by immediate sensorial experience. For the Native Americans, man must constantly try to break through these screens and look beyond the semi-realities imposed in the name of a basic perception of things. And in this, he can be helped by the otter's agility in moving from one realm to another, by the penetrative strength of arrowtips, by the power of thunderbirds and water panthers, and finally, by the absolute freedom brought by the visual language of abstraction.

a foodstuff that, notionally at least, could be kept forever. Here we come back to the idea of the vital principle suspended in time – providing, of course, that one draws on it only as a last resort, when in a state of need. Once again, what we have here is the interplay between life and death.

Beyond the dialectic of figurative and abstract

These four types of bags constitute what, in his analysis of myths, Lévi-Strauss calls a "permutation group", that is to say, a set of elements, linked by a series of simple formal transformations, involving inversion or amplification, which affect certain components of each entity, but at the same time preserving the structure of the whole. As we have just seen, whether "shamanic" or apparently "profane" like the parfleche, all these bags relate to the question of life and death. They are flat. In this sense, they obey the logic of the image more than that of containing. The permutational continuity between these bags is manifested, first of all, by their shape: otter skin bags and spear-pattern bags on the one hand, rec-

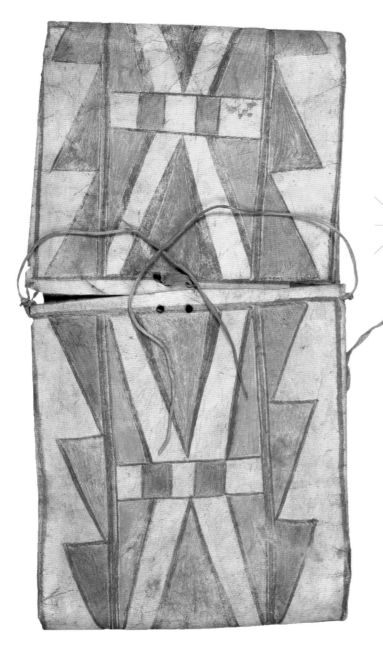

ill. 6 ✳ **Detail of a winter coat**

painted buffalo skin with porcupine quills
representing battle scenes
Blackfoot Indians, Great Plains
United States, 18th or 19th century
Musée du Quai-Branly

In the Plains, the men, unlike the women,
practice a figurative form of art which refers
to the "narration" of past events: hunting
adventures or exploits of warriors, activities
in which death either caused or experienced,
is omnispresent.

Sacred Bags of Ancient Mexico

✳   "Bundle: a number of things or a quantity of material gathered or loosely bound together [...] something wrapped or tied for carrying." Such is the definition given in the Collins English Dictionary.

While the bundles carried by men and women in ancient Mexico generally had a secular function – they were used for carrying clothes or goods by travelers and merchants – some also seemed to have had a sacred function. This was the case from the beginnings of the powerful empire later fought by the Spaniards, where bundles were used to hold either relics or divine attributes, or perhaps the presumed remains of the divine ancestors of the reigning dynasties, or again, human remains, made sacred by the divine attributes with which they were invested. These bundles appear in the pictographic manuscripts produced by two of the great Mesoamerican cultures in existence at the time of the Spanish conquest; the Mexicas, centering on the Mexico Valley, and the Mixtecs, a mosaic of small kingdoms to the west of the current state of Oaxaca. Even today, certain types of bundles are venerated in many regions of Mexico.

Ill. 1 ✳   opposite
The Codex Azcatitlan (extract)

Ill. 1a ✳   opposite, bottom left
Carrier of the cloth bag
of the God Huitzilopochtli

Ill. 1b ✳   opposite, bottom right
The elements of a sacred cloth bag:
head and foot of a humming bird,
a piece of cloth

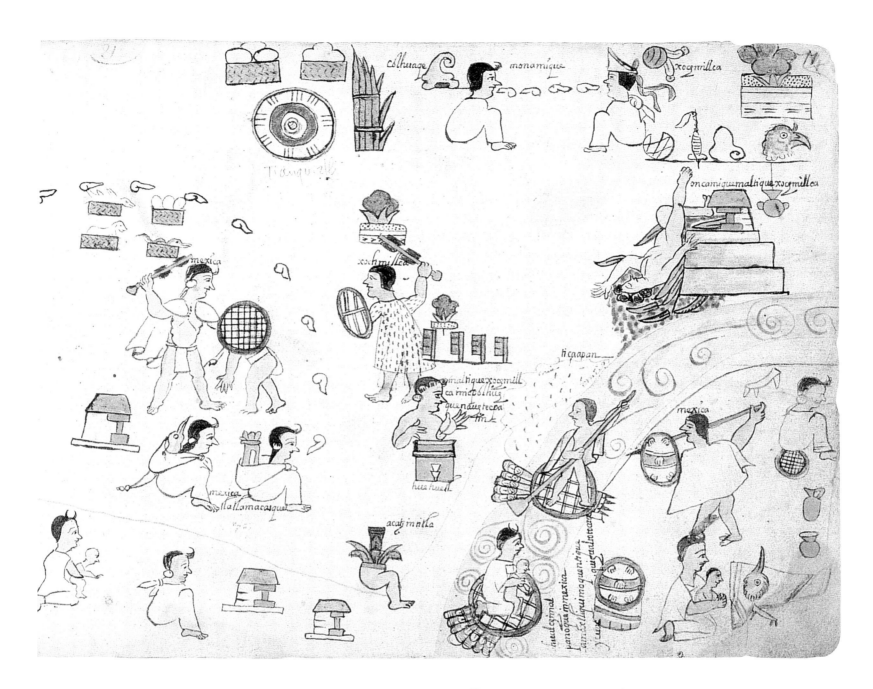

According to most sources, these were carried by the four figures known as *teomamaque* ("god-bearers" in Nahuatl), as identified by the glyph[1] that transcribes their name or that of the group to which they belonged. These figures acted as religious and political guides to the migrant populations. It was they who carried the bundles throughout the long, dangerous march that began in 1116 AD, in Aztlán, the mythical place of origin, and culminated with the foundation of Tenochtitlan in 1345.[2] In less than two centuries, this people rose from poverty to build a great power.

The Mexicas called the sacred bundle the *teoquimilli*, "sacred packet",[3] or *tlaquimilolli* (referring to the action of "tying a knot"). The examples listed here were found in two manuscripts: the *Codex*

Azcatitlan[4] and the *Tira de la Peregrinacion*,[5] made in the 16th century. The former belongs to an indigenous tradition on which the influence of European drawing is already in evidence; the latter is free of that influence.

The bundle was tied either around the neck (ill. 1a, 5a, 6a) or below the shoulders (ill. 2a, 3a, 3b, 3c, 4), much the same way as a mother carried her children. The form and material (fabric or deerskin) varies with the different manuscripts, and in accordance with the social status of the bearer. In the *Codex Azcatitlan* the bundle is made from simple, supple white cloth (ill. 1a, 5a, 6a) when the bearer is anonymous (not accompanied by a name glyph). When the bearer is a historical figure (and therefore accompanied by a name glyph) the bundle is like a kind of rigid quiver, placed on supple white material whose ends are knotted at the front. In most cases there is a fringe running along the base of the quiver, which itself is decorated with black signs (ill. 3a, 3b, 3c). In the *Tira de la Peregrinación*, the bundle is always simple, in plain-colored material, even when carried by a historical figure (ill. 4). The gods are represented by their essential attributes. Huitzilopochtli (from *huitzilin*, "hummingbird"

ill. 2 ✳
The Codex Azcatitlan (extract)

ill. 2a ✳
Lord Apantecatl ("He who wears water headdress), carries the bag of Tlaloc, God of Rain

ill. 3 ✳ ***The Codex Azcatitlan*** (extract)

left to right

ill. 3a ✳ Lord Huitzcoatl
("Thorn of cactus-snake") carries
the bag of Tezcatlipoca,
God of darkness and disorder

ill. 3b ✳ Lord Citlalcoatl ("Star-snake")
carries the bag of Huitzilopochtli,
God of War

ill. 3c ✳ Lord Yayauhqui Xihuitl
("Black gem")

ill. 3d ✳ Lord Xochitl ("Flower")
carries the bag of Chicomecoatl
("7 Snake"), Goddess of Corn

ill. 4 ✳
Tira de la Peregrinación (extract)

left to right

• Noble lady Petlachimatzin
("She who wears a plaited shield)

• Lord Apantecatzin ("The Lord
who wears a water headdress")

• Lord Cuauhcoatzin
(Lord eagle-snake")

• Lord Texcacoatzin ("Snake Lord
covered with volcanic glass")
and carrier of the sacred cloth bag
of the god Huitzilopochtli

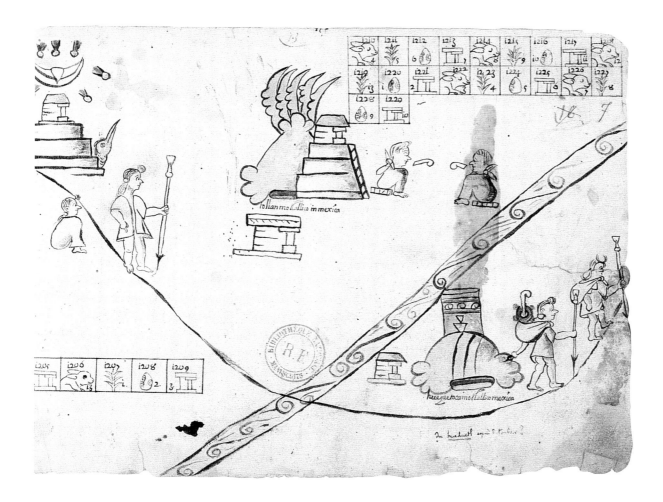

and *opochtli,* "left-handed") is the Mexicas' tutelary god and god of war. At the moment of conquest, he shares the heart of the sacred enclosure at Tenochtitlan with Tlaloc, the god of rain. When the Mexicas set off from Aztlán, it was he who guided them with his orders and prophecies of their future. In the *Codex Azcatitlan* Huitzilopochtli is represented by the head of a hummingbird, which is the pictographic transcription of the first part of his name. In illustration 1b, we can see the various elements required for his bundle, before this is tied up: the piece of material and the long-beaked head of the hummingbird. In illustration 3b, we can see the hummingbird being carried by the lord of the Malinalca, Citlalcoatl,[6] a figure whose importance is all the greater because he wears the *temilotli,* a headdress reserved for valiant warriors, and a rich coat. In illustrations 1a and 6a the god is represented by the hummingbird head, and by the tail of a rattlesnake. In the *Tira de la Peregrinación* (ill. 4), the god speaking (we see two lines of words scrolling out of his mouth) to his bearer, the lord Tezcacoatl ("Reflecting serpent") is represented by a human face emerging from the open beak of the hummingbird.

Tezcatlipoca,[7] or "Smoking mirror," the elusive, malevolent, omnipotent and ubiquitous god of night appears twice in the

ill. 5 ✳
The Codex Azcatitlan (extract)

ill. 5a ✳
Carrier of the cloth bag
of the God Tezcatlipoca

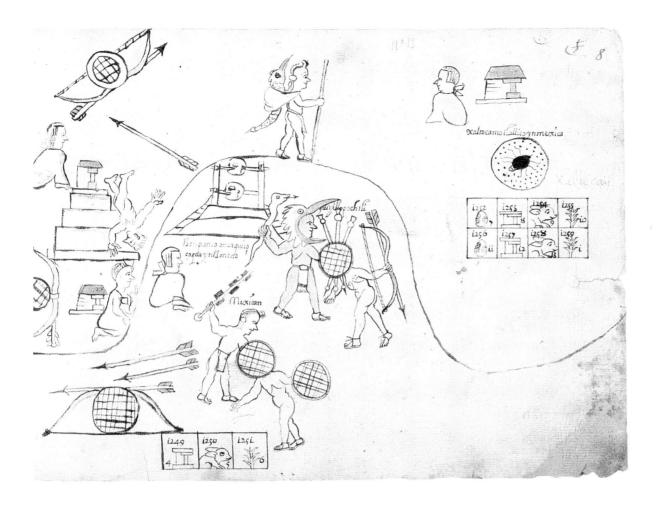

Codex Azcatitlan. The first time (ill. 3a), he is identified by the pictographic transcription of his name, a simple red ring representing the mirror, with two curls of smoke coming from it. The bundle is carried by the lord Huitzcoatl, who is identified by his name glyph;[8] chief of the Chichimec, he wears the *temilotli* on his head and has a rich coat. In another representation (ill. 5a), the glyph of "Smoking mirror" comprises a red ring decorated with four circles, and the image also shows a rattlesnake tail emerging from the bottom of the bundle. A curl of smoke is coming out of the mirror.

Tlaloc (ill. 2a), the god of beneficial and maleficent rain, is represented in the *Codex Azcatitlan* by one of his main attributes: the snake above his upper lip. He is carried by a male figure known, according to Barlow, as Tezcacoatl.[9]

Chicomecoatl, "7 Snake," [10] the goddess of ripe corn (ill. 3d) is represented here by her name glyph, which comprises a snake with seven circles of numbers, carried by a male figure called "Flower," who wears the *temilotli* headdress.

ill. 6 ✳
The Codex Azcatitlan (extract)

ill. 6a ✳
Carrier of the cloth bag
of the God Huitzilopochtli

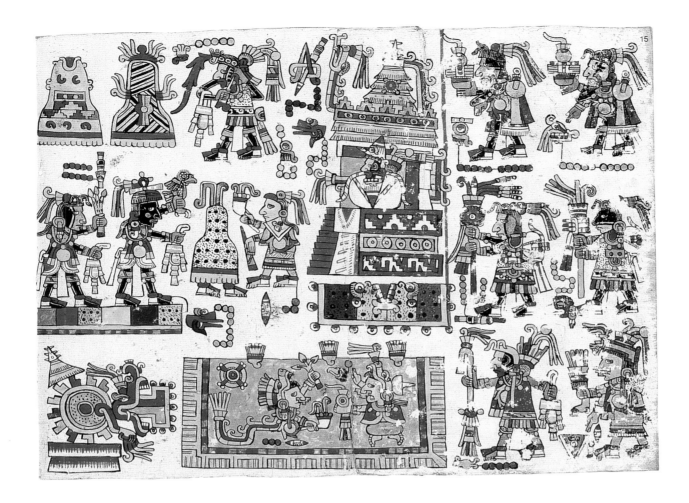

The manuscripts of the Mixtec tradition

In the *Codex Nuttall*,[11] as in most Mixtec manuscripts, there are two kinds of bundles: the ones that contain the attributes of the gods and are placed on temple platforms or on mountaintops, and those containing human remains and invested with divine attributes.

The benevolent god Quetzalcoatl ("Plumed serpent") was the symbol of the golden age, the inventor of the calendar, of writing, of penitence and of many other blessings. In various Mixtec manuscripts, he appears as the ancestor of powerful dynasties and is represented in the form of a god of wind, and as such is always accompanied by his name glyph "9 Wind Quetzalcoatl", especially in the *Codex Vindobonensis*,[12] where he is said to have been born in a flint. This glyph is none other than his calendar name, "9 Wind," comprising the figure 9 (nine small circles) and the glyph of the day "wind," a bearded human face and a face mask in the shape of a bird's beak. The sacred bundle of Quetzalcoatl appears twice in the *Codex Nuttall*. White, almost spherical, it is carefully tied using braided cords. The representations of the god are positioned vertically on one side of the bundle. They are identical and

ill. 7 ✳
The Codex Nuttall (extrait)

ill. 7a ✳
Sacred bag of the God Quetzalcoatl ("Snake-quetzal") under his calendrical name "9 Wind"

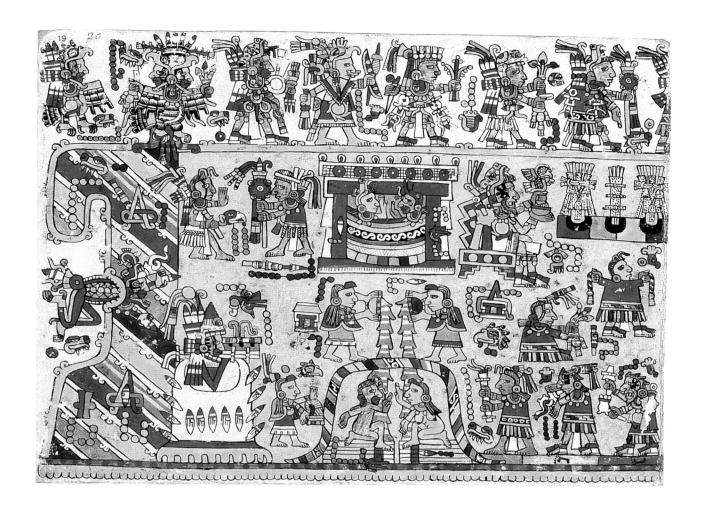

partial: we see a face covered with paint in two colors, lodged in a slot made in the sacrificial knife that also serves as his helmet. This knife, which is generally an attribute of Itztapaltotec ("Our Lord of the knife"), one of the gods of agriculture, in turn simulates a "human" face seen in profile, with, in the upper part, an eye, and, around the slit that serves as its mouth cavity, open lips showing a row of teeth which are partly red.

In the first representation, Quetzalcoatl's bundle (ill. 7a) is placed at the top of the steps to the "temple of the plumed serpent" of the city-state identified by Alfonso Caso[13] as Texupan. Leaning against one side of the bundle, which is tied with braided white string, the ends of which hang down its sides, the god is carrying on his back a kind of "quiver", probably containing instruments of self-sacrifice and, on his right, a commander's stick, of which we can see only the plumes at its top. A small sacrificial knife, perhaps indicating a nose, is placed below the eye in the face, this being simulated by the flint knife.

In the second representation (ill. 8a), the bundle is placed not on a temple but on an element in the landscape which is a transcription of the place name "White Flint Mountain". The god has a quiver on his back which seems to contain three flint knives and

ill. 8 ☀
The Codex Nuttall (extract)

ill. 8a ☀
Sacred bag of the the God
Quetzalcoatl ("Snake-quetzal")
under his calendrical name "9 Wind"

which is surmounted by a big plume of feathers. Behind Quetzalcoatl, placed on the bundle, are a white object (perhaps a roll of paper) and the notched stick used to light fires, as represented here by two curls of smoke.

Xipe Totec ("Our Lord who is flayed") is the god of agriculture and war. In Mesoamerican society, it was customary for all important figures to be burned after death. When the death was a sacrificial one, the bundles bore the attributes of the divinity to whom the victim had been sacrificed. Here, on the white bundle (ill. 9), around which, on the left, a priest is preparing to sacrifice a quail, and, on the right, another is using a long brand to light the fire, we see the skull and two long bones (probably the thigh bones) of the person sacrificed, along with parts of Xipe Totec's customary red and white costume. Part of the sacrificial coat, cape and loin cloth were put on by the victim for the sacrifice. According to Caso,[14] this would have been "10 Dog" or his brother "6 House."

This quick overview of holy bundles allows us to venture a few hypotheses. We can say that the cults devoted to Huitzilopochtli, Tezcatlipoca, Tlaloc and Chicomecoatl began well before the construction of the impressive temples devoted to them at Tenochtitlan. Also, that the gods were venerated at a tribal level before becoming national deities. And finally, that the cult of sacred bundles was probably the oldest cultual form.

This cultual form evolved. Just before the Spanish conquest it had reached a high level of sophistication, especially among the Miztecs. By now, bundles were only occasionally moved around. Instead, they tended to be exhibited for all to see on the platforms of the city-states' major temples.

The sacred bundle withstood the impact of evangelization. Indeed, its use became increasingly widespread, precisely because of persecution: it was easier than a statue to hide and carry from one secret place of worship to another. The minutes of the Inquisition's trials of the Indians tend to confirm this, since they contain frequent reference to these bundles (as proof of the owners' idolatry).

Nowadays, bundles containing holy objects are venerated all over Mexico. In the mountain region of the State of Guerrero,[15] local communities make cloth bundles for religious festivals. These contain incense, flowers, garlands of leaves and flowers, candles, cotton and incense. The bundle and its contents are carried to the place of worship and destroyed by fire during the celebrations.

ill. 9 ✴ *The Codex Nuttall* (extract)

opposite

Mortuary cloth bag carrying
attributes of the God Xipe Totec

1   The name glyphs of divine or human characters or ethnic groups
that feature in Mesoamerican pictographic manuscripts consisted of
a calendar date or a proper name, or sometimes both together (ill. 3).
2   Nigel Davies, *The Aztecs*, London: Macmillan, 1973, p. 2-3.
3   Alfonso Caso, *Reyes y Reinos de la Mixteca*, Mexico City: Fondo de Cultura
Económica, "Seccion de obras de antropologia" collection, 1979, Vol. II, p. 60-64.
4   *Codex Azcatitlan,* introduction by Michel Graulich, commentary by Robert
Barlow, updated by Michel Graulich, French. Trans. by Dominique Michelet, Paris:
Bibliothèque Nationale de France, 1995, 2 vols.
5   *Tira de la Peregrinación,* commentary by Joaquin Galarza
and Krystyna M. Libura, Mexico City: Ediciones Tecolotes, 1999.
6   *Codex Azcatitlan, op. cit.,* vol. I, p. 51.
7   On Tezcatlipoca, see Olivier Guilhem, *Moqueries et métamorphoses d'un dieu aztèque
Tezcatlipoca, le "Seigneur au miroir fumant,"* Paris: Musée de l'Homme, "Mémoires de
l'Institut d'ethnologie/Muséum national d'histoire naturelle" collection, 1997.

8   *Codex Azcatitlan, op. cit.,* Vol. I, p. 51.
9   *Ibid.,* p. 47.
10   Calendar name of the adult goddess of corn,
born on the seventh "snake" day.
11   Zelia Nuttall, *The Codex Nuttall, a Picture Manuscript
from Ancient Mexico*, introduction by Arthur Miller, New York:
Dover Publications, 1975.
12   *Codex Vindobonensis,* commentary by Otto Adelhofer, Graz:
Akademische Druck und Verlagsanstalt, 1974, p. 49-IV.
13   Alfonso Caso, *op. cit.*, p. 63.
14   *Ibid.,* p. 246.
15   According to Danièle Dehouve.

The Bag of Tales

chat

verb

transmission

message

manifesto

slogan

expression

address

inventory

ill. XLV **Laura James,** *People Waiting in the Sun*, 1997, private collection

ill. xlvi "**This is not a bag**", Spring/Summer 1990 collection, paper, cotton, Moschino Italie collection

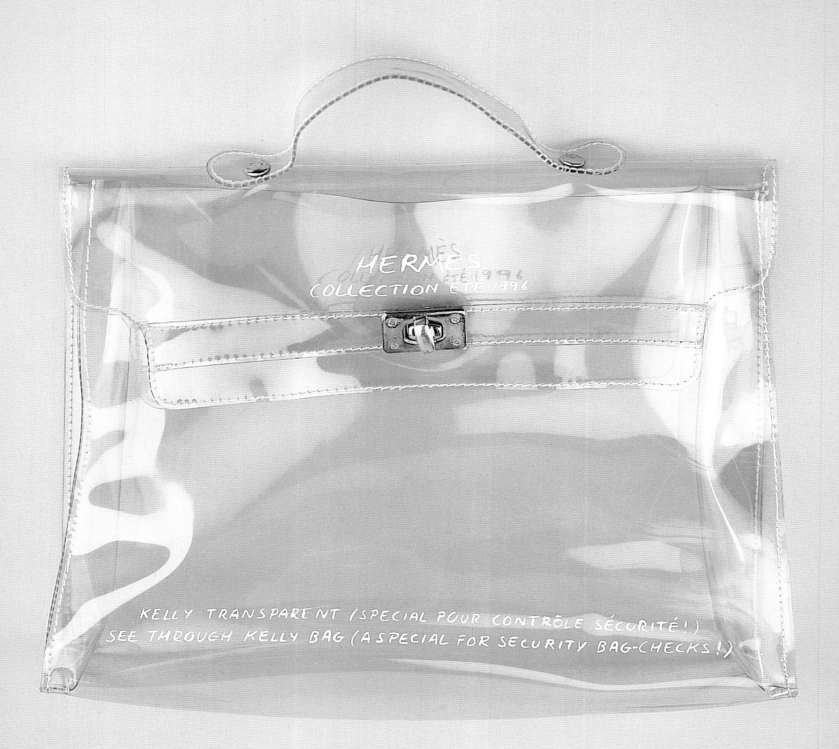

ill. XLVII **Transparent Kelly bag** ('special design for security checks!'), Hermès, distributed at the presentation of the Spring/Summer 1996 collection, private collection

Ce sac contient, un billet d'avion pour Dakar, un peigne bleu,

... photo de moi bébé, un mouchoir noué, le chéquier de mon patron, un pistolet Baretta chargé de deux balles, le N° de téléphone de Jack Lang – ma brosse à dents – un slip de rechange – une photo de Marcel l'odeur d'un parfum renversé 4 alka seltzer – un briquet rouge,

How Snakes Became Poisonous
A Native American Tale

When the world was still young and everything was different, there was no night anywhere on earth. The sun shone constantly in the sky, and neither people nor animals could sleep. If by chance they closed their eyes, the blazing heat of the sun would immediately awaken them. Only the snakes felt well; they were always fresh and composed, and for good reason. They were the keepers of night and darkness.

But one day, that came to an end. When the Indians heard that the snakes were the custodians of night and darkness, they sent their greatest chief to the Supreme Chief of the Snakes to ask him to give them at least a small bit of night and darkness.

The great Chief of the Indians disappeared far into the depths of the forest, where Chief Snake lived. Chief Snake welcomed him loudly, but not very politely:

"Who dares disturb my rest?"

"I am the Great Chief of all the Indians, "answered the visitor," and I come to ask for a little night and darkness. In exchange, I'm offering you our best bow and arrows."

"Just how would I use them? I have no hands! Give me something else!"

The Great Chief of the Indians went back home empty-handed. He called together the Grand Council, and told them what had happened. They decided to offer a rattle to Chief Snake, because a great chief always needs a rattle to preside over ritual dances. Then the Indian chief disappeared for the second time into the depths of the forest. Chief Snake was expecting his visit. When he saw the rattle, he shook his head:

"That's a good and beautiful rattle, but what could I do with it? I, who have no hands?"

"If you like," said the Indian Chief, *"I can fasten it to your tail."*

And so he fastened it there. Chief Snake waved his tail and the rattle buzzed, although rather faintly. That was good enough.

"This is not exactly what I would have wished for, but all the same I can give you a little night and darkness."

And he had a small leather bag brought to the Indian Chief.

"Thank you, Great Chief Snake, for this bit of night and shadow. But tell me, what would it take for you to give us the whole night and complete darkness?"

"The entire night and total darkness? That," the Great Snake replied, *"would be very expensive. A rattle is far from sufficient. You will have to bring me a large jug of the poison with which you coat your arrows."*

The Indian Chief did not see why snakes needed this poison, but he did not ask any questions. He carried away the small bag, and the minute he arrived at his village, he opened it.

Night and darkness spread over the world and all the Indians enjoyed a delicious rest. But it was too short; the bag contained such a small amount of night and shadow that soon the sunlight came to wake them up. And it began all over again – the long days and short nights. As soon as animals and people savored a brief moment of sleep, the sun returned with a new day. The Indians, who had not figured on this, convened their Grand Council, which decided to collect the poison the snakes had requested. What a lengthy task! They could only collect the poison drop by drop; but finally, they managed to fill a large jug. Then the Great Chief of the Indians disappeared for the third time into the depths of the forest. The Great Serpent was expecting his visit, and said:

"I knew you would return. I have filled this bag with complete night and darkness. Surely that will satisfy you."

The Chief of the Indians handed over the jug of poison to the Great Snake, and said:

"Thank you, Great Snake. But I would like to know why you need this poison."

"Because," the Great Snake answered, *"most of my people are small and weak. The whole world persecutes them. When we have poison, we will be able to defend ourselves. Go now, but do not open the bag before you arrive at your village. If you open it too soon, darkness will spread over the world before I can distribute the poison equally among all the snakes. And nothing good for your people or my people will come from that."*

The Indian Chief promised not to open the bag before arriving at home, and ran, completely satisfied, toward his village. But on his way, he met a parrot, whose cries echoed through the forest:

"The great Indian Chief is coming back from the snakes' home, bringing a long night and total darkness back in his bag!"

At the cries of the parrot, all the forest animals rushed up and begged the Great Chief to open his bag right away, to release total night and darkness. The Chief tried to reason with them:

"Wait a moment, until I have reached my village. I promised the Great Snake!"

But the animals did not want to listen; they would not wait one minute more. They snatched the bag out of his hands and opened it. Immediately, the world was nothing but night and darkness. This was the very moment the Great Snake had chosen to distribute the poison to his people. But in the dark night, he could not see what he was doing. The snakes, who were jostling each other, upset the jar, and the poison spilled out. Several snakes made off with a great amount of poison, while others only got a small amount, and still others got nothing at all.

From then on, some snakes were poisonous, but other snakes were not. The family of the Great Chief belongs to the poisonous snakes, but everyone knows where they are — because they all have rattles on their tails.

ill. 1 : opposite
Griot at a wedding
River region, Senegal, 2003
photograph by Catherine
and Bernard Desjeux

The griot sings the newlyweds' praises
with references to their ancestry.

Bags of Words:
African Oral Literature

"What is left in the bag is superior to what has been taken away."
Mossi proverb [1]

! The abundance of water skins and bags of all kinds in African myths, tales and proverbs, reflects the rich symbolic resonance of these receptacles in the traditional societies that use them. They are intimately bound up with two fundamental notions: fecundity and speech. Starting from Christiane Seydou's definition of the bag as "a container whose contents are not invisible, and that can be opened or closed only from outside," [2] I would like to consider several other properties of this object, in order to show how they relate to these two notions.

The primary quality associated with a bag is, I think, its suppleness, which immediately sets it apart from the clay *canari*, the straw basket or the round, rigid calabash. The heroes of certain tales sometimes hide a bag under their clothes, pressing it against their body. For example, Moro, the cunning hero of a Bobo tale (Burkina Faso) wins the king's daughter, by hiding under his clothes, bags full of water that enable him to triumph in an otherwise impossible challenge (he must drown the village rock with his sweat). [3] And in a Moba fable (southern Togo), a child who is "more wily than the chief" manages to strike down an ox, with the help of a friendly viper hidden in his bag. [4]

This quality, linked to the bag's form and material – when it is made of skin – is what often causes it to be associated with certain parts of the animal or human body.

The belly is the most common association. Indeed, it has been shown that the "men with bags" that are a recurrent feature of the European imagination (think of bogeymen, the sandman or even Father Christmas) are attenuated representations of the ogre and dragon, those fantastic creatures that swallow up children.[5] Here, the bag becomes the creature's external belly. Throughout sub-Saharan Africa we find this "classic" theme of the hero enclosed against his will in a bag by a king, a chief or an animal such as a hyena, that "great beast with its big bag" as one Rwandan tale puts it.[6] The hero in question can be a child (the "Cunning Child" or "Terrible Child" tales of Mali), an adult (the Dogon of Mali and the Mossi in Burkina Faso) or an animal (often, in these savanna lands, the hare, a creature that is physically weak but noted for its intelligence and cunning). Whatever else, this hero will have a particular talent: that of being a good talker. Indeed, one of them is called the "Prince of Liars".[7] Thanks to this gift of the gab, the prisoner will manage to get out of the bag. For one way in which the bag differs from other containers is that it doesn't stifle the voice. Though shut in, the hero can dialogue with his jailer, who is always curious or gluttonous, and it is his voice that will make him free – usually his skill as an orator, but sometimes his talent for imitation. In some cases, the hero will pretend to be nibbling peanuts, or scoffing honey: "I've eaten so much honey", says one, "that my stomach hurts".[8] Such is his professed delight, his pleasure in eating that his exclamations impel his captor to open the bag in order to share the feast.

The "belly bag" can also be quite simply the womb of a pregnant woman in those tales where the unborn child speaks to its mother and gives her advice, from this interior that it wants to leave, often well before term. "Mummy? Rub coal on your thigh to make me come out, I hate the usual place for coming out", orders the precocious boy, in a story recorded in 1970 from Syebèrkè Biyès, a Tenda storyteller in eastern Senegal.[9] Here, the child masters the method needed to at last get out of the bag – in other words, to be born. And when it emerges, it does so complete "with a bow, a knife and a little bag", rather like the child hero of a Mossi tale, whose unusual birth, carrying a knife and with a hide bag over his shoulder, heralds an equally exceptional destiny.[10]

Conversely, if we look to southern Africa, for some of the San, the act of entering a bag in antelope leather is equivalent to going inside the animal itself. The smell of antelope leather also plays a role here, conferring supernatural powers. This is not a mere metaphor, but a genuine metamorphosis which enables the man who has, in a state of trance, "entered into the animal" to be transformed into an antelope.[11] This metamorphosis also occurs frequently in myths and tales, in conjunction with the passage into another world, another kingdom. The hero may be transformed, or simply slip into the skin of an animal and, thus disguised, can travel to the other side, go over to "the other shore".

From the bag as belly, let us now move to male sexual attributes. In several African languages, as indeed in French,[15] the word for a purse or pouch (*bourse*) can also be used to refer to the testicles. The bellows of sub-Saharan smithies, whether itinerant or located in a single village, are often made with bags in skin which, by association, may stand for the testicles of the blacksmith (as in Bambara), or even for the blacksmith himself (as in Dogon society, where he is called *jemene*, i.e., "big bag" or "testicles").[16] In Bambara society, it is also a striking fact that the cobbler suffers from the same affliction as the blacksmith in Dogon society: a "hernia of the scrotum", an illness traditionally associated with an inability to hold one's tongue. The cobbler is "talkative, he has no verbal restraint; he is a liar, he is a man who cannot be trusted".[17] This same cobbler is also the maker of bags, he is the *garāke*, the man who prepares the envelope of knowledge" or *bala*, the wise man's bag; or the leather bag that will protect and contain *sebew*, those amulets that are so much a feature of the Mandingo world.

In his study of this passage theme in European folk literature, Vladimir Propp relates it to the funerary practices of ancient Egypt, but also to those of certain cattle-rearing peoples of the Americas and Africa. He sees it as expressing "an old idea of identification with the animal after death",[12] a form of the totemism that so fascinated the first anthropologists. Without wishing to generalize here, or to bring in totemism, we can however note that in certain African societies, when important people died, all or part of their body was wrapped up in pieces of hide. For example, when a king of the Mundang (Chad) dies, the many manipulations involved in the funerary ceremonies included wrapping his skull in a piece of skin from a sacrificed ox. Important figures are "buried naked except for this garment of skin[13] [from a ram offered by the heir]". Likewise, in the ancient Empire of Mali, the sovereign would always be seated on the skin of three-year-old bull and, when he died, would be wrapped in it for burial.[14] These few examples show the close relation between this wrapping in a skin – entering the bag – and the passage into the other world. For the San, it is a matter of a symbolic death, for the Mundang and Mandingo, a real one.

Can this be taken any further? The place allotted to bags in African myths and tales is often that of a frontier space, a place of transition between life – the "belly-bag" from which one must emerge in order to be born – and death – the "envelope-bag" that the deceased enters before departure.

Let us now come back to this second term, which we have already touched on: speech. As men who manipulate and make bags, the blacksmith and cobbler both have problems with language: they are voluble and mendacious, their speech is disorderly and excessive. And yet it is to the cobbler that goes the task of making those bags of knowledge that only old men have the right to carry,[18] those bags which contain orderly and therefore measured speech, speech that not all men can master. For another characteristic of the bag is its opacity: its contents are not accessible to all, and sometimes one must know the words that will make them fruitful. Which brings us to another recurrent theme in these tales: the bag as source of wealth that becomes active only when the magic formula is spoken. "Bag full to the brim with millet", repeats the hero of one Dogon tale, thus managing to ward off famine.[19] Proper use of the formula becomes "evidence that the initiate has acquired the knowledge he has come looking for; he has discovered the hidden meaning of things, and as this has become clear to him, so he has gained power over them".[20] And just as a man must know how to talk to the bag, so one must be able to make the bag talk. Remaining within the vast region once covered by the Mandingo Empire (Mali, Guinea, Senegal and Gambia), we can note that divination and stories both involve bags. The Mande seer, an accomplished hunter, is the only person to own a *sassa*, the hunting bag from which he will take twelve cowry shells in order to look into the future of the kingdom.[21] As for the *griot*, he readily enters into the game of metaphor: "We are bags of words, we are the bags that hold centuries-old secrets", explains one of them, Djeli Mamadou Kouyaté, before starting to tell the story of Soundiata Keita, the heroic founder of the Empire of Mali in the 13th century.[22] For the *griot*, talking means opening this "bag" that he possesses, agreeing to shed light on the contents known to him alone. He is the master of knowledge of the past, just as the seer is the master of knowledge of the future. The words contained in the bag come out and are revealed as they are spoken by the man who can make "his" bag talk.

A tale is more than just a story told after sundown to amuse or help listeners sleep. And this is even more true of myth. These two forms are used to pass on values, to enter into a vision of the world, to show youngsters the way ahead. To borrow Christiane Seydou's terms, because of its association with both the "*ex-* and the *in-*" the bag is particularly "good for thinking with" in that it is credited with the fundamental characteristic of being neither inside nor outside (or both at the same time). It is a cultural object made of animal skin, and thus very much an intermediary place that must be passed through, or whose contents must be mastered, in order to achieve an understanding of the world.

1 Doris Bonnet, *Le Proverbe chez les Mossi du Yatenga (Haute-Volta)*,
Paris: CNRS-ACCT, 1982.

2 Christiane Seydou, "Une dialectique de l'ex- et de l'in- ou le motif du 'sac'
dans les contes de l'Enfant terrible," Veronika Görög, Suzanne Platiel, Diana
Rey-Hulman and Christiane Seydou, *Histoires d'enfants terribles: Afrique noire,
étude et anthologie*, preface and conclusion by Geneviève Calame-Griaule,
Paris: G.-P. Maisonneuve et Larose, "Les Littératures populaires de toutes les
nations" collection, 1980, p. 215.

3 Marcel Guilhem, *Cinquante contes et fableaux de la savane*,
Paris: Ligel, 1962, Vol. II, p. 7-10.

4 Denise Paulme, *La Mère dévorante, essai sur la morphologie des contes
africains*, Paris: Gallimard, "Tell" collection, 1986 (1976), p. 194.

5 Nicole Belmont, *Comment on fait peur aux enfants*,
followed by *Les Croquemitaines, une mythologie de l'enfance?*,
Paris: Mercure de France, "Le petit Mercure" collection, 1999.

6 Pierre Smith, *Le Récit populaire au Rwanda*,
Paris: A. Colin, "Classiques africains" collection, 1975, p. 361.

7 Gaston Canu, *Contes mossi actuels, étude ethno-linguistique*,
Dakar: Mémoires de l'Institut Fondamental d'Afrique Noire,
No. 82, 1969, p. 150-183.

8 Denise Paulme, *op. cit.*, p. 56.

9 Marie-Paule Ferry, *Les Dits de la nuit: contes tenda (Sénégal oriental)*,
Paris: Karthala, "Contes et légendes" collection, 1983, p. 286.

10 Denise Paulme, *op. cit.*, p. 199-200.

11 David Lewis-Williams, "Image des San et art san. Une dialectique
potentiellement créatrice en Afrique australe," *Ubuntu*,
Paris: Réunion des Musées Nationaux, 2000, p. 186.

12 Vladimir Propp, V., *The Theory and History of Folklore*, Minneapolis:
Minnesota University Press, 1984 (original Russian edition: 1946).

13 Alfred Adler, *La mort est le masque du roi. La royauté sacrée des Moundang
du Tchad*, Paris: Payot, "Bibliothèque scientifique" collection, 1982, p. 199.

14 Massa Makan Diabaté, M.M., *L'Aigle et l'épervier, ou la Geste de Sunjata*,
Paris: Pierre-Jean Oswald, "Poésie, prose africaine" collection, 1975, p. 24.

15 The word "bourse" (purse) can refer both to a particular kind of bag and
to the testicles. Sometimes, indeed, the latter are used to make the former:
"Sa bourse fut faicte de la couille d'un Oriflant, que luy donna Her Pracontal
proconsul de Lybie," Rabelais, "La Vie tres horrificque du grand Gargantua"
(His penis was made of an elephant's testicle, which had been given to him
by Herr Pracontal, procurator of Lybia.), ch. VIII, in *Œuvres complètes*,
Paris: Gallimard, "Bibliothèque de la Pléiade" collection, 1994, p. 26.

16 Christiane Seydou, *op. cit.*, p. 223.

17 Dominique Zahan, *La Dialectique du verbe chez les Bambara*,
Paris: Mouton, 1963, p. 132.

18 *Ibid*, p. 131.

19 Geneviève Calame-Griaule & Veronika Görög-Karady, "La calebasse et le
fouet : le thème des objets magiques en Afrique occidentale",
Cahiers d'études africaines, 45, Vol. XII, 1st book, 1972, p. 18.

20 *Ibid.*, p 71.

21 Djibril Tamsir Niane, *Soundjata ou l'épopée mandingue*,
Paris: Présence africaine, 1976 (1960), p.19.

22 *Ibid.*, p. 9.

I am a *griot*, a storyteller. I, Djeli Mamadou Kouyaté,
son of Bintou Kouyaté and of Djeli Kedian Kouyaté,
am a master in the art of speaking.
From time immemorial, the Kouyaté family has served
the Kéita princes of Mandingos; we are the word-bags,
the bags that hold innumerable earthly mysteries.
For us, the art of words has no secrets; without us,
the names of kings would be lost in oblivion,
for we are the memory of men. Through words,
we give life to events and to the heroic deeds of the kings
who came before the people of today.[1]
[...] Well, one day when the king, as was his custom,
was sitting in state under the great kapok tree
surrounded by his retinue, there appeared before him
a man dressed as a hunter. He wore the tight pants
of the devotees of Kondolon-Sané[2], and the cowries
sewn onto his shirt indicated that he was a master hunter.
The entire audience turned toward the stranger,
whose bow, polished by use, gleamed in the sun.
The man walked right up to the king,
whom he recognized among his courtiers.

The Legend of Sundjata (Mali)

1   Text excerpted from Djibril Tamsir Niane, *Soundjata ou l'épopee
mandingue*, Paris: Présence Africaine, 1976 (1960), pp. 9-19. In his foreword,
Djibril Tamsir Niane pays homage to Djeli Mamadou Kouyaté: "an obscure
griot from the village of Djeliba Koro in the Siguiri district in Guinea. I owe
everything to him" (p. 5).
2   "Kondolon is a divinity of the hunt. She has Sané as an inseparable
companion. The two divinities are always joined, and are invoked together.
This double divinity has the ability to be everywhere at once, and when
she reveals herself to a hunter, it is often a sign that he will find game"
(Djibril Tamsir Niane, *op. cit.*, p. 15, No. 4).
3   "All the traditions acknowledge that the small village of Niani was the first
capital of Mandingo. It was the residence of the first kings. Soundjata is said
to have built a great city there. It is also called Nianiba, or greater Niani.
Today, it is a small village with some hundreds of inhabitants on the
Sankarani, one kilometer from the border with Sudan" (*ibid.*, p. 17, No. 1).
4   "Literally, Sïmbon is the hunter's whistle. But Sïmbon is also an
honorific term which serves to designate a great hunter" (*ibid.*, p. 15, No. 3).
5   "This is a hunter's bag [*sassa*]. The *sassa* is one kind of bag or another;
it may appear in many versions. In general, hunters have a small *sassa*
for their personal fetishes" (*ibid.*, p. 19, No. 2).

He bowed and said:

"I greet you, king of Mandingo, and I greet all the people of Mandingo; I am a hunter in pursuit of game, and I come from Sangaran. An intrepid doe led me up to the very walls of Nianiba[3]. Through the magic of my great master Sïmbon[4], my arrows hit her, and she lies not far from your walls. As is only right, your Majesty, I come to bring you your share."

He drew a haunch out of his leather bag; but then Gnankouman Doua, the king's storyteller, seized the haunch and said:

"Stranger, whoever you are, you shall be the king's guest, for you are respectful of traditions. Come, take a place on the mat beside us. The king rejoices, because he loves honorable men."

The king nodded his head, and all the courtiers agreed.

The griot began again, in a more familiar tone:

"You who come from Sangaran, the country of the devotees of Kolondon-Sané, you who have doubtless had a learned master, would you open your bag of knowledge for us, would you teach us with your words, because you have obviously visited many lands?"

The king, silent as usual, nodded his head. A courtier added:

"The hunters of Sangaran are the best soothsayers.
If the Stranger is willing, we can learn much from him."

The hunter came to sit next to Gnankouman Doua, who gave him one end of the mat. He said:

"Storyteller of the king, I'm not one of those hunters whose tongue is more skillful than his arms. I am not a teller of great adventures, and I don't like to take advantage of the credulity of good people; but thanks to the knowledge that my master has bestowed on me, I can boast of being a seer among seers."

Out of his fetish bag[5], he took twelve cowries, which he threw onto the mat. The king and his entire entourage now turned toward the Stranger, who began to knead the twelve luminous shells with his rough hand.

Mothers of the fair and brave
Heavy is the debt you owe
For the suffering of the slave
And thro an age of pain and woe

But a brighter day is near
Blessings by your Justice given
Faithful wives & children dear
And the hope of Joy in Heaven

Shall your sons wish freedom blest
Be the oppressors of your race
As I plead, each noble breast
Kindles at the foul disgrace

Torn from Afric's sunny plain
By your fathers cruelty
We have groaned in heavy chains
We have pined in misery

We shall bless your holy zeal
In our lisping girls & boys
For we have a heart to feel
All a parents anxious joys

We shall see the harvest wave
And the sweets of science know
Freemen — at the name of Slave
Shall our souls indignant glow

ill. 1 (opposite) and 2 :
The Slave's Address
to British Ladies
bag with a anti-slavery poem
attributed to Suzannah Watts
and published by the Female Society
of Birmingham in 1828
19th century
Great Britain, Wilberforce House
Hull City Museums and Art Galleries

Bag Gab

! The word *bag* is small, a single syllable of three letters, where two end consonants, a labial and a velar stop, encircle the vowel *a*. If *a* is the thing contained, then *b*, through its labial explosion, puffs itself into a volume that is immediately defined, jerked shut, and given closure by the velar stop *g*.

Like its three letters, a bag has three defining features: 1) it is a receptacle 2) it is made up of various flexible materials, and 3) it can only be opened or closed on top.

Each bag's material circumstances convey shades of meaning for the word *bag* to take on. Let's examine the various bits of language that encircle it. Often, other nouns join on to make a compound that suggests function by describing what the bag contains: *garbage bag, mailbag, cosmetic bag, laundry bag, sports bag.* Nouns describing the professions of persons who carry them also adhere to their bags: *messenger bag, doctor's bag.* Still other nouns remind us what the bag is made of: *leather bag, plastic bag, brown paper bag.* And others emphasize its magnitude or capacity: *tote bag, mini bag, duffel bag.*

Some bags do more than simply contain. A *bagpipe* expels the air contained in it to make a musical drone. An *intravenous (IV) bag* transfers its contents to a hospital patient, drop by drop. Other bags meet their nouns in prepositional phrases, like the *bag of waters* that nourishes and protects the baby in the womb. The preposition "of" indicates contents, which may be as atmospheric as the wind or, more rarely, abstractions such as a *bag of tricks.* There is a clear enough difference between a *bag of wind* and a *windbag*, but what is the difference between a *bag of sand* and a *sandbag*?

The third criterion, "open only on top", allows more to be carried than the hand can hold, and guarantees the contents won't be spilled unless the bag is

GAB

BAG

turned upside down. Just so, the word *bag* may carry inside it an arsenal of derivatives based on its root: *baggies, baggage*. Because they are open on top and made of flexible or soft material, many bags take their forms from what they carry. When empty, a bag is flat or folded. "An empty bag", Benjamin Franklin's Poor Richard remarks, "cannot stand upright". When full, it takes on the shape its bulky contents express.

In this sense, bags are mutable objects, as are all the words that issue from their many folds. This malleable, adaptive character makes the bag useful as a human metaphor. Early on, hunting man used it; we speak of *bagging* a deer, or even a woman, though we may mean no more than that she has agreed to a date. This hunting-gathering idea leads to more sinister applications, as in the gangland phrase *to sandbag* a victim, and dump the body, thus enclosed, in the river.

Paradoxically, we may use the word *bag* to imply great achievement or confidence, announcing of a forthcoming event that *it's in the bag*, that the formless has been given shape. Yet what others might assume to be in the bag (ourselves, perhaps?) can of course slip out through the top, which is what we mean by *giving school* or job *the bag* and going to the beach on a sunny afternoon. Those who do not accompany us to the beach are left behind *holding the bag*; responsible for the tasks we have escaped. Employers, irate that we have *bagged our work*, can turn about and do the same thing to us. By *giving us the bag*, firing us, they are putting us into a sack to be drowned, and emptying our pockets as well. We may each have our *bag*, a knowledge or mastery that defines us, like playing

all the hot air it contains until not a whisper remains. And when we empty a vacuum cleaner bag, we learn the whole story about the detritus that surrounds us.

A bag may have a distinct shape, but unless we look within, we may never know its contents. Most bags hide their freight, whether good or bad. In this sense, a bag can have a secret or hermetic side; hence the name of the firm Hermes, so called after the Greek messenger-god. That peddler carrying a bag over his shoulder who is he but the devil with his collection of human souls? Rigoletto, hero of the eponymous opera, believes his enormous bag contains the body of the Duke of Mantua, when the sound of the duke's voice makes him look into the bag to find that he is about to drown the body of his beloved daughter. Any number of unpleasantnesses may be let out of bags, like a wild cat, clawing and snarling. In far-off times, miscreants might be sewn in a bag with a pair of leopards and left to spin for our edification, instead of being hung or defenestrated.

A bag may also be a pouch, and in this sense, we lament the black or blue *bags under our eyes*. More privately, it can represent that most intimate of female bags, the vagina, accompanied (by way of epithet) by her walking condoms, the *dirt bag* and the *scumbag*. In this feared sense, we may refer to an old crone as an *old bag*, or a prostitute as a *baggage*. When recycled into blood pudding or sausage, offal becomes *bag pudding* or *bags of mystery,* tasty until the trusting diner inquires about the ingredients. And the troubled history of an otherwise attractive date? Unprocessed trauma, failed relationships: the contents of *emotional baggage*.

ill. 1 and 2 : opposite
Philibert-Louis Debucourt

An 6. Costume Parisien. (47)

Voile à l'Iphigénie. Mantelet Blanc. Sac à devise. Champs élysées.

Ever versatile, bags hold precious things, as well as the unspeakable or unmentionable. Masses of bags may be required to organize the treasure in a pirate's ship or Ali Baba's cave. An army surrenders totally, *bag and baggage*, before a city and its entire contents are sacked, just as a roommate absconds with the contents of an apartment, bag and baggage. In the reconstruction era after the American Civil War, war profiteers, who arrived carrying suitcases made of recycled carpets, came to be known as *carpetbaggers*. The ultimate filler of bags is, of course, money, and a *moneybag* is thought to contain an almost infinite supply. Would it be nice to marry such a bag, or to be a moneybags oneself? A guy *with his bags full* is, by comparison with the likes of us, fabulously rich. The prospect of heavenly riches, long held out to the poor who have not yet inherited the earth, was not strong enough to hold one Demas, who in the 16th century "gave religion *the bagge*, when the world offered him the purse".

A bag is a visible extension of the person to whom it belongs, i. e., a sailor's bag or a woman's handbag. As a symbol of the person thus extended, it defines profession while simultaneously indicating style. With that in mind, we may reverse the word bag, seeing it as content rather than container. Enclosing, it is itself enclosed. Thus turned around, the *gab bag* clarifies itself by showing what defines it and gives it flavor.

Bag ladies and bag people do not apply here, but the Baganda do, a Bantu people inhabiting the province of Bugunda in Uganda. Baghdad is not the city of a thousand and one bags; it was the city of a thousand and one gardens, from the Persian *bagh*. Most germane to the spirit of any festive occasion is that musical or verse trifle the *baga*telle, something to be tossed off, like a bag used and then discarded. We stuff *bag*els and ruta*bag*as into the sacs that are our stomachs,

though the *bag*uette, that long white stick French husbands carry insolently over their shoulders, one hand on the handlebars as they pedal home for lunch, is often more palatable. As for less festive occasions: a *bag*arre happens when two gangster *bag*men start hurling more than words at one another.

Small wonder, then, that writers have incorporated *bag* into names for their folksy characters: Bushy, *Bag*ot, and Green, the three assassins in Shakespeare's Richard II, and the well-known Hobbit, Frodo *Bag*gins, who wants to return his gold to the earth's dark purse.

Since the bases of baseball are called bags (from sandbags), it is fitting that an eminence of the modern game should be Jeff *Bag*well, the Cardinal first baseman. Among writers, Enid *Bag*nold's novel *National Velvet* eventually disgorged the twelve-year-old Elizabeth Taylor. Last, but certainly not least is the American poet Robert *Bagg*, who claims that his name derives from German Bach or Scottish Beck, but wears only *Oxford bags* — for in *grab-bags* of this sort, nothing is accidental.

This ubiquitous word, *bag*, draws beauty from its every metamorphosis. A Japanese proverb says it all: *The bag of desires is bottomless.*

Bag Time *

I spit on my life. I dissociate myself
From it. Who isn't better than his life.

* *La Vie dans les plis*, Paris, Gallimard, 1949

It began in my childhood. There was a large overbearing adult.

How to revenge myself on him? I put him in a bag.

There I could beat him whenever I pleased.

He screamed, but I didn't listen. It didn't interest me.

I've wisely hung onto this childhood habit.

I didn't trust the possibilities of intervention

acquired as an adult; for one thing, they didn't go far enough.

You don't offer a chair to someone who is in bed.

As I was saying, I've sensibly maintained this habit,

and until now, I've kept it secret. That was the safest thing.

The inconvenience — for there is one — is that thanks to this habit,

I find it too easy to tolerate impossible people.

I know that I lie in wait for them with a bag.

That gives me extraordinary patience.

On purpose, I let the most ridiculous situations drag on,

squeezing the last drop from them.

The joy I would feel in showing them the door in reality is dwarfed

at the moment of action by the utterly delightful prospect

of stuffing them in the bag. In the bag where I beat them black

and blue with impunity, with an ardor that would tire

ten strong men one after the other.

Without this little knack of mine, how would I have gotten through

my discouraging life, often poor, always elbowed around by everyone?

How would I have been able to continue for decades through so many

setbacks, under so many masters near and far, under two wars,

two long occupations by a warlike people who believed in smashing us

like tenpins, and countless other enemies?

But my liberating habit saved me. Barely, it's true,

and I fought against a despair that seemed likely to leave me nothing.

Mediocrities, bores, the bully I could have gotten rid of a hundred times.

I'm saving time in my bag for them all.

Translated by Robin Magowan

A Brief Lexicon of Bags

ACCORDÉON (19th century, from the German *Akkord*)
A lady's bag made of two or three pouches side by side, fastened to each other by stitching, snaps, or slide fasteners to allow expansion or contraction of the bag, according to its desired capacity. The entire bag may be closed by a flap. Seen from the side, it resembles the bellows of the musical instrument that shares its name.

ALOIÈRE (from *alleier/aloier*, from Latin *allegare*, to combine)
Another name for the *aumonière*. A purse made of leather or any kind of fabric, hung from the belt.

AUMÔNIÈRE [alms purse] (12th century, from low Latin *alemos(i)na*, ecclesiastical Latin *elecmosina* (alms), from Greek *elemosyne*, compassion)
A free-form purse worn on their belts by men and women in the Middle Ages, originally containing money intended for alms. Made up in leatherwork or fine fabrics, often richly embroidered, alms purses were often donated by the noble women who had decorated them. In the 15th century, a metal clasp gradually replaced the cord used to close the bag, which then assumed the name "money bag" or "game bag".
"Elisabeth decided to unfasten her husband's belt and began to search through the alms purse which was attached to it." (Montalembert, *Histoire de Sainte Elisabeth de Hongrie*.)
Saracen almoners, the name given to these purses during the Crusades, were often richly ornamented, and were also worn on the belt by the Arabs.
In its widest sense, a small lady's handbag in the form of a purse for objects in current use. "An alms purse, the name which some women still give to their little purses."(H. Estienne, *Précellence*.)

BAGUETTE (SAC-)
A small, long, narrow bag with a shoulder strap, carried under the arm. A descendant of bags elongated in order to carry oblong items, it was revived as a fashionable handbag in the 1970s.

BAL(L)ANTINE (from Greek *balantion*, purse)
A type of purse made of leather, fabric, or metal, suspended from a long cord, which may be wound around the wrist or the arm. The bal(l)antine swings back and forth at knee height as you walk. See also *réticule*.

BAL(L)UCHON [bundle]
A primitive bag of hide or woven cloth, with all four corners knotted together, carried on the end of a pole.

BAVOLET [athletics bag]
Sports bag consisting of three compartments. The central section, generally the largest, is closed by a clasp or zipper. The other two compartments on either side of the bag are identical to each other. Occasionally these two sections are larger and closed, abutting a smaller, open, central section. This bag usually has a handle on each side, and a shoulder strap or a hand grip at either end of its zipper.

BESACE (13th century, from low Latin *bisacia*, from *bis* "twice" and *saccus*) or **BISSAC** (15th century) [beggar's bag, scrip, shoulder bag, pilgrim's wallet]
Originally an elongated bag of soft material with an opening in the middle, which is thrown over the shoulder to form two pouches, one in front, the other behind. It is normally used to carry food.
Thus, by analogy, a bag worn slung over the shoulder, with two symmetrical sides, which are rounded at the bottom and waisted at the top.
It may be closed by a central flap or a zipper.
The bissac is a type of bag that opens down the middle, shaped so that it forms a double bag, and is hung on either side of the shoulder or mount.

BOUGE (in use from the 12th through 18th centuries, from Latin *bulga*)
Leather or canvas bag, often leather and canvas, or cowhide reinforced with steerhide. Straps, chains, and hinges are added to it; locks are seen occasionally, which was an innovation. The bouge is the equivalent of a traveling trunk, used for moving house.

BOUGETTE (12th century, from *bouge*)
An oblong bag closed by a chain. The descriptions given in dictionaries are imprecise, often designating a satchel locked by a key, a small suitcase, or a portmanteau bag. In their statutes, saddlers had the right to manufacture bougettes. Until the 17th century, some bougettes were mounted on wood.

BOURSE [purse] (12th century, *bolse* from *bursa*; *byrsa*; in Provençal, *bolse*; *borse* in the 16th century)
A small bag closed by a cord or a spring, intended for tokens, seals, stamps, a rosary, relics, money... If the purse is double, it's known as a "peasant's buttocks." Robert's French Dictionary cites some visual or literary uses:
"Lodge the devil in your purse" – to have a heavy but flat purse, to be penniless.
"Of a man who has no credit or other resource,
It is said that the devil lives in his purse,
That is to say nothing lodges there."
(La Fontaine, *Fables*.)
"Friend of my wallet."
"This worshipful fellow was warned
That you fleeced me of all my money
And that my purse had a big abscess."
(Clément Marot, *Au roi pour avoir été dérobé*.)

BOURSE DE MARIAGE [marriage purse]
This purse contains the gold coins presented by the groom on his betrothal. In the Middle Ages, it was part of the marriage ceremony, a practise that continued into the 18th century.

ill. 1 : *Viator ad Aerarium*
purse belonging to an official of the Roman Treasury
relief, 1st century, Italy
Rome, Museo della Civiltà Romana
The tax collector put the money he amassed into this purse to take it (*viator* means traveler) to the Treasury (*aerarium*).

BOURSELLE
A small bag that is hidden in the pocket instead of being worn externally.

BOURSETTE
Often made of velvet, it slips into a pocket.

BOURSICAUT or **BOURSICOT**
A little purse for saving small sums or holding them in reserve.
"She put on an expression of looking for her purse… 'We were not still there', he said, 'when you were making a fuss about your purse.' "
(George Sand, *François le Champi*.)

CABAS [two-handled bag, tote bag, shopping bag]
(14th century, from Provençal *cabas*; low Latin *capacius*, from *capax*, that which contains much)
A flat bag of flexible material, capacious, with two arching handles, carried in the hand or over the arm. Originally, the cabas was a rush basket designed to carry fruits or supplies.
"They went to the market with a cabas to offer to carry the provisions the burghers had bought."
(Lesage, *Histoire de Guzman d'Alfarache*.)
"Félicité removed slices of cold meat from her cabas and we lunched in an apartment next to the dairy."
(Flaubert, *Un Coeur Simple*.)

CARNASSIÈRE (18th century, from Provençal *carnassiero*) or **CARNIER** (18th century, from Provençal *carnier*, from Latin *carnarium*, "place where one preserves meats")
A string bag, with a shoulder strap, used to carry dead game.

CARTABLE or **CARTON D'ÉCOLIER** [schoolbag, school satchel] (from low Latin *cartabulum*, a receptacle for paper, derived from *carta*, paper)
A type of satchel with handles, slung over the shoulder or on a strap, made of leather, cardboard, or other materials, in which schoolchildren place their books, notebooks, and crayons… Also called "musette," "portfolio," "briefcase," or "satchel"…
In the medieval period, when printed books were still rare, schoolchildren are portrayed carrying wax-surfaced wooden writing tablets on their belts.
In the 19th century, with the birth of compulsory public education, schoolchildren often had a long walk to the nearest school; they began to use the satchel, the *musette*, the beggar's bag, or the game bag fastened to a shoulder strap or carried on the back. The peddlers' catalogs that circulated at the beginning of the 19th century present classic models, which excited the envy of Alphonse Daudet's hero, nicknamed by his schoolmaster and classmates "Petit Chose" (little thing). It occurs to him, many years afterward, that the suffering he experienced over the course of his school years "was not only because my smock was different from the other children. The others had beautiful schoolbags of yellow leather, inkwells of sweet-smelling boxwood, notebooks with cardboard covers, and new books with many footnotes…" Petit Chose's schoolbag, constructed by his brother Jacques, who "did as well as he could" with thick cardboard and strong glue, is admittedly very practical, "with no end of compartments", but odd-looking all the same, and "exhaling an embarrassing smell of glue."
(Alphonse Daudet, *Histoire d'un enfant: le petit Chose*.)
In the very popular work of 19th-century German children's literature *Struwwelpeter* (Shock-headed Peter or Slovenly Peter) by Heinrich Hoffmann, we are told about the misadventures of Johnny Head-in-Air, an absent-minded young schoolboy: he walks very elegantly, holding his schoolbag proudly under his arm like a minister's briefcase, before tumbling into a river where his schoolbag is carried far away by the swift current.

CARTOUCHIÈRE [cartridge bag]
A leather box or pouch that contains a soldier's ammunition. It replaced the 16th-century shoulder bag and the old cartridge pouch, and is made of leather – black for the infantry, fawn for the cavalry. The interior structure evolved over the years and according to its function: first a simple gusseted pouch, it was later divided into small compartments, each holding a cartridge. The cartridge bag of a regimental medic contained various medicines and implements for dressing wounds. For hunting, the cartridge bag becomes a belt fitted out with small cases or pockets into which cartridges are slipped. Today, the term denotes a small, stiff, rectangular, upright bag of thick leather, fitted with a flap, and worn on a shoulder strap.

CAVOUR
The base and sides of a bag formed out of a single stiff strip.

CHÂTELAINE (19th century, from Latin *castellanus*, relating to castle)
A type of fastener more or less finely worked, consisting of chains in gold or silver that hold a watch, keys, sewing equipment, and so forth, which women attached to their waistbands at the end of the 18th century, and on into the Romantic period.
"The girl took one of the charms that hung from her châtelaine, that cascade of jewelry that women wore hanging on a hook from their waistbands…" (J. de la Varende.)
A small lady's bag in fabric or leather, rectangular in form, closed by a clasp.

COUFFE, COUFFIN, SCOUFIN, or **COUFFLE** (17th century, from Provençal, *coufo*; Arabic *quffa*; Spanish *alcofa*; Latin *cophinus*, basket). [coffer, basket]
A type of large basket used to carry merchandise.
"The baker dropped three huge loaves of brown bread as well as a bag of bran into the coffer on the right, and then he offered a handful of wheat to the donkey, who ate it politely out of his hand."
(Bosco, *L'Ane culotte*.)
The contents of a coffer: a coffer of figs.
"While passing by the store, he took a coffer of raisins and an ewer of clean water." (Flaubert, *Salammbô*.)

ESCHARPE or **ÉCHARPE** (early 12th century)
A bag hung by its neck from a shoulder-belt or baldric worn slantwise across the body.

ESCARCELLE [money bag] (13th century, but rare before the 16th century, from Italian *scarcella*, from *scarso*, Latin *scarsus*, miser. Montaigne speaks of a *echarse*, or thrifty, life)
A large purse often fitted with a lock, sometimes in combination with a strongbox, specially intended for silver. Worn at the waist until the 16th century, it is differentiated from the alms purse by its hinge.
The escarcelle should also be distinguished from the *escharce*, which is a money box.
"Luxury and Folly inflate his wealth. To make a long story short, he is proud of his money bag."
(La Fontaine, *Fables*.)
"When will we get married? When will we have in-laws? My good man, it's really necessary, do you hear, necessary to rifle through the money bag! While saying these words, he makes her acquaintance. He invites her to sit down beside him. Takes her hand, her arm, and lifts a corner of his handkerchief." (La Fontaine, *Fables*.)
"Many a pistol slips into the moneybag of our man, He will send the devil to Rome."
(La Fontaine, *Contes en vers*.)

FOURRE-TOUT [hold-all, carry-all]
Similar in form to the *cabas*, but smaller and without an interior pocket. An inexpensive, utilitarian bag, flexible and practical, generally made of leather or coarse canvas. Its construction is very simple: a container and a pair of handles.

GERLE
A kind of beggar's bag.

GIBECIÈRE [hunting bag, game bag] (13th century, from *gibiez*, early French variant of *gibier* [game], perhaps also from *gibe*, meaning thigh)
A large bag with a flap, ordinarily of leather, worn on a shoulder strap or on a belt. Originally used by soldiers to carry grenades and by hunters to hold ammunition and prey, it was also carried by farmers and fishermen. A mesh game bag was attached to the front.
"An immense hunting bag, held on the shoulders by a large strap of yellow leather, bumped against the small of his back." (Barres, *La Colline inspirée*.)

"In his hunting bag, he had cheese and bread, potatoes, and nuts, according to the season."
(Ch. L. Philippe, *Père Perdrix*.)
In *Eve et David*, Balzac conjures up "that leather bag made into a hunting bag, divided into three compartments, so familiar to travelers (…)"
Another version of the game bag, made of woven willow, appears in *La Vieille fille*: "Suzanne concealed the pouch in a fine willow game bag which she carried on her arm…"
As a fashion accessory, the hunting bag was wide and flat. At first worn in front, by the 17th century, it had moved to the small of the back, sometimes in velvet, ornamented with pearls, and with or without a hinge. The name and the object itself went out of style at the end of the 17th century.
In the 19th century, *gibecière* could also refer to the leather bag that schoolchildren carried on their shoulders, and to the bag used by magicians. One turn of the bag signified one magic trick: "He has more than one trick in his bag" (up his sleeve).

GLADSTONE BAG (after the 19th-century British prime minister W. E. Gladstone) or "twin" bag.
A bag with two equal-sized hinged compartments, opening symmetrically. Two belts keep the bag closed. It corresponds to a *valisette*, or light traveling bag.

GORGE
The interior fold of a bag's flap.

GOUSSET [fob, coin pocket, watch pocket]
A small purse, worn at first under the armpit, but then, much later, fastened inside the waistband of trousers.
"A poor innocent philosopher, floundering in the shadows of calamity, with his empty coin purse reverberating against his hollow belly."
(Victor Hugo, *Notre-Dame de Paris*.)
A small pocket in the waistband of trousers, a waistcoat, or a jacket. *Fish in your fob; pull your watch from your watch pocket.*
"Not one word more, if you please, said M. de La Seiglière, drawing from the watch pocket of his black satin trousers a little string purse which he slipped furtively between the fingers of M. Des Tournelles."
(Jules Sandeau, *Mlle. De La Seiglière*.)

HAVRESAC [haversack]
A knapsack of hide or cloth that contains the effects of an infantryman (uniforms, boots).

INDISPENSABLE
A nickname for the reticule or the *ballantine* during the reign of the "Merveilleuses", elegant society women of the Directoire period.

MONTAGE DE SACS [bag assembly]
Method of joining the various pieces that make up a bag. Several techniques are used:

MONTAGE SELLIER [saddle stitching]
The flat assembly of two clean-cut sides, top-stitched by machine or hand. Excellent method for sports bags.

MONTAGE MAROQUINIER [Moroccan method]
The application of a piece of finished leather over the edge of another piece of leather, thus concealing the raw edge. This operation is followed by a seam.

MONTAGE REMBORDE CONTRE-COLLÉ [counter-glued assembly] Luxury method, generally used for suede. This technique involves preparing the two sides that are to be assembled, folding them to the line of the trim, and gluing them together. A straight stitch (by machine or hand) will secure them.

MONTAGE RETOURNÉ [turned-back assembly]
Two sides stitched wrong sides together, and then turned inside out to conceal the seam, which is now on the inside. Often embellished by piping (a thin strip of leather folded in half) inserted between the two sides.

MIDINETTE
Small lady's bag of the carry-all type.

MUSETTE
A small cloth bag worn on a shoulder strap; named for its similarity to the rustic wind instrument that resembles a bagpipe. It appears in the early 19th century to carry provisions. In peddlers' catalogs of the time, it is referred to as "the student's musette".

PANETIÈRE (13th century, from *pain* [bread])
A kind of satchel in white canvas, worn hanging on the left side, in which shepherds and travelers (especially pilgrims) placed bread and provisions.

POCHETTE [clutch bag] (diminutive of *poche* [pocket], from Frankish *pokka*)
A small lady's bag with neither handle nor shoulder strap, but sometimes with a grip on the back.

POCHON
Bag, sachet, pouch.

POLOCHON (origin uncertain, perhaps from middle Dutch *poluwe*)
Small flexible cylindrical baggage carried horizontally, provided with a slide fastener and two handles.

POMPADOUR (in the taste or style made fashionable by the Marquise de Pompadour in the 18th century)
Small pouch of velvet or lace, worn hanging from a cord, and used to carry smelling salts, a perfumed handkerchief, a notebook, or money.

RABAT [flap]
The part of the bag that folds over to close it, sometimes augmented by a clasp.

RÉTICULE [reticule, string bag, mesh bag, net bag]
(from Latin *reticulum*, small string bag)
A string bag carried in antiquity as a container for provisions or tools. Under *reticulum*, Diderot's *Encyclopédie* provides a description: "this word means a small snare or net, or a racket for playing real tennis (because it is webbed), and last, a net or webbed bag to carry bread while traveling. Varro says *panarium*, which is why St Augustine calls a supply of bread *annonam reticam*, because it is carried in string bags, whereas the market basket in common usage among the poor was made from palm leaves, rush, or willow, and was called *cumera*. As for *reticula* or net bags: they were well and widely used in ancient Greece and Rome. In *The Acharnians* of Aristophanes, there are onions in net bags; small net bags are also used to carry flowers. In this manner, Cicero paints a delightful portrait of Varrus at a feast: '*Ipse coronam habebat unam in capite, alteram in collo, reticulum quae ad nares sibi apponebat, tenuissimo lino, minutis maculis, plenum rosae.*' ('He wore a garland on his head, and another around his neck; and he breathed from time to time the scent of a mass of roses which he had placed in a bag of linen string, a tissue of fine knots.') That was the string bag of Varrus; but not all *reticula* were made of fine linen knotted into a mesh of tiny squares. They were often woven of rush, without much style. Nevertheless, some were magnificent, threaded with ivory or silver. In Hippolochus' description of the feast of Carunus, which Athenaeus has preserved for us, there are string bags for bread made from strips of ivory, and even bread bags made of silver strips."
After the French Revolution, fashionable merchants revived the reticule in the form of a small bag suspended from a fine chain or a cord. It was immediately adopted by the flirts of the Palais-Royal, who had had to dispense with the services of the personal handkerchief-holders who had hitherto carried their small effects. The Classical revival set the tone, inspiring fashion in both interior design and clothing. The fashion for dresses that clung to the body made a small bag, which could be hung from a wrist or an arm, a welcome substitute for the numerous pockets that had been tucked away in the voluminous skirts of the Ancien Regime.
The reticule was also called *ballantine*, because it balanced, swinging back and forth beside the legs; or *ridicule*, in mockery. It was considered ridiculous to show off by dangling these "pockets" conspicuously from the hand. Under the Directoire, the reticule in fine mesh lined with silk saw a lively success in France.

SAC [sack] (from *sakkos/saccus*; Chantraine sees a definite Semitic loanword, probably Phoenician – perhaps Hebrew – *saq*, which refers to a rough material in goathair or packing canvas, *akkadrer* – *saqqn* – a traveling word)
A general term referring to a container intended to carry a great variety of objects or materials.

In the 18th century, Diderot's *Encyclopédie* gave the following definition: "a species of pocket made from a piece of leather, canvas, or other fabric, sewn at the sides and base so that a single opening remains at the top. Sacks are usually deeper than they are wide. One uses sacks to carry many kinds of goods, such as wool, woad dye, saffron, wheat, oats, flour, peas, flat beans, lime, coal, and many similar things. [...] The shopping bag is a kind of case made of fabric without a wooden frame, in which one can put one thing or another; there are bags for books, or small bottles, and larger bags to accommodate ladies' books, and for travelers."

SAC À DOS [rucksack, backpack]
A bag worn on the back, usually held in place by two buckled straps, and closed by a drawstring, which is sometimes concealed under a flap.

SAC À LA MALICE, SAC À MALICE [bag of tricks]
The suitcase from which conjurers suddenly pull the objects with which they execute their magic tricks. Figuratively, the place from which one takes the objects necessary to realize certain amazing procedures: a well-filled strongbox is a miraculous bag of tricks.

SAC À MAIN [handbag]
A feminine accessory that holds money, papers, and cosmetics. It came into general use after World War I. With handle(s) or shoulder strap, in shapes and materials that vary according to use, the handbag defines itself variously by function as city bag, evening bag, sport bag, carry-all... or by its form, as baguette bag, bucket bag...

SACOCHE (17th century, from Italian saccoccia, little bag)
A double bag. In leather, the saddlebag, which was composed of two bags joined together by straps, was a useful accessory for messengers and travelers for transporting papers or valuables. The two parts of the saddlebag counter-balanced each other when placed over the back of a mount, with one bag hanging down either side.
Louis Sébastien Mercier in *Le Tableau de Paris* (1781) recalls canvas saddlebags carried over the shoulder by bank tellers who would fill them with gold and silver coins: "deep bags of heavy cloth, suitable for accommodating the scattered limbs of Lord Million, used by money messengers, who, alas, are none the wealthier for it."

SAC-SEAU [bucket bag]
A women's carry-all bag, cylindrical or flared, with a stiff base. Usually open, but sometimes closed by a flap with a loop to protect against prying eyes. The bucket bag was inspired by fire buckets, the earliest of which were leather. It may have one or two handles, or a shoulder strap.

SERVIETTE [attaché case, briefcase] (from Latin *servire*, to be a slave, submissive)
A rectangular bag with a flap secured by one or more clasps; with bellows to separate interior compartments; and with or without handles. It serves to carry documents (lawyer's briefcase, minister's briefcase, diplomat's briefcase...)

SOUFFLETS (from 12th-century term for bellows, from the Latin *soufflare*)
Pieces that are joined at the side to form a flexible, collapsible base for a bag, intended to increase or decrease capacity. Bellows may be flexible, folded in half, to draw up the base...

SQUARE MOUTH
A vivid name referring to a suitcase characterized by its very large opening. It is fitted with a metal frame that spans its entire width and ends at the sides in two spreading "jaws," which open horizontally, permitting maximum accessibility. Carried with the help of handles mounted on each side, it is reminiscent of the antique form of doctors' bag.
The French term is *excelsior*, as opposed to *City* or *Magenta*, whose "jaws" open vertically in a "V."

TASSE or TASCHE (14th century, from German *taska* for pocket)
A very ornate purse worn at the side by men until the beginning of the 17th century.

TUCK
A metal accessory that secures the mouth of the bag, consisting of a hinged piece, the *mentonnet* or hasp, which folds over and clasps under a small projection. Used mainly in school satchels and briefcases.

VANITY-CASE
A small hard suitcase in the form of a stiff rectangle or cylinder, equipped with a handle, designed to carry and protect feminine toiletries. A mirror is usually attached to the inside of the lid. Internal compartments and loops prevent the bottles and other contents from moving around and colliding with each other.

BIBLIOGRAPHY

Only articles with a bibliography are included here

Introduction
Magic Bags, Farid Chenoune
- **Gaston Bachelard**, *Poétique de l'espace*, Paris,
Presses universitaires de France, 1957.
- On the *bilum* bag: **Christian Kaufmann**, « Maschenstoffe und ihre
gesellschaftliche Funktion am Beispiel der Kwoma von Papua-Neuguinea »,
Tribus (No 35, December 1986, p. 127-175), Stuttgart Linden-Museum, 1986

CARRYING ON

The High Fashion Bag,
Olivier Saillard
- **Vanda Forster**, *Bags & Purses*, London, B. T. Batsford Ltd, 1982
- **Nathalie Hambro**, *The Art of the Handbag*, London,
Contemporary Collection, 1999.
- **Geneviève** and **Gérard Picot**, *Le Sac à main : une histoire amusée et passionnée*,
Paris, Éditions du May, 1993.
- **Laird Borrelli** and **Valerie Steele**, *Sacs. Langages du style*, Paris,
Éditions du Collectionneur, 1999.
- **Claire Wilcox**, *Un Siècle de sacs, symboles de l'élégance*,
London, Serge Media, 1997.
- **Claire Wilcox**, *Bags*, London, Victoria & Albert Museum, 1999.

Sylvie Fleury's Shopping Bags,
Laurent Goumarre
- **Éric Troncy**, "The better you look", in *Sylvie Fleury*, Paris, Réunion des musées
nationaux, Dijon, Les Presses du Réel, "Art contemporain" collection, 2001.

The Destiny of a Plastic Bag,
Farid Chenoune
- **Claude Closky**, *Mon Catalogue*, Limoges, Éditions Frac Limousin, 1999.

NOMADS AND VOYAGERS

The Carpetbag: Packing the Essential,
Ménéhould du Chatelle
- **Henri d'Alméras**, *Au bon vieux temps des diligences*, Paris, Albin Michel, 1931.
- **Henry Havard**, *Dictionnaire de l'ameublement et de la décoration depuis
le XIIIᵉ siècle jusqu'à nos jours*, t. IV, Paris, Ancienne Maison Quantin, 1887-1890.

Among the Tuareg,
Edmond Bernus
- **Edmond Bernus**, *Touaregs nigériens. Unité culturelle et diversité régionale d'un
peuple pasteur.* Paris, Orstom, "Mémoires" collection, No 94, 1989 ; 2nd edition:
Paris, L'Harmattan, 1993, 507 p.
- **Père Charles de Foucauld**, *Dictionnaire touareg-français, dialecte de l'Ahaggar*,
Paris, Imprimerie nationale de France, 4 Vol., 2022 p.
- **Jean Gabus**, *Au Sahara : arts et symboles.* Neuchâtel, Éditions de la Baconnière,
1958, 407 p.
- **G. de Gironcourt**, "L'art chez les Touareg", in *Missions de Gironcourt en Afrique
occidentale. Documents scientifiques*, Paris, Société de géographie, 1920,
p. 269-291.
- **Théodore Monod**, *Méharées. Explorations au vrai Sahara.* Paris, Je Sers, 1937,
303 p. ; rééd. Actes Sud, "Babel" collection, 1994.
- **Nicolaisen Johanès**, *Ecology and Culture of the Pastoral Tuareg, with Particular
Reference to the Tuareg of Ahaggar and Ayr*, Copenhagen, National Museum,
1963, 548 p.
- **Nicolas Francis**, *Tamesna, les Ioullemmeden de l'Est ou Touâreg Kel Dinnik, cercle
de T'âwa, colonie du Niger.* Paris, Imprimerie nationale, 1950, 279 p.
- **Petites sœurs de Jésus**, *Contes touaregs de l'Air*, Introduction by L. Galand,
commentary by G. Calame-Griaule, Paris, SELAF, CNRS, 1974, 266 p.
- **Yves Urvoy**, "L'art des Touareg du Sud-Est et des Oulliminden de l'Est",
in *L'Art dans le territoire du Niger, Études nigériennes n° II*, Centre IFAN,
gouvernement du Niger, 1955, 68 p.

- **Jean Vercoutter**, "Cui", "Égypte", in *Dictionnaire archéologique de techniques*,
Paris, Éditions de l'Accueil, 1963, 2 Vols., t. I, p. 344.

Exhibition Catalogues:
- Musée d'Ethnographie et de Préhistoire du Bardo (Alger), *Planches, Album n° I*,
published under the direction of L. Balout, preface by R. Capot-Rey, captions
Marceau Gast, Paris, Arts et Métiers graphiques, 1959.
- *Touareg*, Album of photographs & exhibition catalogue, royal museum
of Central Africa, Tervuren, 1994, 158 photos.
- *Tuareg. Nomadas del desierto*, Ethnographic Museum, Neuchâtel-Fundacion
"la Caixa", Barcelone, 2001, 94 plates.

WORKS AND DAYS

Sewing Bags,
Stéphane Laverrière
- *Encyclopédie ou Dictionnaire raisonné des sciences, des arts et des métiers*,
Neufchastel, Samuel Faulche & Compagnie, Libraires et Imprimeurs, 1765.
- **Henri Havard**, *Dictionnaire de l'ameublement et de la décoration depuis
le XIIIᵉ siècle jusqu'à nos jours*, Paris, Librairies-Imprimeries Réunies, 1901.
- **Jacques Savary Des Bruslons**, *Dictionnaire universel de commerce, d'histoire
naturelle et des arts et métiers*, Copenhague, C. and Philibert, new edition, 1760.
- *Livre-Journal de Lazare Duvaux, marchand-bijoutier ordinaire du Roy,
1748-1758…*, Paris, Société des bibliophiles français, 1873.
- **Caroline-Stéphanie-Félicité Du Crest, comtesse de Genlis**, *Dictionnaire critique et
raisonné des étiquettes de la cour… ou L'Esprit des étiquettes et des usages anciens,
comparé aux modernes*, Paris, P. Mongie Aîné, 1818, 2 Vol.

Bags of New Holland and Van Diemen's Land,
Gabrielle Baglione
- **Nicolas Baudin**, *Mon voyage aux terres australes. Journal personnel du commandant
Baudin*, transcription J. Bonnemains, Paris, Imprimerie nationale, 2000.
- **Joseph-Marie de Gérando**, *Considérations sur les diverses méthodes à suivre dans
l'observation des peuples sauvages*, [1799].
- **Jean Jamin**, "Faibles sauvages… corps indigents : le désenchantement de
François Péron", *Le Corps enjeu*, éd. Jacques Hainard et Roland Khaer, Neuchâtel,
Musée d'ethnographie, 1983.
- **Pierre-Bernard Milius**, *Voyage aux terres australes*, éd. Jacqueline Bonnemains et
Pascale Hauguel, Le Havre, Société havraise d'études diverses et Muséum
d'histoire naturelle du Havre, 1987.
- **Howard Morphy**, *Aboriginal Art*, London, Phaidon, 1998.
- **François Péron**, "Île Maria – Suite des observations de phisique [sic] et
d'Histoire naturelle, ventôse an X", 1802, Le Havre, Muséum d'histoire
naturelle, manuscrit No 18 042.

Wicker Fish Baskets,
François Blary
- **François Blary**, "Les fortifications du château de Château-Thierry des derniers
comtes herbertiens au premier duc de Bouillon", in *Congrès archéologique
de France 1990, Aisne méridionale*, Société française d'archéologie, t. I, 1994.
- **François Blary**, *Château-Thierry. Des comtes de Vermandois aux ducs de Bouillon :
contribution à l'étude des phénomènes urbains*, thèse d'histoire et d'archéologie
médiévale, université de Paris I Panthéon-Sorbonne, 2001 (due out late 2004).
- **François Blary** and **V. Durey-Blary**, "L'art culinaire dans un château aux
XIVᵉ et XVᵉ siècles. L'exemple de Château-Thierry (Aisne)", in *Actes du VIᵉ congrès
international, L'innovation technique au Moyen Âge – Bourgogne, 1996*, Société
d'archéologie médiévale, 1998.

MONEY, POWER AND CEREMONY

Ceremonial Bags,
Monique Blanc
- **Julia Fritsch**, *Objets du voyage et du commerce au Moyen Âge*, Un mois,
une œuvre, musée national du Moyen Âge, Thermes et Hôtel de Cluny,
January 2004.
- **Verena Kessel**, *Studien zu Darstellungen von Taschen und Beuteln im 14. und*

15. Jahrhundert, Jahrbuch des Museums für Kunst und Gewerbe, Hambourg,
Vol. III, 1984.
- **Jean-Paul Leclercq**, *Monture d'escarcelle,* La Vitrine du mois, Paris,
musée des Arts décoratifs, April 2003.
- **Véronique Montembault**, "Les chaussures et autres objets en cuir",
in Christiane Prigent (dir.), *Art et société en France au xvᵉ siècle,* Paris,
Maisonneuve et Larose, 1999, p. 669-673.
- *The Secular Spirit, Life and Art at the End of the Middle Ages,*
New York, The Metropolitan Museum of Art, p. 74-91.

Money Bags,
Ménéhould du Chatelle
- *Dictionnaire des dictionnaires. Encyclopédie universelle des lettres, des sciences
et des arts...,* Paul Guérin (dir.), Paris, A. Picard, 1884, p. 202.
- **Pierre Chaunu**, *Le Temps des Réformes,* Paris, Fayard,
"Le Monde sans frontière" collection, 1975.
- **Simon Schama**, *L'Embarras des richesses, une interprétation de la culture
hollandaise au siècle d'Or,* Paris, Gallimard,
"Bibliothèque illustrée des histoires" collection, 1991.

SECRETS OF THE GODS

Medieval Relic Pouches,
Vivianne Huchard
- **Eugène Chartraire**, "Les tissus anciens du trésor de la cathédrale de Sens",
Revue de l'Art chrétien, Paris, Honoré Champion, 1911.
- **Victor Gay**, *Glossaire archéologique du Moyen Âge et de la Renaissance,* Paris,
1887-1928 ; reprint Nendeln (Lichtenstein), Kraus reprint, 1967.
- **Henri Havard**, *Dictionnaire de l'ameublement et de la décoration depuis
le xiiiᵉ siècle jusqu'à nos jours,* Paris, Librairies-Imprimeries Réunies, 1901

Beaded Bags of Africa,
Etienne Féau
Generalities on beads and beadwork:
- **W. G. N. Van der Sleen**, *A Handbook on Beads,* Liège, Association internationale
pour l'histoire du verre, librairie Halvart, 1973.
- **Margret Carey**, *Beads and Beadwork of East and South Africa,* London,
Shire Ethnography, 1986.
- **Margret Carey**, *Beads and Beadwork of West and Central Africa,* London,
Shire Ethnography, 1991.
On Yoruba beads:
- **Ulli Beier**, *Yoruba Beaded Crowns : Sacred Regalia of the Olokuku of Okuku,*
London, Ethnographica Lagos, National Museum, 1982.
- **Henry John Drewal** and **John Mason**, *Beads, Body and Soul : Art and Light in the
Yoruba Universe,* Los Angeles, UCLA Fowler Museum of Cultural History, 1998.
- **William Fagg**, *Yoruba Beadwork,* New York, Rizzoli, 1980.
- **Alison Hodge**, *Nigeria's Traditional Crafts,* London, Ethnographica, 1982.

Native American Bags,
Emmanuel Désveaux
On the notions of structure and transformation:
- **Claude Lévi-Strauss**, *Mythologiques,* Paris, Plon, 4 volumes : *Le Cru et le cuit,*
1964, *Du miel aux cendres,* 1966, *L'Origine des manières de table,* 1968,
L'Homme nu, 1971.
On the broad application of the notion of transformation, notably to objects
and on the Amerindian conception of reproduction:
- **Emmanuel Désveaux**, *Quadratura Americana, essai d'anthropologie
lévi-straussienne,* Geneva, Georg éditeur, 2000.
On feminine abstraction in the art of the Plains:
- **Emmanuel Désveaux**, "Les forêts du Nord-Est et les plaines : le figuratif et le
géométrique", in *Le Grand Atlas de l'art,* Paris, Encyclopeadia Universalis,
p. 370-371.
On the Midewiwin brotherhood:
Walter J. Hoffman, "The Midewiwin or 'Grand Medicine Society', of the
Ojibwa", in *7ᵗʰ Annual report of the Bureau of American Ethnology for the years
1885-1886,* Washington, Smithsonian Institution, p. 143-300.

On parfleches:
- **Gaylord Torrence**, *The American Indian Parfleche: a Tradition of Abstract Painting,*
Washington, University of Washington Press, 1994.
On Sauk, Fox and Potawatomi bags, called "panelbags":
- **Ruth B. Phillips**, *Patterns of Power / vers la force spirituelle,* Kleinburg, Ontario,
Mc Michael Canadian Collection, 1984.

Sacred Bags of Ancient Mexico,
Anne-Marie Vié-Wohrer
- *Codex Azcatitlan,* introduction by **Michel Graulich**, commentary by **Robert
Barlow**, updated by **Michel Graulich**, French translation by **Dominique Michelet**,
Paris, Bibliothèque nationale de France, 1995, 2 Vol.
- *Codex Vindobonensis,* commentary by **Otto Adelhofer**, Graz, Akademische
Druck und Verlagsanstalt, 1974
- *Tira de la Peregrinación,* commentary by **Joaquin Galarza**
and **Krystyna M. Libura**, Mexico, Ediciones Tecolotes, 1999.
- **Alfonso Caso**, *Reyes y Reinos de la Mixteca,* Mexico, Fondo de cultura
económica, "Seccion de obras de antropologia" collection, 1979.
- **Nigel Davies**, *The Aztecs,* London, Macmillan, 1973.
- **Olivier Guilhem**, *Moqueries et métamorphoses d'un dieu aztèque Tezcatlipoca,
le "Seigneur au miroir fumant",* Paris, musée de l'Homme, "Mémoires
de l'Institut d'ethnologie/Muséum national d'histoire naturelle" collection, 1997.
- **Zelia Nuttall**, *The Codex Nuttall, a Picture Manuscript from Ancient Mexico,*
introduction by Arthur Miller, New York, Dover Publications, 1975.

THE BAG OF TALES

Bags of Words: African Oral Literature,
Katia Kukawa
- **Alfred Adler**, *La mort est le masque du roi. La royauté sacrée des Moundang
du Tchad,* Paris, Payot, "Bibliothèque scientifique" collection, 1982.
- **Nicole Belmont**, *Comment on fait peur aux enfants,* followed by: *Les
Croquemitaines, une mythologie de l'enfance ?,* Paris, Mercure de France,
"Le petit Mercure" collection, 1999.
- **Doris Bonnet**, *Le Proverbe chez les Mossi du Yatenga (Haute-Volta),*
Paris, CNRS-ACCT, 1982.
- **Geneviève Calame-Griaule** and **Veronika Görög-Karady**, "La calebasse et le
fouet : le thème des objets magiques en Afrique occidentale", *Cahiers d'études
africaines,* 45, Vol. XII, 1ᵉʳ cahier, 1972.
- **Gaston Canu**, *Contes mossi actuels, étude ethno-linguistique,* Dakar,
Mémoires de l'Institut fondamental d'Afrique noire, No 82, 1969.
- **Massa Makan Diabaté**, *L'Aigle et l'épervier, ou la Geste de Sunjata,* Paris,
Pierre-Jean Oswald, "Poésie, prose africaine" collection, 1975.
- **Marie-Paule Ferry**, *Les Dits de la nuit : contes tenda (Sénégal oriental),* Paris,
Karthala, "Contes et légendes" collection, 1983.
- **Marcel Guilhem**, *Cinquante contes et fableaux de la savane,* Paris, Ligel, 1962.
- **David Lewis-Williams**, "Image des San et art san. Une dialectique
potentiel-lement créatrice en Afrique australe", in *Ubuntu,* Paris, Réunion
des musées nationaux, 2000.
- **Djibril Tamsir Niane**, *Soundjata ou l'épopée mandingue,* Paris, Présence africaine,
1976 (1960).
- **Denise Paulme**, *La Mère dévorante, essai sur la morphologie des contes africains,*
Paris, Gallimard, "Tel" collection, 1986 (1976).
- **Vladimir Propp**, *Les Racines historiques du conte merveilleux,* translated from the
Russian by Lise Gruel-Apert, preface by Daniel Fabre and Jean-Claude Schmitt,
Paris, Gallimard, 1983 (1946).
- **Christiane Seydou**, "Une dialectique de l'ex et de l'in ou le motif du 'sac' dans
les contes de l'Enfant terrible", in *Histoires d'enfants terribles (Afrique noire),*
Paris Maisonneuve et Larose, 1980.
- **Pierre Smith**, *Le Récit populaire au Rwanda,* Paris, A. Colin,
"Classiques africains" collection, 1975.
- **Dominique Zahan**, *La Dialectique du verbe chez les Bambara,* Paris, Mouton, 1963.

FRONT COVER CAPTIONS

From left to right, starting at the top, the bags are numbered from 1 to 25
1. Small size horsehide bag, Hermès, Conservatoire des créations Hermès
2. see ill. 5 p. 250
3. 1930s clutch bag, France, attributed to Robert Mallet-Steven,
Paris, documentation center of the Musée de la Mode et du Textile
4. see ill. 2 p. 283
5. Bag-suitcase, Hermès, 1923, python, sand-grain morocco, lambskin,
nickel-plated brass, Conservatoire des créations Hermès
6. see ill. 18 p. 41
7. see ill. 10 p. 162
8. "Henri Ier, Comte de Champagne" alms purse, France, 14th century
silk-embroidered red velvet, Troyes, cathedral treasury
9. see ill. 11 p. 190
10. see ill. x
11. Handbag, France, circa 1820, embossed cardboard, brass sequins,
steel clasp and chain, taffeta, Paris, Musée de la Mode et du Textile, UCAD collection
12. see ill. xix
13. see ill. 8 p. 61
14. Bag with set, Hermès, special order, 1980, black calfskin, lined with red shagreen H,
gold-plated brass, cut crystal, Conservatoire des créations Hermès
15. see ill. 3 p. 156
16. Laundry bag, Hermès, 1960, unbleached linen H and brown calfskin,
Conservatoire des créations Hermès
17. see ill. 5 p. 35
18. Tall bag with straps that belonged to Humphrey Bogart, Hermès, 1950,
natural cowhide, canvas and light cotton, polished brass, Conservatoire des créations
Hermès, gift of Madame Lauren Bacall
19. Bilum bag, Papua New Guinea, Marie-José Guigues
20. "Clio" handbag, Hermès, 1952, calf box lined with dipped lambskin,
gold-plated brass, collection of the Conservatoire des créations Hermès
21. Pullman automobile handbag, Hermès, 1940, box calf lined with lambskin,
silver-plated brass, collection of the Conservatoire des créations Hermès
22. see ill. iii
23. see ill. 2 p. 127
24. see ill. vii
25. see ill. 3 p. 58

COPYRIGHTS AND PHOTOGRAPHY CREDITS

Numbers refer to plates.
© Agence Vu : 7 p. 61, 6 p. 78, xxxii
© AKG : 9 p. 37, 27 p. 46, xxiv, 4 p. 210, 6 p. 239
© Alberto Sorbelli : 3 p. 72
© Antoine Jarrier : xx
© Archives Martin Margiela : 2 p. 57
© Ashmolean Museum, Oxford : 3 p. 19
© BnF : 25 p. 46, 1 p. 137, 7 p. 143, 6 p. 160, 7 p. 160, 8 p. 160, 3 p. 185, 5 p. 185, xxxvii,
7 p. 215, 11 p. 219, 12 p. 220, 15 p. 226, 2 p. 262, 1 p. 330, 2 p. 331
© Bridgeman Art Library : 1 p. 126, 4 p. 128-129, xxiii, 1 p. 154, 2 p. 155, 1 p. 231, 5 p. 238,
4 p. 269, xlv, 1 p. 326, 2 p. 327
© Bibliothèque municipale de Lyon/Didier Nicol : 5 p. 211
© Bibliothèque Muséum du Havre : 2 p. 175, 3 p. 175
© Bibliothèque publique de Genève : 4 p. 237
© Cahiers du Cinéma : p. 87
© Catherine and Bernard Desjeux : 1 p. 63, 2 p. 67, 2 p. 139, 3 p. 139, 4 p. 139, 5 p. 139,
6 p. 142, p. 319
© Claudine Doury/Agence VU : xii
© Cl. musées de Sens / L. de Cargoüet : 9 p. 217, 1, 2, 3, 4, p. 271
© Cl. musées de Sens / E. Berry : 10 p. 217
© Collection particulière : 6 p. 251
© Contact Press Images : xvii
© Courtesy of Vogue Paris : 20 p. 45, 22 p. 45
© Dagli Orti : 1 p. 16-17, 2 p. 18, 2 p. 125, 6 p. 212, 8 p. 243, 11 p. 247, xlii, p. 334
© Denis Darzacq/Agence VU : vi
© Denis Vinçon / CPI : xxv
© Don Cole / UCLA Fowler Museum of Cultural History : 2 p. 283, 3 p. 284, 6 p. 287, couv. 4
© E. Tramolada : 3 p. 69
© Eugen Schwarz / Mission des Archives, Bâle : 3 p. 249
La Beauté en voyage © Éditions Cercle d'Art, Paris 2003. Photo : Guy Lucas de Peslouan:
2 p. 127, 3 p. 127, 9 p. 135, couv. 23
© Farid Chenoune : 4 p. 76
© FLC, ADAGP Paris, 2004 : 15 p. 40
© Getty Images : 2 p. 75

© Harvard Business School, Boston : 2 p. 232
© INAH, Mexico : 1 p. 121
© Jean-Marc Tingaud / Ucad : v, viii, ix, x, xi, 1 p. 33, 2 p. 34, 3 p. 34, 4 p. 35, 5 p. 35, 6 p. 35,
7 p. 35, 10 p. 37, 14 p. 39, 16 p. 41, 17 p. 41, 18 p. 41, 35 p. 48, 1 p. 56, 5 p. 59, 6 p. 59, 8 p. 61,
xviii, xix, xxii, xxxv, 3 p. 156, 9 p. 161, 10 p. 161, 9 p. 188, 10 p. 189, xxxiv, xxxv, 17 p. 229,
18 p. 229, xliv, xlvi, xlvii, xlviii, couv. 1, 5, 11, 14, 16, 18, 20, 21
© J.-C. Dartoux : 2 p. 185
© Jean-Pierre and Bonnie Chaumeil : 1 p. 289, 2 p. 290
© Julien Lévy : 31 p. 46
© Laurent Sully Jaulmes / Ucad : 13 p. 39, 1 p. 164, couv. 3
© Leemage : 19-20 p. 42, 24 p. 46, xxx
© Laurent Bremaud : 36 p. 48
© Madeleine Vionnet : 11 p. 38, 12 p. 38
© Magnum Photos : 29 p. 46, 3 p. 76, 5 p. 77
© Marie-José Guigues : 4 p. 58, xxix, xxxix, xl, couv. 19
© Martine Plantec / LP3 Conservation : 8 p. 216
© Mission du patrimoine photographique : i
© M. J. Watts / musée d'Ethnographie, Genève : 1 p. 248, 2 p. 248, 4 p. 250, 5 p. 250,
1 p. 275, 2 p. 276, 3 p. 277, 4 p. 281, couv. 2
© Monique Manceau, reporter, photographe : 5 p. 112
© musée Alfred-Bonno, Chelles : 1 p. 207
© musée des Beaux-Arts, Angoulême/Philippe Mazère : 5 p. 285
© musée de Bretagne, Rennes : 2 p. 180, 3 p. 180
© muséum d'Histoire naturelle de Toulouse : 3 p. 58, couv. 25
© musée de Londres : 1 p. 179
© musée de la Marine, Paris / P. Dantec : 17 p. 197, 18 p. 197, 19 p. 197
© musée du Quai-Branly, Paris : 1 p. 282, 4 p. 285, 6 p. 299
© musée Thomas-Dobrée, Nantes : 16 p. 228
© musée de Troyes / Didier Vogel : 5 p. 272, couv. 8
© musées du Vatican, Rome : 3 p. 264-265
© Museum für Volkerkunde, Berlin : 5 p. 299
© Olivier Goulet : 9 p. 61
© Patrick Ageneau, Muséum, Lyon : xxxiii
© Peter Horner, Museum der Kulturen, Bâle : iii, xxvi, couv. 22
© Pierre Boisson : i
© Pierre David / musées d'Angers : 2 p. 296
© Pierre Sportolaro : 7 p. 79
© Philippe Sebert : ii, 5 p. 130, 6 p. 130, 7 p. 132, 8 p. 133, 6 p. 186, 8 p. 187, 11 p. 190,
12 p. 191, 13 p. 192, 14 p. 193, 15 p. 194, 7 p. 241, 10 p. 246
© Rapho : xiv, 1 p. 185, 4 p. 185, 7 p. 186
© Raymond Depardon/Magnum Photos : vii
© RMN : 8 p. 36, 4 p. 157, 5 p. 158-159, 1 p. 167, 2 p. 170, 3 p. 209, 14 p. 224, 3 p. 234-235,
1 p. 261, 6 p. 273,
© RMN / Hervé Lewandowski : xxxviii
© Robert Bresson : p. 89
© Robert Doisneau / Rapho : 28 p. 46
© Roger-Viollet : 26 p. 46, xv, 2 p. 165
© Seeberger : 23 p. 46
© Serge Lieb / Documentation Tallandier : 21 p. 45
© Sotheby's / AKG : 9 p. 244
© Steve Miller : 2 p. 51
© Tallandier : xiii, xxi, 16 p. 195
© The Detroit Institute of Arts, 1992 : 1 p. 294, 3 p. 297, 4 p. 297
© V. Terebenine : 1 p. 107, 2 p. 109, 3 p. 110, 4 p. 111, 6 p. 114, 7 p. 115
© 2002 The Metropolitan Museum of Art, New York : 13 p. 223

All rights reserved: 32 p. 47, 33 p. 47, 34 p. 47, 37 p. 49, 2 p. 57, 1 p. 70, 2 p. 71, 1 p. 74,
p. 84, p. 85, p. 86, p. 88, p. 90, p. 91, p. 92, p. 93, p. 94, p. 95, xvi, xxviii, xxxi, xxxvi, 1 p. 173,
1 p. 182, 2 p. 182, 2 p. 208, xli, xliii, 6 p. 301 à 308

- The text "My Life in 128 cubic inches", by Christine Martin, was published under the
title "Mon sac et moi", signed Camille Fervaques, in Mixt(e), No 12,
December 2000-January-February 2001, Excelsior Publications. All rights reserved.
- The text by Henri Michaux entitled "Bag Time" is taken from his book
La Vie dans les plis, Paris, éditions Gallimard, 1949. All rights reserved.
- How Snake Became Poisonious. Native American tale. All rights reserved.<
- The text by Djeli Mamadou Kouyaté entitled "The Legend of Soundjata (Mali)" is taken
from the book by Djibril Tamsir Niane, Soundjata ou l'épopée mandingue, Paris, Présence
africaine, 1960; 2nd edition, 1976. All rights reserved.

Printed and bound in Italy by Mondadori